PRE

English 2200, *English 2600*, and *English 3200* are the original programmed courses in grammar, usage, sentence-building, capitalization, and punctuation. Since the introduction of the series in colleges in 1963, it has proved effective in teaching the elements of English to more than a million students of all abilities in a wide range of institutions: state and private universities, community, junior, and four-year colleges, vocational and technical institutes, and business colleges.

The Self-Teaching Method

Like their predecessors, the 1994 College Editions of the series are self-pacing, self-correcting, thorough, and flexible. They are programmed to make the learning of grammar and usage a positive, success-oriented experience. Each lesson in *English 2200*, *English 2600*, and *English 3200* contains twenty to forty sequential learning "frames." Each frame has three elements: an easy-to-understand explanation of a small but significant step in the mastery of the lesson topic; a question or statement about the topic to which the student must respond; and the answer to the preceding frame's question. Students perform and correct their work individually, at their own pace. Correct responses are immediately reinforced and incorrect responses are corrected at once. This step-by-step format, based on decades of in-class testing and refinement, provides the immediate positive reinforcement and encouragement students need to maximize learning.

Three Parallel, Graduated Programs

English 2200, *English 2600*, and *English 3200* are parallel in approach and design and may therefore be used cumulatively. As their titles indicate, they vary in length according to the number of frames, and they vary in emphasis. *English 2200* and *English 2600* focus on the parts of speech and how they are combined into correctly punctuated sentences. In *English 2200*, students are introduced to words that make up and enrich sentences. In *English 2600*, they expand on this knowledge by studying the function of verbs, subjects, and modifiers, as well as the patterns of simple sentences. *English 3200* guides students directly from one unit on the simple sentence to six units on more sophisticated ways of handling sentences. It treats compound and complex sentences, devices of subordination, and techniques for writing sentences with variety and smoothness.

Pedagogical Flexibility

College instructors have found that the cumulative programmed format of the series offers an extraordinary degree of pedagogical flexibility. They have used the same book as a basic text for an entire class, as an independent course of study for individuals, as a review for groups outside the classroom, and as a remedial text for individuals or groups. These last two uses have made the series especially attractive to writing laboratories and learning centers. Further, because the three programs in the series cover the same principles of grammar and usage, they may be used sequentially in three graduated courses or even together in a single class. For example, using the results of the diagnostic Pre-Test for *English 2600*, instructors may assign students either *English 2200*, *English 2600*, or *English 3200*. Instead of spending many class hours on details of grammar and usage, instructors assigning these self-teaching programs are free to devote more time to the teaching of writing, vocabulary, spelling, and other skills.

The Writing Applications

The writing applications in the second part of this book correspond to the units on grammar, sentence-building, usage, and punctuation in the first part. They are designed to complement the programmed instruction so that students can use the information already learned in their writing. The writing applications give students the opportunity to apply directly the principles of grammar and usage mastered in the first part of the book.

Each writing application asks the student to write about a topic, using a six-stage process, called the *writing process*. Learning to use the writing process will enable the student to plan, compose, and revise more quickly, easily, and accurately.

Indexes

A detailed index, useful to both instructors and students, follows each programmed course. Every entry in the index is followed by the frame number and the page, in parentheses, on which the frame appears. The frames indexed are those containing key concepts, definitions, or illustrations. For example, under the entry "fragment" in the index to *English 3200* are eleven subentries; these entries direct students to various kinds of fragments, as well as to methods for correcting them. Students may turn to particular entries to answer their own questions about specific points of grammar and usage. Besides offering a handy reference, however, the index is a useful aid for planning remedial and review exercises. When students reveal that they have not yet mastered a particular concept, the instructor, by consulting the index, can guide them to review the appropriate frames. Students who require help in correcting specific errors when revising a composition may be alerted to frames that show them how to identify and remedy those errors.

Test Booklets and Answer Keys

A 60- or 64-page test booklet for each volume in the series is provided free to college instructors in class quantities, one booklet for each textbook ordered. Additional copies of the test booklets are sold separately and may be ordered from the

English 2600
with Writing Applications

A PROGRAMMED COURSE IN GRAMMAR AND USAGE

Sixth College Edition

Joseph C. Blumenthal

English 2600 with Writing Applications, Sixth College Edition
Joseph C. Blumenthal

Publisher: Ted Buchholz

Acquisitions Editor: Stephen T. Jordan

Project Editor: Nancy Lombardi

Cover Designer: Diana Jean Parks

Production Managers: Kelly Donaldson, Erin Gregg

© 1994, 1981, 1973, 1969, 1962, 1960 Wadsworth, Cengage Learning. Copyright renewed 1990, 1998 by Margaret W. Blumenthal.

ALL RIGHTS RESERVED. No part of this work covered by the copyright herein may be reproduced, transmitted, stored or used in any form or by any means graphic, electronic, or mechanical, including but not limited to photocopying, recording, scanning, digitizing, taping, Web distribution, information networks, or information storage and retrieval systems, except as permitted under Section 107 or 108 of the 1976 United States Copyright Act, without the prior written permission of the publisher.

For product information and technology assistance, contact us at **Cengage Learning Customer & Sales Support, 1-800-354-9706**

For permission to use material from this text or product, submit all requests online at **www.cengage.com/permissions**
Further permissions questions can be e-mailed to **permissionrequest@cengage.com**

Library of Congress Control Number: 92-83969

ISBN-13: 978-0-15-500862-5

ISBN-10: 0-15-500862-5

Wadsworth
20 Davis Drive
Belmont, CA 94002-3098
USA

Cengage Learning is a leading provider of customized learning solutions with office locations around the globe, including Singapore, the United Kingdom, Australia, Mexico, Brazil and Japan. Locate your local office at **international.cengage.com/region**

Cengage Learning products are represented in Canada by Nelson Education, Ltd.

For your course and learning solutions, visit **academic.cengage.com**

Purchase any of our products at your local college store or at our preferred online store **www.cengagebrain.com**

Printed in the United States of America
24 25 26 27 28 23 22 21 20 19

The College Series

English 2200

English 2600

English 3200

TESTS FOR ENGLISH 2200

TESTS FOR ENGLISH 2600

TESTS FOR ENGLISH 3200
Alternate Tests for English 3200

ANSWER KEY FOR EACH TEST BOOK

About the Author

Joseph C. Blumenthal received his A.B. and A.M. degrees from the University of Michigan. He also did graduate work at the University of Chicago and at Columbia University. From 1938 to 1959 he was head of the English Department at Mackenzie High School in Detroit. Among his writings are the *Common Sense English* series, the *English Workshop* series (with John F. Warriner and others), and *The English Language* series (with Louis Zahner and others).

About the Sixth Edition

This edition retains the index that is intended to make *English 2600* more useful to students and instructors by giving them ready access to the entire body of material treated in the text. Each entry is indexed by frame and page numbers to facilitate reference.

New to this edition is a writing applications section, designed to move students from mastering skills to using those skills in real writing situations.

The Test Booklet

The 64-page test booklet designed for use with *English 2600* consists of a Pre-Test, two parallel tests for each of the twelve units, two Halfway Tests, and a Final Test.

publisher. An alternate test booklet, parallel in form and content to the original, is available for *English 3200*. When placing orders for *English 3200*, instructors should indicate whether they wish the original or the alternate test booklets. In addition, an Answer Key for each of the test booklets is available to instructors.

Each test booklet contains a diagnostic Pre-Test, two parallel Mastery Tests (labeled A and B) for each unit in the textbook, two parallel Halfway Tests, and a Final Test.

This testing apparatus considerably enhances the flexibility of the series. Whether a test is given to individual students or to an entire class at the same time depends on how the textbook itself is used. If students proceed at their own rate until they complete the entire book, individual testing will be necessary. If the class waits until all students complete a given unit before proceeding to the next unit, the class may be tested simultaneously. The Pre-Test enables instructors to determine a student's overall grasp of fundamentals, to identify his or her strengths and weaknesses, and to plan an individualized program while avoiding material the student has already mastered.

The inclusion of parallel Mastery Tests offers flexibility in meeting the needs of a specific class in providing for various classroom situations. For example:

1. Test A may be used as a pre-test for every unit and Test B as a final test.

2. Test A may serve as a practice test and Test B as the official test.

3. Test A or B may be used as a makeup test for students who did not achieve satisfactory scores on their first test.

4. Tests A and B may be used with different classes or with alternate rows in the same classroom.

No matter how the tests are used, one idea, basic to the method of programmed learning, should be kept in mind: a response should have an immediate reinforcement.

To the Student

English 2600 is a programmed course in grammar, sentence-building, correct usage, and punctuation. A feature of this edition is an index that can help you locate a particular topic quickly when you need it for reference or review.

If this is your first experience with a programmed textbook, you may be puzzled by its appearance. As you leaf through its pages, you may wonder why it looks so different from other books you have studied.

Why the zebra-like pages with alternating bands of gray and white?

Why is the material divided into small bits, or *frames*?

Why don't you read the pages from top to bottom as you do other books?

Why are the answers printed in the marginal strips where they can be so easily seen?

English 2600 looks so different because it is built upon some modern learning principles. For many years, the problems of learning have been studied scientifically in colleges and universities all over the country. As a result, new discoveries have been made that can make learning faster, surer, more thorough (and, we hope, more fun). *English 2600* is based on some of the most important of these discoveries.

1. In a programmed course, often called simply a *program*, the material is broken down into very small and carefully arranged steps—approximately 2,600 in this book—through which you reason your way, one step at a time. There is no separation between explanation and exercise, as in other language textbooks; the two are tightly interwoven. Every step, or *frame*, calls for a written response, which requires both *thinking* and *concentration*. The advantages of "reasoning your own way" instead of "being told" have been known to good teachers ever since the days of Socrates. By thinking your way through the program, you are likely to understand better and to remember longer.

2. Programs are constructed to prevent mistakes before they happen. The psychologists call this "errorless learning" and have proved its importance by scientific experiment. The steps are so small and their arrangement is so orderly that you are not likely to make many errors. When an error occurs, you catch it immediately by turning the page for the answer. You are corrected before a wrong habit can become established. You spend your time *learning*—not *unlearning*. Using a programmed textbook is like having a private tutor who watches you as you work and who sets you back on the track the moment you wander off.

3. A very important factor in this method is what the psychologists call *reinforcement*. Its importance in learning cannot be stated too strongly.

With the usual textbook, you first study the lesson (which you may or may not understand completely). Then you apply what you have studied to an exercise. Unfortunately, you do not find out until some time later (often the next day) whether you did the exercise correctly. With *English 2600* you discover immediately whether your answer is right or wrong. At this point something very interesting and mysterious happens. The instant you find out you are right, the idea "takes root," so to speak, in your brain. This does not happen as successfully when time (even a moment or two) is allowed to elapse before you discover that you are right.

Finding out immediately that you are right is called *reinforcement*, and the quicker and more often this happens, the better you learn and remember. A reinforcement is something like a reward; and if you have ever taught a dog tricks, you know from experience how the biscuits speed up learning.

4. With programmed instruction you can advance at your own speed. Since you work by yourself, no one needs to wait for you, and you don't need to wait for anyone else. Many students complete an entire course of study in a fraction of the time usually required by the traditional textbook method. The time you save by this method can be used profitably in other language activities.

How to Use *English 2600*

Each step, or frame, requires that you perform some operation. For example, in many of the frames you will do one of two things:

1. If there is a blank line, write in the missing word or letter.

   Example: Jones is the name of a ***person*.**

2. If there are two or more words or letters in parentheses, underline the correct answer.

   Example: Jones is the name of a *(person, place)*.

(Note: Your instructor will tell you whether to write your answers in this book, in a notebook, or on sheets of paper.)

The first work frame is Frame 2 (on page 3). After you complete Frame 2, turn to Frame 3, *in the same position* on the next *right-hand* page (page 5). In the column to the left of Frame 3, you will find the correct answer to Frame 2. If your answer is not correct, turn back and correct it before doing Frame 3. You will always find the answer to a frame in the column to the left of the frame that you are to do next. Thus you find the answer to Frame 3 to the left of Frame 4, the answer to Frame 4 to the left of Frame 5, and so on.

Go completely through the book, taking only the top gray frame on each *right-hand* page (3, 5, 7, 9, 11, and so on) until you reach the end. When you reach the end of the book, turn back to page 1 and follow the second band—a white one—through the book, still working only on the *right-hand* pages. Then proceed to the third horizontal band, which is gray, going through all the *right-hand* pages. Continue in this way through the fourth, fifth, and sixth bands. When you come to the last white band on the last *right-hand* page (Frame 1320), turn back to page 2 and start reading the gray bands at the top of the *left-hand* pages. Continue through the book, following each horizontal band through the *left-hand* pages. The last frame is 2633 on page 436.

The alternating bands of white and gray will make it easy for you to stay on the same horizontal band as you advance through the book. Since both frame and answer are numbered (each in the lower right corner), you will always know where you are and where to go next.

The Writing Applications

The writing applications in the second part of this book correspond to the units on grammar, sentence-building, usage, and punctuation in the first part. They are designed to complement the programmed instruction so that you can use the information you have already learned in your writing. The writing applications give you the opportunity to apply directly the principles of grammar and usage you mastered in the first part of the book.

Each writing application asks you to write about a topic, using a six-stage process, called the *writing process*. Learning to use the writing process will enable you to plan, compose, and revise more quickly, easily, and accurately.

How to Use the Writing Applications

Preceding the writing applications is a basic introduction to the writing process. Read this information carefully before you complete your first writing application. Then use this section for reference whenever you want to review the basic concepts and stages of the writing process.

Following the introduction to the writing process are the writing applications. There are two or three writing applications for each unit. Your teacher will tell you exactly which writing applications to complete and when.

Each writing application follows a specific order that will enable you to practice using the stages of the writing process. Each application begins with an introductory paragraph and examples of a particular writing skill that you will be asked to demonstrate. Following this information is a writing assignment, which gives you the opportunity to plan and write your first draft.

Since evaluation is an important stage in the writing process, each writing assignment is followed by an evaluation checklist. The checklist will enable you to analyze your writing for weaknesses. Thus you always have the opportunity to revise your writing before you prepare a final version. The writing applications and the programmed instruction, although different in several ways, are alike in that they have you follow a step-by-step process that enables you to evaluate your own progress.

Each application concludes with steps for revising, proofreading, and writing a final version.

Getting the Most from *English 2600*

1. Whenever you are unsure about the correct answer to a frame, read the frame again very carefully, looking for clues. You will generally find a clue that guides you to the right answer. As the lesson advances, fewer and fewer clues will be given; so if you make a mistake, you will need to go back a few frames to try to correct your thinking. If you still don't understand where your mistake lies, ask your instructor for help.

2. Take as much time as you need in figuring out your answer. But once you write your answer, turn immediately to the next frame to check its correctness. Scientific experiment has proved that the more quickly you check your answer, the better you learn. *Even the delay of a few seconds makes a big difference.*

3. Don't cheat yourself out of the valuable experience of thinking. Don't look at the answer in the next frame until *after* you have figured it out for yourself. Thinking things through takes effort, but it is this kind of effort that results in the most effective kind of learning. You are not working for grades on these lessons because the lessons will not be scored. In fact, you will always end with a perfect score because you are expected to correct each error immediately (and you will probably make very few). However, your instructor may want to evaluate your work by administering and scoring the tests that accompany *English 2600.* "Peeking ahead" for the answer will not give you the reasoning ability you will need to pass the tests.

If you use *English 2600* in the mature way in which it is designed to be used, you may discover that, working at your own pace, you have achieved a better command of the fundamentals of your language—and in a much shorter time. You may also find that you have developed your ability to think and concentrate in ways that will help you in your other studies. You will have profited from letting science help you with its most recent and exciting discoveries about how people learn.

Contents

UNIT 1: **THE VERB AND ITS SUBJECT**

Lesson 1 What Makes a Sentence?

[Frames 2–32]

---

bath

220

Luis invited . . . (Whom?)

Luis invited his best friend.

The word that completes the meaning of the verb **invited** is

______________.

221

---

feels, looks

440

A linking verb must always be completed by a subject complement.

A subject complement is so called because it completes the meaning of the verb and describes or identifies the

______________.

441

---

b

660

If you can move a modifier to another position in the sentence, it is likely to be an (*adverb, adjective*).

661

---

map

880

Here, again, are the **pronouns** that can be used as clause signals to start **adjective clauses:**

ADJECTIVE CLAUSE SIGNALS: **who (whom, whose), which, that**

Are these the same signal words that start adverb clauses? (*Yes, No*)

881

S F

1100

Slipping through a hole in the fence. The rabbit disappeared.

____ ____

1101

sits

1320

To set means "to put or to place something." Never use this word unless you name the "something" that is put or placed somewhere (or use a pronoun in its place).

You can set (put) the bag on the floor.

What is the "something" that you can **set** (put) on the floor?

It is the ______.

1321

---

are

1539

The trees on the hillside (*prevent, prevents*) **soil erosion.**

1540

---

most

1758

With some words, we have the choice of forming the second degree by adding either **-er** or **more** and of forming the third degree by adding either **-est** or **most.**

Let's play a livelier game.

or: **Let's play a ________ lively game.**

1759

Karen's

1977

Yours writes better than Gails.

Which underlined word does *not* require an apostrophe because it is a pronoun? ____________

1978

~~C~~aptain, ~~M~~ajor

2196

Cross out each capital letter that is not correct:

Rosa's Mother asked my Father to drive Juan to school.

2197

March,

2415

We shall be at the Fongs' house in Houston from June 18 to the end of the month.

2416

Here is a *complete sentence* of only two words:

Birds fly.

We know what this sentence is about. It is not about *dogs* or *horses*. It is about ________.

2

---

friend

Some verbs can be either complete or incomplete, depending on the sense in which they are used.

a. **The weather changed.**

b. **Bob changed the tire.**

In which sentence does the verb **changed** require a noun to complete the intended meaning? ___

221 222

---

subject

a. **Carmen's favorite instrument is the** *guitar*.
b. **Carmen played the** *guitar* **at the party.**

In which sentence is *guitar* a subject complement? ___

441 442

---

adverb

A preposition is a word that shows the ____________ between the noun or pronoun that follows it and some other word in the sentence.

661 662

No

Use **who (whom, whose)** to refer to **persons.**

Underline the correct pronoun for the clause signal:

The witness (*which, who*) *had seen the accident* **could not be found.**

881 882

F S

A passer-by, seeing our difficulty. Came over to our car.

___ ___

1101 1102

bag 1321	Once again, **to sit** means "to take a sitting position" or "to be in place." In which of the following sentences does this definition fit —*a* or *b*? a. **I prefer to . . . in the balcony.** b. **Don't . . . the hot pan on the table.** 1322
prevent 1540	**One of the women** (*remind, reminds*) **me of my mother.** 1541
more 1759	**This is the pleasantest spot in the park.** or: **This is the ________ pleasant spot in the park.** 1760
Yours 1978	**My friends car was behind ours.** Which underlined word does *not* require an apostrophe because it is a pronoun? ____________ 1979
~~M~~other, ~~F~~ather 2197	In this and the following frames, copy only the words that require capitalization, adding the needed capitals: **Langston Hughes's poem "mother to son" is very moving.** ________________________________ 2198
None 2416	**We will be staying at Columbine Lodge Denver from Monday July 1 through Saturday July 6.** (Add five commas.) 2417

birds

Birds . . .

Birds fly is a sentence, but the word **birds** by itself is not a ______________.

2 | 3

---

b

Fred laughed.

Fred tore . . .

Both verbs—**laughed** and **tore**—show actions.

Which of these action verbs fails to make a *complete* statement about the subject **Fred?** ______________

222 | 223

---

a

1 ⟶ 2

a. **Howard polished his** ______________.

1 ⟵ 1

b. **Howard was our best** ______________.

Which sentence would be completed by a subject complement? ____

442 | 443

---

relationship

The noun or pronoun that follows a preposition is called its (*object, subject*).

662 | 663

---

who

Use **which** to refer to **things** or **animals.**

Underline the correct pronoun for the clause signal:

A dog (*which, who*) *has been properly trained* **will not chase cars.**

882 | 883

F F

John Neihardt wrote *Black Elk Speaks.* **A book about a Sioux Holy Man.**

____ ____

1102 | 1103

a 1322	**I prefer to . . . in the balcony.** The meaning we want is "to take a sitting position." Therefore, the correct word is ______. 1323
reminds 1541	**The car with many extras** *(cost, costs)* **$15,000.** 1542
most 1760	Never use both **-er** and **more** or both **-est** and **most** with the same word. This is needless duplication. a. **Let's play a more livelier game.** b. **Let's play a more lively game.** Which sentence is wrong because both **-er** and **more** are used with the same word? ___ 1761
ours 1979	Which words can show ownership without the use of apostrophes—*nouns* or *pronouns*? ____________ 1980
Mother, Son 2198	Copy the words that require capitals: **His father is a close friend of superintendent Andrews and mayor Sanders.** ____________________ 2199
Lodge, Denver, Monday, July 1, Saturday, 2417	**Jack Karr of Baltimore will wrestle Sam Lutz of Chicago at Soldiers' Field Chicago.** 2418

sentence

3

The word **birds** by itself merely *names* a topic that we might talk about. To make a sentence of it, we must *tell* something about ________.

4

---

tore

223

Fred tore . . . (What?)

What did Fred tear—his hair, his sock, or his shirt? The sentence fails to tell *what* received the action of the verb **tore.** Therefore, the meaning of the sentence is (*complete, incomplete*).

224

---

b

443

a. **The Chungs were frequent** *visitors* **in our home.**
b. **My parents invited many** *visitors* **to our home.**

In which sentence is the italicized word a subject complement? ____

444

---

object

663

A group of words that begins with a preposition and ends with its object is called a ________________ *phrase.*

664

---

which

883

Use **that** to refer to anything—**persons, things,** or **animals.** Underline the correct pronoun:

The clerk (*which, that*) *waited on me* **was very helpful.**

884

S F

1103

Ann Corey, the owner of the boat. Gave us permission to use it.

____ ____

1104

sit

1323

Here are the forms of the verb **sit:**

PRESENT	SIMPLE PAST	PAST WITH HELPER
sit (on chair)	**sat**	**have sat**

The two past forms of **sit** are (*different, alike*).

1324

---

costs

1542

The printing on these sheets (*come, comes*) **out in the wash.**

1543

---

a

1761

a. **The de luxe model is fancier than the standard.**
b. **The de luxe model is more fancy than the standard.**
c. **The de luxe model is more fancier than the standard.**

The above sentences are correct except for sentence ____.

1762

---

pronouns

1980

a. **Our's was parked in front of our neighbors house.**
b. **Ours was parked in front of our neighbor's house.**

Which sentence is correct? ____

1981

Superintendent,
Mayor

2199

This morning father Sanchez and sister Magdalene visited our class.

____

2200

Field,

2418

Eleanor Grayson of 310 Fulton Street was elected mayor of Gotham City.

2419

birds

4

Birds fly.

In this sentence, the word that *tells* something about **birds** is ______.

5

---

incomplete

224

Fred tore his shirt.

Now the meaning of the sentence is complete. We know *what* Fred tore. He tore his **shirt.**

Which word *receives the action* of the verb **tore?** ______

225

---

a

444

a. **Marian Anderson won great** *fame* **all over Europe.**
b. **Marian Anderson became** *famous* **all over Europe.**

In which sentence is the italicized word a direct object?

____

445

---

prepositional

664

A prepositional phrase can be used either as an adjective or an adverb. (*True, False*)

665

---

that

884

The main point to remember is never to use **which** to refer to **persons.**

Underline the correct pronoun:

the teacher (*who, which*)

885

F F

1104

Ann Corey is the owner of the boat. She gave us permission to use it.

____ ____

1105

alike

1324

PRESENT	SIMPLE PAST	PAST WITH HELPER
sit (on a chair)	**sat**	**have sat**

Ernie ________ in the same seat all semester.

1325

---

comes

1543

Lesson 50 Words That Mean One

[Frames 1545–1573]

---

c

1762

a. **This was the most happiest day in my life.**
b. **This was the happiest day in my life.**

Which sentence is right because it avoids duplication? ____

1763

---

b

1981

Make a special effort to hold back your apostrophes whenever you write these words:

POSSESSIVE PRONOUNS

his	**its** (**its** name)	**yours**
hers	**ours**	**theirs**

Which of the above pronouns means "belonging to it"? ________

1982

Father, Sister

2200

I received gifts from my uncle George, aunt Helen, and my two cousins.

____

2201

None

2419

Every address in the United States has a ZIP Code number. Write this number after the state with no comma between them. The state and ZIP Code number form a single unit. Supply the necessary commas:

You can write Pete at 5225 Cornelius Avenue Indianapolis Indiana 46208 until July 15.

2420

fly 5	**Birds fly.** This sentence doesn't tell us that birds *eat, sleep,* or *sing.* It tells us that birds ______. 6
shirt 225	**Wilt Chamberlain praised the coach.** Which word *receives the action* of the verb **praised?** _____ 226
a 445	a. **The President gave a medal to the** *astronaut.* b. **The President gave the** *astronaut* **a medal.** In which sentence is the italicized word an indirect object? ____ 446
True 665	A prepositional phrase that modifies a noun or pronoun is called an ________________ *phrase.* A prepositional phrase that modifies a verb is called an ________________ *phrase.* 666
who 885	Underline the correct pronoun: **the elephant** (*who, which*) 886
S S 1105	**Being interested in music. I made my report on Paul Robeson. A great American singer of the twentieth century.** ____ ____ ____ 1106

sat

1325

Ernie sat in the same seat all semester.

If we added the helper **has** to the verb, would we need to change the word **sat?** (*Yes, No*)

1326

The words **each, every, either,** and **neither** can be used as adjectives and (except for **every**) also as pronouns.

Each **one** *Either* **boy**
Every **house** *Neither* **road**

When these words modify nouns or pronouns, they are used as ______________.

1545

---

b

1763

In this and the following frames, underline the correct form of the adjective or adverb:

Personality is (*importanter, more important*) **than good looks.**

1764

---

its

1982

Do not confuse the possessive (ownership) pronoun **its** with the contraction **it's (= it is).**

a. **What is its name?**
b. **It's time to eat.**

In which sentence does the underlined word show ownership? ____

1983

Uncle, Aunt

2201

Lesson 71 Capitals—Not Too Many, Not Too Few

[Frames 2203–2226]

Avenue,
Indianapolis,
46208,

2420

Supply the necessary commas:

I wrote to Ebony 820 South Michigan Avenue Chicago IL 60605 for a back issue of the magazine.

(Remember that the state and ZIP Code number which follows it are a single unit.)

2421

fly 6	To tell about something means to make a statement about it. **Birds fly.** The word **fly** makes a statement about ________. 7
coach 226	Sometimes the word that completes the verb *receives the action.* At other times, it *shows the result of the action.* **Arthur prepares his own breakfast.** Which word *shows the result of the action* of the verb **prepares?** ________ 227
b 446	Words that are used to connect words or groups of words are called ____________. 447
adjective adverb 666	A phrase that is separated by other words from the word it modifies is likely to be an (*adjective, adverb*) *phrase.* 667
which 886	Underline the correct pronoun: **any store** (*that, who*) 887
F S F 1106	Lesson **36** **Run-on Sentences: Three Guilty Words** [Frames 1108–1137] *page 13*

No

1326

To set means "to put or to place something."

You can't just put—you have to put *something*. Unless the sentence names this "something," this is not the word you want.

Don't set the hot pan on the table.

The "something" in this sentence is __________.

1327

adjectives

1545

Each **comes in a box.**
Either **fits you well.**
Neither **plans to go.**

When these words are used in place of nouns, they are _______________.

1546

more important

1764

Is Mark (*older, more older*) **than Floyd?**

1765

a

1983

a. **What is its name?**
b. **It's time to eat.**

In which sentence is the underlined word a contraction for the two words **It is?** ___

1984

Too many capitals are as bad as too few. Let's look at some groups of **common nouns** that should *not* be capitalized.

ANIMALS: **collie, spaniel, tiger, panther**
BIRDS: **robin, pheasant, woodpecker, crow**

Supply the missing letters:

At the zoo we saw ___lephants and ___iraffes.

2203

Ebony, Avenue, Chicago, IL 60605,

2421

Lesson 78 Unit Review

[Frames 2423–2441]

page 14

birds 7	A group of words that both names something and makes a ________ about it is a **complete sentence.** 8
breakfast 227	A word in the predicate that *receives the action* or *shows the result* of this action is called a **direct object.** **Mom repaired the bicycle.** The noun **bicycle** *receives the action* of the verb **repaired** and is therefore a ________ ________. 228
conjunctions 447	Three common conjunctions are ______, ______, and ______. 448
adverb 667	a. **I learned about boats from my aunt.** b. **The letter from my aunt contained a check.** In which sentence is the underlined prepositional phrase an adverb phrase? ____ 668
that 887	Underline the correct pronoun: **the nurse** (*which, who*) 888
	Erving made a free throw. **The crowd went wild.** These are two separate and complete sentences. A period shows where the first sentence ends, and a ________ letter shows where the second sentence begins. 1108

pan 1327	PRESENT SIMPLE PAST PAST WITH HELPER **set** (put) **set** **have set** Does the word **set** change in any of the verb's three forms? (*Yes, No*) 1328
pronouns 1546	The following words are singular. We know this because we can use the word *one* with each of them. **each (each** *one***)** **either (either** *one***)** **every (every** *one***)** **neither (neither** *one***)** In the sentence below, which verb agrees with the singular subject **one?** ______ **Each one** (*is, are*) **in its place.** 1547
older 1765	**Our new house is** (*more comfortable, comfortabler*) **than our old one.** 1766
b 1984	**It's** (= **It is) time to eat.** The apostrophe in the contraction **It's** takes the place of the missing letter ____. 1985
e, g 2203	The name **collie** would apply to *any* dog of this breed. The name of a *particular* dog might be **Lassie** or **Prince.** **The name of our collie was blondie.** In this sentence, capitalize (*collie, blondie*). 2204
	In this and the following frames, supply the necessary commas. Not every sentence requires a comma. Some sentences require commas according to more than one rule. **Can you come to my graduation Shirley on Friday June 21?** 2423

statement

8

Birds fly.

This little sentence is like most sentences because it has ________ parts: a *naming part* and a *telling part.*

9

---

direct object

228

The cashier made a mistake.

Because it *shows the result of the action* of the verb **made,** the direct object is the noun ________________.

229

---

and, but, or

448

a. **One of my brothers washed and wiped all the dishes.**
b. **Andrea and my brother washed all the dishes.**

Which sentence has compound verbs? ____

449

---

a

668

Underline *two* prepositional phrases:

The future of our country depends on its schools.

669

---

who

888

Now we shall continue to combine sentences by changing one of them to an adjective clause.

Jenny had an *uncle. He* **was very kind to her.**

First, we find a word in the second sentence (*He*) that means the same as a word in the first sentence (________).

889

---

capital

1108

Erving made a free throw. **The crowd went wild.**

Erving made a free throw, *and* **the crowd went wild.**

We have now combined these two sentences into a single (*complex, compound*) sentence.

1109

No

Mother . . . the pie on the window sill to cool.

This sentence names the "something" that was put somewhere. It was a **pie.**

Therefore, our verb should be a form of (*sit, set*).

1328 | 1329

---

is

a. **Each one is in its place.**

b. **Each is in its place.**

The subject of sentence *a* is the pronoun **one.**

The subject of sentence *b* is the pronoun ________.

1547 | 1548

---

more comfortable

The weather gets (*more cold, colder*) **at night.**

1766 | 1767

---

i

Write the contraction of the words **It is.** ________

1985 | 1986

Blondie

There never was a cocker more affectionate than duke.

In this sentence, capitalize (*cocker, duke*).

2204 | 2205

---

graduation,
Shirley, Friday,

Add any necessary commas:

Joe Louis a worker in a Detroit automobile plant became the world's heavyweight champion in 1937.

2423 | 2424

two

9

Flowers fade.

In this sentence, __________ is the *naming part,* and __________ is the *telling part.*

10

---

mistake

229

A direct object receives the __________ of the verb or shows the __________ of this action.

230

---

a

449

a. **Mrs. Yashido showed** *Mother* **and** *Rayna* **her beautiful garden.**
b. **Mrs. Yashido showed them her** *house* **and** *garden.*

In which sentence are the italicized words compound indirect objects? ____

450

---

of our country, on its schools

669

UNIT 4: **BUILDING BETTER SENTENCES**

Lesson 23 Recognizing Compound Sentences

[Frames 671–707]

---

uncle

889

who

Jenny had an *uncle.* ~~**He**~~ **was very kind to her.**

Next, we change the second sentence into an adjective clause by putting the clause signal *who* in place of the word __________.

890

---

compound

1109

Erving made a free throw, *and* **the crowd went wild.**

The two statements of this compound sentence are held together by the conjunction ________, with a comma before it.

1110

set

1329

Mother set the pie on the window sill to cool.

If we added the helper **had** to the verb, would we need to change the word **set?** (*Yes, No*)

1330

Each

1548

a. **Either one is a bargain.**

b. **Either is a bargain.**

The subject of sentence *a* is the pronoun **one.**

The subject of sentence *b* is the pronoun ______________.

1549

---

colder

1767

It is the (*beautifullest, most beautiful*) **car I have ever seen.**

1768

It's

1986

a. **See if its ready.**

b. **Where is its mother?**

In which sentence should **its** be written *without* an apostrophe because it is a possessive pronoun? ____

1987

Duke

2205

After tweety escaped, Father never wanted another parakeet.

In this sentence, capitalize (*tweety, parakeet*).

2206

Joe Louis, plant,

2424

Add any necessary commas:

An aluminum screen will not rust or warp or swell under any weather conditions.

2425

Flowers (naming part)
fade (telling part)

10

Glass breaks.

In this sentence, ____________ is the *naming part*, and ____________ is the *telling part*.

11

---

action, result

230

PATTERN 2:

Subject—Action Verb → Direct Object

This, our second sentence pattern, consists of three parts.

The hot weather in July drove many people to the beaches.

The third part of the framework of this sentence is the direct object ______________.

231

---

a

450

a. **The heavy rain flooded** *streets* **and** *basements.*
b. **Two certainties of life are** *death* **and** *taxes.*

In which sentence are the italicized words compound subject complements? ___

451

Glen | buys old cars.

This sentence can be divided into two major parts: the **complete subject** and the **complete pred__________.**

671

He

890

a. **He was very kind to her.**
b. *who was very kind to her*

We changed *a*, which is a sentence, to *b*, which is a ____________.

891

---

and

1110

a. **Erving made a free throw, and the crowd went wild.**
b. **Erving made a free throw, the crowd went wild.**

Which sentence is wrong because there is no conjunction to hold the two statements together? ___

1111

No

1330

Here are the two verbs to compare:

PRESENT	SIMPLE PAST	PAST WITH HELPER
sit (on a chair)	**sat**	**have sat**
set (put)	**set**	**have set**

The simple past form of **sit** is ______, but the simple past form of **set** is ______.

1331

Either

1549

Neither (*is, are*) **a bargain.**

Which verb agrees with the subject **Neither?** ______

1550

---

most beautiful

1768

Rhode Island is the (*smallest, most small*) **state in the Union.**

1769

---

b

1987

a. **It's not in its cage.**
b. **Its not in it's cage.**

Which sentence is correct? ____

1988

Tweety

2206

Here are some more common nouns that should *not* be capitalized:

TREES: **pine, maple, oak, birch**
FLOWERS: **rose, orchid, aster, dandelion**

Supply the missing letters:

There was a bed of ____oses around the ____ine tree.

2207

None

2425

In the early days of the industry each automobile was practically made by hand and the price of cars was very high.

2426

Glass
(naming part)
breaks
(telling part)

11

Water freezes.

In this sentence, **Water** is the ______________ *part,* and **freezes** is the ______________ *part.*

12

---

people

231

When a sentence includes a direct object, as well as a subject and an action verb, it has three parts.

a. **The driver of the other car accepted the blame.**
b. **The driver of the other car apologized.**

Which sentence is built around a *three-part* framework—*a* or *b*? ____

232

---

b

451

A verb that is used before the main verb to express our meaning more exactly is called a ______________ verb.

452

(pred)icate

671

Glen and Rosa | **buy old cars.**

Although the complete subject now contains two simple subjects, the sentence can still be divided into ______ major parts. (How many?)

672

---

clause

891

Jenny had an uncle *who was very kind to her.*

The clause *who was very kind to her* is an adjective clause because it modifies the noun ____________.

892

---

b

1111

WRONG: **Erving made a free throw, the crowd went wild.**

This sentence is wrong because a comma by itself can't hold the two statements of a compound sentence together.

A ______________________ is needed after the comma.

1112

Answer	Frame
(sit) sat (set) set 1331	**to sit** **to set** Which of these verbs means "to take a sitting position" or "to be in place"? __________ 1332
is 1550	The singular words **each, every, either,** and **neither** are often followed by an **of** phrase with a plural noun. Do not let this plural noun trick you into using a plural verb. A verb does not agree with the object of a preposition. It agrees with its __________. 1551
smallest 1769	**Lucille ordered the** (*most expensive, expensivest*) **sandwich on the menu.** 1770
a 1988	Underline the correct word in each pair: **Amy put** (*her's, hers*) **in with** (*their's, theirs*). 1989
r, p 2207	Capitalize a proper adjective that modifies a common noun. **French poodle** **African violet** **Scotch pine** **One sees very few russian wolfhounds.** In the above sentence, capitalize (*russian, wolfhounds*). 2208
industry, hand, 2426	**I wrote to the Sterling Stamp Co. 1600 Jefferson Ave. Buffalo NY 14208 for their latest price list.** 2427

naming, telling

12

A complete sentence usually has ______ parts. (How many?)

13

---

a

232

The driver of the other car accepted the blame.

The noun **blame** is the ______ ______ of the verb **accepted.**

233

---

helping

452

a. **surely, soon, always, really, not**
b. **must, will, should, may, could, might**

Which group consists of helping verbs? ___

453

---

two

672

Glen and Rosa | buy old cars and rebuild them.

Now the complete subject has two parts connected by the word **and,** and the complete predicate also has two parts connected by the word ______.

673

---

uncle

892

The paper printed a *notice.* **Few people saw** *it.*

The pronoun *it,* in the second sentence, means the same as the noun ______ in the first sentence.

893

---

conjunction

1112

WRONG: **Erving made a free throw, the crowd went wild.**

A sentence like this is called a **run-on sentence.**

In a run-on sentence, one sentence "runs on" into another without a conjunction to connect them or a period and a capital to *sep*______ them.

1113

to sit 1332	In this and the following frames, underline the correct verb in each pair: **There was no place to** *(sit, set)* **down and wait.** 1333
subject 1551	**One is a bargain.** **Every one is a bargain.** Both sentences have the same subject—the pronoun ____. 1552
most expensive 1770	**Ralph ordered the** *(most cheap, cheapest)* **sandwich on the menu.** 1771
hers, theirs 1989	*(It's, Its)* **too late for** *(it's, its)* **nap.** 1990
Russian 2208	**The oaks were draped with spanish moss.** In this sentence, capitalize *(oaks, spanish, moss)*. 2209
Co., Ave., Buffalo, NY 14208, 2427	**When we first met Rosemary had dark brown hair and wore glasses.** 2428

two

13

We often use the word **subject** to mean *topic;* for example, "What subjects (topics) did you discuss?"

In grammar, we call the *naming part* of a sentence the **subject** because it names the topic that the sentence is about.

Water freezes.

Water is the sub________ of this sentence. 14

---

direct object

233

a. **The argument finally ended.**

b. **Dad finally ended the argument.**

Which sentence is built around a two-part framework—*a* or *b*? ___ 234

---

b

453

A helping verb can be separated from the main verb by another word. (*True, False*) 454

---

and

673

Glen and Rosa | buy old cars and rebuild them.

Because the complete subject has more than one part, we say the subject is **compound.**

Because the complete predicate also has more than one part, we say that the predicate is ______________. 674

---

notice

893

The paper printed a *notice.* **Few people saw ~~it~~.** *which*

which **few people saw.**

First, we change *it* to *which.*

Then we move *which* to the (*beginning, end*) of the clause, where the clause signal belongs. 894

(sep)arate

1113

Erving made a free throw the crowd went wild.

Erving made a free throw, the crowd went wild.

Both sentences—the one with the comma and the one without the comma—are (*correct, run-on*) sentences. 1114

sit

1333

Don't (*sit, set*) **the dish so near the edge of the table.**

1334

---

one

1552

Every one is a bargain.

One is the subject of this sentence.

Can any prepositional phrase that we put after it change the fact that **one** is the subject? (*Yes, No*)

1553

---

cheapest

1771

In this and the following frames, underline the word that will avoid duplication. If you use **more,** don't also use **-er;** if you use **most,** don't also use **-est,** and vice versa.

Aluminum is (*lighter, more lighter*) **than steel.**

1772

It's, its

1990

Does he want to borrow (*yours, your's*) **or** (*ours, our's*)?

1991

Spanish

2209

Do not capitalize—

DISEASES: **flu, mumps, pneumonia, diabetes**

After recovering from tonsilitis, Judy caught the asiatic flu.

In this sentence, capitalize (*tonsilitis, asiatic, flu*).

2210

---

met,

2428

Yes I have complete faith ladies and gentlemen in our democratic form of government.

2429

(sub)ject

14

In grammar, we call the *telling part* of a sentence the **predicate.**

Water freezes.

The **predicate** of this sentence is ________________.

15

---

a

234

a. **The tree behind our garage died.**

b. **Our dog chases cars.**

Which sentence is built around a three-part framework—*a* or *b*? ____

235

True

454

In one of the following sentences, the complete verb is interrupted by a word that is not a verb.

Underline each word of the verb in this sentence only.

The ship will soon be crossing the equator.

The author of this article must have lived in Japan.

455

---

compound

674

Glen and Rosa | buy old cars and rebuild them.

Although both the subject and the predicate are compound, we can still divide the sentence into two parts: the **complete subject** and the **complete** ________________.

675

---

beginning

894

The paper printed a notice *which few people saw.*

The clause *which few people saw* modifies the noun **notice.** It is therefore an ________________ *clause.*

895

---

run-on

1114

As Erving made a free throw, **the crowd went wild.**

This sentence is right. It is not a run-on sentence.

The word group (*before, after*) the comma could not stand by itself as a complete sentence.

1115

set

1334

You can *(sit, set)* **next to us.**

1335

No

1553

Every one (of these suits) is a bargain.

Now a plural noun—**suits**—has appeared between the subject and the verb.

The plural noun **suits** is not the subject. It is the object of the preposition ______.

1554

---

lighter

1772

I was more *(hungrier, hungry)* **than the other boys.**

1773

---

yours, ours

1991

(It's, Its) **mother knows that** *(it's, its)* **crying.**

1992

Asiatic

2210

The Weather Bureau gives each hurricane a person's name to identify it—like **Carol** or **Bob.** However, we do not give each particular case of **measles** or **mumps** a special name like **Barry** or **Winifred.**

Since **measles** or **mumps** means any case of measles or mumps, it *(is, is not)* capitalized.

2211

Yes, faith, gentlemen,

2429

Dale of course apologized to Mr. Bromley and he accepted his apology very graciously.

2430

freezes

15

Predicate is a long word. Let's break it up into three syllables and learn to spell it:

pred-i-cate

The third syllable of **predicate** is ________.

16

---

b

235

Don't mistake other words that may follow the verb for a *direct object.*

To be a *direct object,* a word must either receive the ____________ of the verb or show the ____________ of this action.

236

---

will be crossing

455

UNIT 3: **THE WORK OF MODIFIERS**

Lesson 16 Meet the Adjective

[Frames 457–481]

---

predicate

675

A sentence that can be divided into two parts—a subject and a predicate—is a **simple sentence.**

A **simple sentence** may have a *compound subject* and/or a *compound* ________________.

676

---

adjective

895

After changing a sentence to an adjective clause, be sure to put it next to the word it modifies in the other sentence.

who

Jack forgot to mention the turn. ~~*He*~~ *gave us our directions.*

Does the clause *who gave us our directions* modify **Jack** or **turn?** ________

896

---

before

1115

As Erving made a free throw, **the crowd went wild.**

The word group before the comma is an *adverb* ________.

1116

sit

Why does Pete (*sit, set*) **around waiting for opportunities to come to him?**

1335 | 1336

of

Every one of . . .

No matter how we complete this **of** phrase, the pronoun **one** will remain the subject of this sentence.

For this reason, the verb in this sentence will need to be (*singular, plural*).

1554 | 1555

hungry

Mr. Chin is more (*friendly, friendlier*) **than Miss Sibley.**

1773 | 1774

Its, it's

1992

Lesson 65 "We Boys" and the "–*self*" Pronouns

[Frames 1994–2015]

is not

The measles was spreading throughout the Wicker school.

In this sentence, capitalize (*measles, school*).

2211 | 2212

Dale, course, Mr. Bromley,

Well you should have heard Coach Frankoski talk to the boys between halves.

2430 | 2431

cate

16

Iron bends.

In this sentence, the subject is __________, and the predicate is __________.

17

action, result

236

Larry drove *recklessly.*
Larry drove the *car.*

What did Larry drive—a golf ball, a tractor, or a car?

Is *recklessly* or *car* a direct object? __________

237

a. **dog** b. **large dog**

Does *a* or *b* give us a clearer picture of a dog? ____

457

predicate

676

My mother is Mexican. **My father is Cherokee.**

Each of the above sentences can be divided into a subject and a predicate.

Therefore, each of the above sentences is a __________ sentence.

677

Jack

896

a. **Jack forgot to mention the turn,** *who gave us our directions.*
b. **Jack,** *who gave us our directions,* **forgot to mention the turn.**

Which sentence makes better sense because the clause comes correctly after the noun it modifies? ____

897

clause

1116

As Erving made a free throw, **the crowd went wild.**

This sentence cannot be separated into two sentences.

This sentence, therefore, (*is, is not*) a run-on sentence.

1117

sit

sat **set**

Which one of these past forms means "took a sitting position" or "was in place"? ______

1336 | 1337

---

singular

Underline the correct verb:

Every one (of these 10,000 stamps) (*is, are*) **for sale.**

1555 | 1556

---

friendly

This melon is (*riper, more riper*) **than the other.**

1774 | 1775

How can you tell which form of the pronoun to use in expressions like "*We* boys" and "*Us* girls"?

By omitting the noun that follows the pronoun **we** or **us,** you will see instantly which pronoun is correct.

(*Us, We*) ~~**boys**~~ **need a rest.**

In the above sentence, choose the pronoun ______. 1994

School

Do not capitalize—

FOODS: **spaghetti, chop suey, pizza, brownies**

GAMES: **football, hockey, bingo, bowling**

After the hockey game, we went to an italian restaurant for pizza.

Capitalize (*hockey, italian, pizza*).

2212 | 2213

Well,

Dr. Otaki excused herself and left the party after she received the telephone call.

2431 | 2432

(subject) Iron
(predicate) bends

17

Milk sours.

In this sentence, **Milk** is the ______________, and **sours** is the ______________.

18

---

car

237

Perry cooks the *dinner.*
Perry cooks *well.*

Is *dinner* or *well* a direct object? __________

238

---

b

457

a. **dog** b. **large dog**

Large dog gives us a clearer picture than just the noun **dog** because the word ________ describes the dog.

458

---

simple

677

a. **My mother is English. My father is Cherokee.**
b. **My mother is English, and my father is Cherokee.**

In b, the two simple sentences are joined into a single sentence by the **conjunction,** or connecting word, ______.

678

---

b

897

which
Our yearbook comes out next week. ~~It~~ *sells for a dollar.*

After we change the second sentence to an adjective clause, we should place the clause after the word it modifies.

What is the article *which sells for a dollar*? It is the (*yearbook, week*).

898

---

is not

1117

a. **Erving made a free throw, and the crowd went wild.**
b. **As Erving made a free throw, the crowd went wild.**
c. **Erving made a free throw, the crowd went wild.**

Which sentence is wrong because it is a run-on sentence—*a, b,* or *c*? ____

1118

sat

We (*sat, set*) **too far back to hear well.**

1337 | 1338

---

is

(Remember that a verb agrees with its subject, not with a noun or pronoun that may follow the subject.)

a. **Each was in its place.**
b. **Each (of the tools) was in its place.**

The subject of both sentence *a* and *b* is the singular pronoun ________.

1556 | 1557

---

riper

We saw the (*most fiercest, fiercest*) **gorilla in captivity.**

1775 | 1776

We

We need a rest.
We boys need a rest.

The subject form **We** is correct because it is the subject of the verb ________ in both sentences.

1994 | 1995

Italian

Later in the evening, Wilma read a book while we played chinese checkers.

Capitalize (*book, chinese, checkers*).

2213 | 2214

None

From this point on, draw circles around any commas that should be omitted. In several sentences, all the commas need to be removed.

Expressways, buses, and airlines, take passenger business away from the railroads.

2432 | 2433

(Milk) subject
(sours)
predicate

18

A sentence usually has two parts.

The grammar names for these two parts are **subject** and ________________.

19

---

dinner

238

José brought . . .

The meaning of this subject and verb is incomplete.

We are waiting to hear *whom* or *what* **José** __________.

239

---

large

458

a. **large dog** b. **large brown dog**

Does *a* or *b* give us a clearer and more detailed picture of a dog? ___

459

---

and

678

My mother is Mexican, | and my father is Cherokee.

Can we divide this sentence into two parts—a subject and a predicate? No, each of its two parts now has *its own* subject and predicate.

Is this a **simple sentence?** (*Yes, No*)

679

---

yearbook

898

a. **Our yearbook comes out next week** *which sells for a dollar.*
b. **Our yearbook,** *which sells for a dollar,* **comes out next week.**

Which sentence makes better sense because the adjective clause is properly placed? ___

899

---

c

1118

Run-on sentences are most likely to occur when two sentences are closely related in thought.

WRONG: **The referee blew her whistle, the game ended.**

No matter how closely related in thought two sentences may be, they are still two separate sentences unless they are connected by the ____________________ **and, but,** or **or.**

1119

sat

1338

You (*sat, set*) **the trap where someone might step on it.**

1339

Each

1557

Each (of the tools) was in its place.

The noun **tools** is not the subject of the verb. It is the object of the preposition ______.

1558

---

fiercest

1776

Jamie was the most (*selfish, selfishest*) **child I have ever seen.**

1777

---

need

1995

Will you drive (*we, us*) **girls to the corner?**

To decide which pronoun to use, omit the noun **girls.**

In the above sentence, choose the pronoun ______.

1996

Chinese

2214

Do not capitalize—

OCCUPATIONS: **engineer, lawyer, minister, plumber**
MUSICAL INSTRUMENTS: **piano, violin, accordion, trumpet**

Our doctor plays the french horn as a hobby.

Capitalize (*doctor, french, horn*).

2215

---

airlines(,)

2433

Draw a circle around each comma that should be omitted:

It is doubtful, by the way, whether John can graduate, and go to college.

2434

predicate

19

The predicate makes a statement about the ________.

20

---

brought

239

José brought home a friend from college.

Whom or *what* did **José** bring—a **home,** a **friend,** or a **college?** ________

240

---

b

459

a. **large dog** b. **large brown dog**

In *a*, there is only one word that describes the **dog.**

In *b*, there are ______ words that describe the **dog.**

460

No

679

Our school is small, but we have good teams.

This sentence was made by joining two simple sentences with the conjunction ______.

680

---

b

899

Dad goes to Dr. Foster. *His office is near our house.*

Underline the clause signal you would put in place of *His* in changing the second sentence to an adjective clause.

which **whose** **who** **that**

900

---

conjunction

1119

a. **When the referee blew her whistle, the game ended.**
b. **The referee blew her whistle, the game ended.**
c. **The referee blew her whistle, and the game ended.**

Which sentence is wrong because it is a run-on sentence—*a*, *b*, or *c*? ____

1120

set 1339	**The scouts** (*sat, set*) **around the campfire and told tall stories.** 1340
of 1558	**Each of the tools was in its place.** The subject of this sentence is the singular pronoun __________. 1559
selfish 1777	**I discovered the** (*most easiest, easiest*) **way of making fudge.** 1778
us 1996	**Will you drive <u>us</u> to the corner?** **Will you drive <u>us</u> girls to the corner?** The object form **us** is correct because it is the object of the verb __________. 1997
French 2215	**This stradivarius violin is owned by a chicago banker.** Capitalize (*stradivarius, violin*) and (*chicago, banker*). 2216
graduate(,) 2434	Draw a circle around each comma that should be omitted: **Their fruits, and vegetables are always fresh, and reasonably priced.** 2435

subject

20

wrote talked melted

Each of these words could be the ______________ of a sentence.

21

---

friend

240

José brought home a friend from college.

The noun **friend** receives the action of the verb **brought.** The noun **friend** is the ______________ ______________ of the verb **brought.**

241

---

two

460

The more words that we have describing a noun, the more (*clear, vague*) our mental picture of it becomes.

461

---

but

680

You must shut the gate, or the dog will get out.

This sentence was made by joining two simple sentences with the conjunction _____.

681

---

whose

900

Dad goes to Dr. Foster. ~~*His*~~ *whose* *office is near our house.*

The clause *whose office is near our house* belongs after the noun (*Dad, Dr. Foster*), which it modifies.

901

---

b

1120

Lisa washed the car. The car was very dusty.

These are two complete sentences, each with a subject and a verb. They should be written (*apart, together*).

1121

sat 1340	(An object can *sit* on a table, desk, or stove just as a person can *sit* on a chair.) **This dictionary always** (*sat, set*) **on Ms. Goya's desk.** 1341
Each 1559	Remember the **"Rule of S"**: When we add an *s* to the subject, we do not add an *s* to the verb. When we add an *s* to the verb, we do not add an *s* to the _______________. 1560
easiest 1778	**This is the most** (*handy, handiest*) **tool I have ever used.** 1779
drive 1997	**He offered the use of the gym to** (*we, us*) **fellows.** To decide which pronoun to use, omit the noun **fellows.** In the above sentence, choose the pronoun _____. 1998
Stradivarius, Chicago 2216	**The minister of Bethel church plays the cello very well.** Capitalize (*minister, church, cello*). 2217
fruits(,) fresh(,) 2435	**I was still holding the king of spades, the queen of spades, and two aces, in my hand at the end of the game.** 2436

predicate

21

bread **pencil** **engine**

Each of these words could be the ________ of a sentence.

22

---

direct object

241

In analyzing sentences, we shall use *S* for *subject*, *V* for *verb*, and *DO* for *direct object*.

Most Americans eat three meals a day.

Label the three-part framework of this sentence:

S ____ ____
Americans **eat** **meals.**

242

---

clear

461

Each of the following two-word phrases gives you a different picture of a dog, doesn't it?

large dog **old dog**
small dog **brown dog**

The word that changes your picture of the dog is the (*first*, *second*) word in each phrase.

462

---

or

681

A sentence made by joining two (or more) simple sentences with the conjunction **and, but,** or **or** is called a **compound sentence.**

The most common conjunctions that connect the two parts of a compound sentence are **and, but,** and ____.

682

Dr. Foster

901

In this and the following frames, combine each pair of sentences by changing the italicized sentence to an adjective clause. Write the full sentence in the blank space.

Ernie had a sore shoulder. *It prevented him from pitching.*

____

____

902

---

apart

1121

It
Lisa washed the car. ~~The car~~ was very dusty.

Since **car** is mentioned in the first sentence, we do not need to repeat the noun **car** in the second sentence.

Therefore we can put the ________ *It* in place of the noun **car** as the subject of the second sentence.

1122

sat

have sat **have set**

Which of these helper forms is a form of the verb **sit,** which means "to take a sitting position" or "to be in place"?

____

1341 | 1342

subject

Every one of these suits (*fit*, *fits*) **you well.**

Since **one,** the subject of this sentence, does not end in *s*, which verb would you choose? __________

1560 | 1561

handy

Lesson 58 One *No* Is Enough!

[Frames 1781–1806]

1779

us

He offered the use of the gym to <u>us</u>.
He offered the use of the gym to <u>us</u> fellows.

The object form **us** is correct because **us** is the object of the preposition ______.

1998 | 1999

Church

Underline the words that require capitals:

Last sunday, my mom played golf with coach Harris at Brookside park.

2217 | 2218

aces (1)

You can read, *Huckleberry Finn,* in one, or two evenings.

2436 | 2437

subject

22

arrives **Henry**

Which word could be used as the subject of a sentence?

____

23

V DO
eat meals

242

The old man always wears his hat in the house.

The framework of this sentence is:

S	V	DO
man	________	________

243

---

first

462

In grammar, we frequently use the word **modify.** *To modify* means *to change*. To modify the body style of a car means to change its style.

After your mother *modifies* a recipe, the recipe is (*the same, different*).

463

---

or

682

______ __________ { **, and** / **, but** / **, or** } ______ __________.

Notice that in a compound sentence there is a subject and a predicate both *before* and *after* the __________, or connecting word.

683

Ernie had a sore shoulder that (which) prevented him from pitching.

902

He gave facts about crime. *They startled everyone.*

____

____

903

---

pronoun

1122

a. **The car was very dusty.**
b. **It was very dusty.**

Both *a* and *b* are complete sentences.

If we were writing only one sentence, without any others, we would write sentence (*a*, *b*). ____

1123

have sat 1342	**You should have** (*sat, set*) **the bottles right on ice.** 1343
fits 1561	**Every one of these stones** (*come, comes*) **from a different state.** Which word is the subject of this sentence—**one** or **stones?** __________ 1562
	Yes is a positive word. **No** is a negative word. **Something** is a positive word. **Nothing** is a __________ word. 1781
to 1999	a. (*We, Us*) **boys decorated the gym.** b. **The gym was decorated by** (*we, us*) **boys.** Is the object form **us** correct in sentence *a* or *b*? ___ 2000
Sunday, Coach, Park 2218	**His brother has been in the Clippert hospital with pneumonia since labor day.** 2219
read(,) Huckleberry Finn(,) one(,) 2437	**Call for your dry cleaning at, 1075 Prentis Avenue, after Tuesday, May 10.** 2438

Henry 23	**elephants** **returned** Which word could be used as the predicate of a sentence? _______________ 24
V DO wears hat 243	**My very best pen recently disappeared.** The framework of this sentence is: S ____________ V ____________ 244
different 463	*To modify* means *to change.* **brown dog** **black dog** When we say that **brown** and **black** modify the noun **dog,** we really mean that they __________ our picture or idea of the dog. 464
conjunction 683	A **simple sentence** *cannot* be divided into two separate sentences. A __________ **sentence** *can* be divided into two separate sentences. 684
He gave facts about crime that (which) startled everyone. 903	**Mr. Dell would not take any money.** *He owns the boat.* ____________________ ____________________ (Be sure to put the clause next to the noun it modifies.) 904
a 1123	a. **The car was very dusty.** b. **It was very dusty.** If the sentence were to follow another sentence that already mentioned the **car,** we would write sentence (*a, b*). ___ 1124

set 1343	**His hat looked as if someone had** (*sat, set*) **on it.** 1344
one 1562	**Every one of these stones** (*come, comes*) **from a different state.** Since **one,** the subject of this sentence, does not end in *s*, which verb would you choose? ________ 1563
negative 1781	a. **some ever something anybody someone either** b. **none never nothing nobody no one neither** Which group of words is negative? ___ 1782
b 2000	**The gym was decorated by us.** **The gym was decorated by us boys.** The object form **us** is correct because **us** is the object of the preposition _____. 2001
Hospital, Labor Day 2219	In this and the following frames, cross out each capital letter that is not correct: **I saw my first Robin this Spring in my Grandmother's back yard.** 2220
at(,) Avenue(,) 2438	**I wrote, and revised, and copied my composition twice before I turned it in.** 2439

returned 24	**answered** **vegetables** **stumbled** Which word could be used as a subject? ________ 25
S V pen disappeared 244	**His good manners won many friends for him.** S V DO ________ **won** ________ 245
change 464	Words that modify nouns and pronouns are called **adjectives. Adjectives** are another *class* of words. The word **adjective** has three syllables: **ad-jec-tive.** An adjective can modify a ________ or pronoun. 465
compound 684	a. **Our class made birdhouses and sold them.** b. **Our class made birdhouses, and the church sold them.** Which sentence has both a subject and a predicate after the conjunction **and?** ____ 685
Mr. Dell, who owns the boat, would not take any money. 904	**He made an announcement.** *None of us heard it.* ________ ________ 905
b 1124	**Lisa washed the car.** *It* **was very dusty.** *It* **was very dusty** is a complete sentence because we know from the previous sentence that *It* means ________. 1125

sat

1344

The painter had *(sat, set)* **the ladders against a tree.**

1345

---

comes

1563

In this and the following frames, underline the verb that agrees with its subject. Remember that **each, every, either,** and **neither** are either singular themselves or modify singular nouns or pronouns.

Each *(was, were)* **with an escort.**

1564

---

b

1782

not	**none**	**never**	**nothing**
nobody	**no one**	**neither**	**nowhere**

Each of these negative words, just like the word **no,** begins with the letter ____.

1783

---

by

2001

The *"–self"* Pronouns

When using pronouns that end with **–self** or **–selves,** be careful not to use words that do not exist.

WRONG: **theirselves, themself** RIGHT: **themselves**

The Beatles played ______________________ **in the film.**

2002

~~R~~obin, ~~S~~pring, ~~G~~randmother's

2220

Cross out each capital letter that is not correct:

Because of his Appendicitis operation, Pete fell behind in his English and Math courses.

2221

---

wrote(,)
revised(,)

2439

If you know what's good for you, you won't cut across Mr. Kronk's lawn, when you deliver his paper.

2440

vegetables

25

kitchen money boiled

Which word could be used as a predicate? ______________

26

S DO
manners friends

245

The price of oranges suddenly jumped.

S ______________ V ______________

246

---

noun

465

brown dog gentle dog
smart dog obedient dog

The adjectives **brown, smart, gentle,** and **obedient** tell us *what kind* of dog and change our picture or idea of it.

In grammar, we say that these adjectives ______________ the noun **dog.**

466

---

b

685

a. **Our class made birdhouses and sold them.**

b. **Our class made birdhouses, and the church sold them.**

Which sentence can be divided into two separate sentences—*a* or *b*? ____

686

He made an announcement that (which) none of us heard.

905

We saw the African Art Exhibit. *It was at the museum.*

____

____

906

---

car

1125

Not only *it* but other pronouns, too, can start a new sentence.

Charo is musical. *She* **plays several instruments.**

She **plays several instruments** is a complete sentence because we know from the previous sentence that *She* means ______________.

1126

set 1345	**You must have** (*sat, set*) **on some wet paint.** 1346
was 1564	**Each of the girls** (*was, were*) **with an escort.** 1565
n 1783	**doesn't haven't can't won't shouldn't** The **n't** at the end of each of these verbs is a contraction of the negative word ______. 1784
themselves 2002	WRONG: **hisself** RIGHT: **himself** **Albert looked at ______________ in the mirror.** 2003
~~A~~ppendicitis, ~~M~~ath 2221	Cross out each capital letter that is not correct: **We bought our Mother a corsage of red Carnations for Mother's Day.** 2222
lawn, 2440	**Very soon, however, I lost my feeling of strangeness, and began to feel at home.** 2441

boiled 26	**Birds fly.** **Water freezes.** **Iron bends.** **Milk sours.** In the above sentences, the subject comes (*before, after*) the predicate. (Underline the correct answer.) 27
S V price jumped 246	**His funny story about the dog amused everybody.** S V DO **story** __________ __________ 247
modify 466	**A sharp stone cut the tire.** *What kind* of stone cut the tire? The __________ **sharp** modifies the noun **stone.** 467
b 686	a. **Our class made birdhouses and sold them.** b. **Our class made birdhouses, and the church sold them.** Which sentence is a compound sentence? ___ 687
We saw the African Art Exhibit that (which) was at the museum. 906	**Pam saw the lightning strike.** *She was standing at the window.* ____________________ ____________________ 907
Charo 1126	**Elephants are intelligent.** *They* **learn tricks quickly.** *They* **learn tricks quickly** is a complete sentence because we know from the previous sentence that the pronoun *They* stands for __________. 1127

sat

They found the baby (*sitting, setting*) in a mud puddle.

1346 | 1347

---

was

Every one (*is, are*) on sale.

1565 | 1566

---

not

One negative word is all we need to make a negative statement. A second negative word is useless duplication and a sign of poor speech.

a. **I could<u>n't</u> see <u>nothing</u>.**
b. **I could<u>n't</u> see <u>anything</u>.**

Which sentence contains two negative words? ____

1784 | 1785

---

himself

WRONG: **yourselfs** RIGHT: **yourselves**

Why don't you boys make ______________ some lunch?

2003 | 2004

~~M~~other, ~~C~~arnations

My Uncle plays the Organ every Sunday at the Highland Community Church.

2222 | 2223

---

strangeness(,)

2441

UNIT 12: **APOSTROPHES AND QUOTATION MARKS**

Lesson 79 Spotting the Apostrophe

[Frames 2443–2484]

page 54

before

27

In most English sentences, we usually first name what we are talking about; then we make a statement about what we have named.

Most English sentences begin with the ________.

28

V
amused

DO
everybody

247

The heavy rains recently destroyed many crops in our state.

S ________ V ________ DO ________

248

---

adjective

467

A tame brown bear approached us.

What kind of bear approached us?

In this sentence, the two adjectives that modify the noun **bear** are ________ and ________.

468

---

b

687

Our class made birdhouses, and the church sold them.

This is a **compound sentence.**

In a compound sentence, place a comma after the first statement. This comma comes before the ________ **and, but,** or **or.**

688

Pam, who was standing at the window, saw the lightning strike.

907

We have a watchdog. *It would lick the face of a burglar.*

____

____

908

Elephants

1127

Elephants are intelligent, *they* **learn tricks quickly.**

This is an incorrect run-on sentence.

One way to correct it is to separate the two sentences with a period and a capital.

Another way is to connect the two separate sentences with the ________ **and.**

1128

sitting

1347

Lesson **43** **Straightening Out *Rise* and *Raise***

[Frames 1349–1380]

is

1566

Every one of these ties (*is, are*) on sale.

(Did you see the word **one** in this sentence? Watch for it, too, in the sentences ahead!)

1567

a

1785

The error of using two negative words instead of one is called a **double negative.**

a. **Jim doesn't want any more.**
b. **Jim doesn't want no more.**

Which sentence is wrong because it contains a **double negative?** ____

1786

yourselves

2004

WRONG: **ourself, ourselfs** RIGHT: **ourselves**

My dad and I built ________________ a workshop.

2005

~~U~~ncle, ~~O~~rgan

2223

Next Summer, my Cousin will graduate as an electrical Engineer from Cornell University.

2224

Here we have two nouns in a row:

boy's bicycle

Which one of these two nouns indicates the owner?

____

2443

subject

28

In analyzing a sentence, we often underline the subject with one line and the predicate with two lines.

EXAMPLES: **Grass grows.** **Dogs bark.**

Underline this sentence to show the subject (one line) and predicate (two lines):

Ice melts.

29

S V
rains destroyed
DO
crops

248

Lesson 9 The Indirect Object Pattern

[Frames 250–279]

tame, brown

468

So far, our adjectives have told *what kind* about the nouns they modify. Adjectives are also used to point out *which one(s)* we mean.

EXAMPLES: **this dog** **that dish** **these houses** **those cars**

The words **this, that, these,** and **those** are ________.

469

conjunction

688

Our class made birdhouses and sold them.

This is not a compound sentence because there is not a subject and predicate, but only a part of the ________, after the conjunction **and.**

689

We have a watchdog that (which) would lick the face of a burglar.

908

a. **who (whom, whose), which, that**
b. **if, as, when, because, after, although**

The words that can be used as adjective clause signals are those in group (*a*, *b*). ____

909

conjunction

1128

a. **Elephants are intelligent. They learn tricks quickly.**
b. **Elephants are intelligent, they learn tricks quickly.**
c. **Elephants are intelligent, and they learn tricks quickly.**

Which sentence is wrong because it is a run-on sentence—*a*, *b*, or *c*? ____

1129

To rise means "to go up" or "to get up."

Farmers rise early.
The curtain rises on time.

The bubbles of air __________ to the surface.

1349

---

is

1567

Don't forget that a final *s* makes a verb *singular* when it expresses present time.

Either one (*look, looks*) **good on you.**

1568

---

b

1786

WRONG: **Jim doesn't want no more.**

This sentence contains a **double negative.**

The first negative word is **doesn't;** the second negative word is ______.

1787

---

ourselves

2005

All the **–self** pronouns are solid words. Don't split them.

I made (*my self, myself*) **a sandwich.**

2006

S̸ummer,
C̸ousin,
E̸ngineer

2224

Our Principal let the members of the Hansberry Drama Club sell Popcorn at the Football game on Thanksgiving Day.

2225

---

boy's

2443

boy's bicycle

Which noun names what is owned? _______________

2444

Ice melts.

29

Underline this sentence to show the subject and predicate:

Mosquitoes bite.

30

In the previous lesson, we studied two sentence patterns:

PATTERN 1: *Subject—Action Verb*
PATTERN 2: *Subject—Action Verb → Direct Object*

Do both patterns include a direct object? (*Yes, No*)

250

---

adjectives

469

a. **tall glass** **empty glass** **green glass** **broken glass**
b. **this glass** **that glass** **these glasses** **those glasses**

Do the adjectives point out *which glass* or *which glasses* we mean in group *a* or *b*? ____

470

---

predicate

689

Our class made birdhouses and sold them.

The conjunction **and** does not connect two sentences.

It connects two parts of the (*subject, predicate*).

690

---

a

909

Never use the pronoun **which** as a clause signal to refer to (*things, persons*).

910

---

b

1129

The word *then* causes many run-on sentence errors.

WRONG: **Ed looked at the clock,** *then* **he went back to sleep.**
RIGHT: **Ed looked at the clock.** *Then* **he went back to sleep.**

Then is not a conjunction like *and, but,* and *or,* which can join two sentences into a (*compound, complex*) sentence.

1130

rise

1349

A person **rises,** a wind **rises,** the sun **rises,** and a price ____________.

1350

---

looks

1568

Every one of these pieces (*fit, fits*) **somewhere.**

1569

---

no

1787

Mr. Platt could <u>not</u> find work (*nowhere, anywhere*).

To avoid using a double negative, we choose the positive word ________________.

1788

---

myself

2006

We were ashamed of (*ourselves, our selves*).

2007

~~P~~rincipal, ~~P~~opcorn, ~~F~~ootball

2225

My Aunt Harriet's Collie and her Persian Cat are the best of friends.

2226

---

bicycle

2444

boy's bicycle

The apostrophe appears in the word that shows (*the owner, what is owned*).

2445

Mosquitoes bite.

Although all are printed as sentences, only *one* of the following pairs of words really is a sentence. Underline this sentence to show the subject and predicate, as you have been doing.

Cold water. **Before noon.** **Snow falls.** **Broken wheel.**

30 | 31

No

Often an action verb requires another word to show *who* or *what* receives its action or to show the result of this action.

This word often needed to complete the meaning of an action verb is called a *direct* ____________.

250 | 251

---

b

Some words can be used as either pronouns or adjectives.

a. **This is the correct address.**
b. **This address is not correct.**

In which sentence is **This** used as an adjective? ________

470 | 471

---

predicate

Our class made birdhouses and sold them.

A comma (*is, is not*) used before a conjunction that connects the two parts of a compound predicate.

690 | 691

---

persons

Ordinarily, an adjective clause should be put right (*after, before*) the noun or pronoun it modifies.

910 | 911

---

compound

Ed looked at the clock. *Then* **he went back to sleep.**

Then is not a conjunction. It is an adverb that tells (*how, when, where*)—just like the other adverbs in the following sentences:

Then **he went to sleep.** *Soon* **he went to sleep.**
Later **he went to sleep.** *Afterward* **he went to sleep.**

1130 | 1131

rises

1350

To raise means "to lift something."
Don't use this word unless you name the "something" that is lifted (or use a pronoun in its place).

This rope raises (lifts) the curtain.

What is the "something" that the rope **raises?** It is the ______________.

1351

---

fits

1569

Neither one of the doors (*was, were*) **unlocked.**

1570

---

anywhere

1788

The baby can hardly walk.

Does **"hardly walk"** mean "walk poorly" or "walk well"?

____

1789

---

ourselves

2007

(*We, Us*) **boys rented the cottage for a week.**

2008

¢ollie, ¢at

2226

Lesson 72 Unit Review

[Frames 2228–2249]

---

the owner

2445

The apostrophe is a mark we use to show *ownership*. To own something means to possess it. We say, therefore, that a word showing ownership is a *possessive* word.

Alice's trophy was in my friend's locker.

The possessive nouns in this sentence are ______________ and ______________.

2446

Snow falls. 31	Only *one* of the following pairs of words is a sentence. Underline this sentence to show the subject and predicate. **Barking dog. Almost ready. Falling rain. Gas explodes.** 32
object 251	S V **Dad gave an orchid.** The meaning of the action verb **gave** is completed by the direct object ______. 252
b 471	Adjectives also tell **how many** and **how much** about the nouns they modify. HOW MANY? **two cars** **most boys** **several trees** HOW MUCH? **no eggs** **some sugar** **enough bread** All the underlined words above are ______. 472
is not 691	a. **Czonka reached for the ball but missed it.** b. **Czonka reached for the ball but he missed it.** Which sentence requires a comma because it is a compound sentence? ____ 692
after 911	Lesson **30** **Using Adjective Clauses to Improve Sentences** [Frames 913–937]
when 1131	a. **We ordered our lunch.** *Then* **we discovered that we had no money.** b. **We ordered our lunch,** *then* **we discovered that we had no money.** Which is correct—*a* or *b*? ____ 1132

curtain

1351

Once again, **to rise** means "to go up" or "to get up."

In which of the following sentences does this definition fit? —*a* or *b*? ____

a. **We must . . . early on weekday mornings.**
b. **Men usually . . . their hats to our bishop.**

1352

---

was

1570

Which one of us (*is, are*) **to blame?**

1571

---

walk poorly

1789

a. **The baby can hardly walk.**
b. **The baby can't hardly walk.**

If **"hardly walk"** means "walk poorly," which sentence says that the baby *can* walk, but poorly? ____

1790

We

2008

They rented the cottage to (*we, us*) **boys for a week.**

2009

Each of these frames will present a problem based on one of the rules of capitalization presented in this unit.

Try to recall the specific rule which applies before you make your decision.

a. **at Niagara falls** b. **at Niagara Falls**

Which item is correctly capitalized? ____

2228

Alice's, friend's

2446

my mom's office **the girls' gym**
a boy's locker **our soldiers' lives**

Examine carefully the four examples above.

Does the apostrophe always come *before* the final *s*? (*Yes, No*)

2447

Gas explodes.

32

Lesson 2 The Complete Subject and Predicate

[Frames 34–64]

orchid

S V DO
Dad gave *Mother* **an orchid.**

Here we find a noun standing between the action verb and its direct object. This noun is ___________.

252 | 253

adjectives

Lynn bought new tires.

The adjective **new** modifies the noun ___________.

472 | 473

b

Czonka reached for the ball, but he missed it.

Would the comma before the conjunction be needed if we dropped the word **he** from this sentence? (*Yes, No*)

692 | 693

We can form a **compound sentence** by connecting two simple sentences with the conjunction *and, but,* or *or.*

The coat was too loose, and the sleeves were too long.

The two parts of this compound sentence are connected by the conjunction _______.

913

a

Another trouble-maker is the adverb *therefore.*

WRONG: **Our tires were old,** *therefore* **we drove slowly.**
RIGHT: **Our tires were old.** *Therefore* **we drove slowly.**

Therefore is not a conjunction. It can't be used like *and* to connect sentences.

Can the adverb *therefore* begin a new sentence? (*Yes, No*)

1132 | 1133

a | **We must . . . early on weekday mornings.**

The meaning we want is "to get up."

Therefore, the correct word is ________.

1352 | 1353

---

is | **Several of the rooms** (*has, have*) **running water.**

1571 | 1572

---

a | a. **I couldn't scarcely stand up.**
b. **I could scarcely stand up.**

Which sentence says that you *could* stand up, but poorly?

____

1790 | 1791

---

us | (*We, Us*) **students always get the blame.**

2009 | 2010

---

b | a. **a Chinese leader**
b. **a chinese leader**

Which item is correctly capitalized? ____

2228 | 2229

No | How do you decide whether to put an apostrophe *before* or *after* the final *s*? The method is very simple.

A <u>boys locker</u> was left open.

Ask yourself, "Who owns the locker?"

The answer is a ________.

2447 | 2448

Until now we have been working with sentences having a one-word subject and a one-word predicate. Usually, however, subjects and predicates have more than one word.

The lock on the front door stuck.

The part of this sentence that has more than one word is the (*subject, predicate*). 34

Mother

253

S V DO
Dad gave *Mother* **an orchid.**

The noun *Mother* is not another direct object like **orchid.**

The thing that Dad **gave** was not *Mother* but an ______. 254

---

tires

473

Lynn bought ________ new tires.

Underline one of the following adjectives which would tell **how many** tires Lynn bought:

expensive good several these

474

No

693

We talked to the jockey and learned a lot about horses.

A compound sentence can be divided into two simple sentences, each with its own subject and predicate.

Is this a compound sentence? (*Yes, No*)

694

---

and

913

A sentence that contains a clause is called a **complex sentence.**

a. **You received a letter which looks important.**
b. **You received a letter, and it looks important.**

Which sentence is **complex** because it contains an adjective clause? ___ 914

Yes

1133

a. **Our tires were old,** *therefore* **we drove slowly.**
b. **Our tires were old, and** *therefore* **we drove slowly.**

Which sentence is correct? ___

1134

rise

1353

Here are the forms of the verb **rise:**

PRESENT	SIMPLE PAST	PAST WITH HELPER
rise (go up)	**rose**	**have risen**

Supply the correct past form of the verb **rise:**

The storm __________ soon after dark.

1354

---

have

1572

Neither of these snapshots (*look, looks*) **a bit like you.**

1573

---

b

1791

The car (*would, wouldn't*) **hardly start.**
The car (*would, wouldn't*) **scarcely start.**

Although the car started with difficulty, the fact is that it *did* start.

Therefore, we choose the word (*would, wouldn't*). 1792

We

2010

What did she say about (*us, we*) **girls?**

2011

---

a

2229

a. **St. Mary's Catholic Church**
b. **a new Catholic Church**

Which item is correctly capitalized? ____

2230

---

boy

2448

Since the answer to your question is **boy,** put the apostrophe after the word **boy.**

A boy's locker was left open.

The apostrophe goes after the letter ____.

2449

subject

34

Diego **graduated.**
My best friend **graduated.**
One of the boys in our club **graduated.**

In how many of the above sentences does the subject have more than one word? ____

35

---

orchid

254

S V DO
Dad gave *Mother* **an orchid.**

The noun *Mother* shows *to whom* Dad gave the orchid. We call such a word an **indirect object.**

The noun **orchid** is the *direct object,* and the noun *Mother* is the ________________ *object.*

255

---

several

474

Lynn bought several new tires.

The noun **tires** is modified by (*one, two*) adjectives.

475

No

694

We talked to the jockey and learned a lot about horses.

Should a comma be inserted after **jockey?** (*Yes, No*)

695

---

a

914

We can often tighten up a weak **compound sentence** by changing one of the statements to an **adjective clause.**

a. **We finally found a restaurant,** *and* **it was still open.**
b. **We finally found a restaurant** *which was still open.*

Which sentence is a complex sentence because it contains a clause? ____

915

---

b

1134

a. **Our tires were old.** *Therefore* **we drove slowly.**
b. **Our tires were old,** *therefore* **we drove slowly.**

Which is correct? ____

1135

rose

1354

PRESENT	SIMPLE PAST	PAST WITH HELPER
rise (go up)	**rose**	**have risen**

The storm rose soon after dark.

If we added the helper **had** to the verb, we would need to change the word **rose** to ________.

1355

---

looks

1573

Lesson 51 The *And, Or,* and *Nor* Problem

[Frames 1575–1596]

---

would

1792

When using the words **hardly** and **scarcely,** do not use a negative word that reverses the meaning.

a. **Little Sandy could hardly reach the shelf.**
b. **Little Sandy couldn't hardly reach the shelf.**

Which sentence is correct? ____

1793

---

us

2011

We wouldn't let (*ourselves, ourselfs*) **believe this rumor.**

2012

---

a

2230

a. **a drifast bathing suit**
b. **a Drifast bathing suit**

Which item is correctly capitalized? ____

2231

---

y

2449

Now suppose that we want to write—

Several <u>boys lockers</u> were left open.

Ask again, "Who owns the lockers?" This time the answer is not **boy,** but ________.

2450

Two

35

Diego **graduated.**
My best friend **graduated.**
One of the boys in our club **graduated.**

In how many of the above sentences does the predicate have more than one word? ________

36

---

indirect

255

S V IO DO
Dad gave Mother an orchid.

The indirect object **Mother** comes (*before, after*) the direct object **orchid.**

256

---

two

475

Joe spilled red paint on himself.

The adjective ________ modifies the noun **paint.**

476

No

695

↓
We talked to the jockey and learned a lot about horses.

Suppose that we added the name **Bob** at the point marked by the arrow. Would it then be correct to insert a comma after **jockey?** (*Yes, No*)

696

---

b

915

a. **We finally found a restaurant,** *and* **it was still open.**
b. **We finally found a restaurant** *which was still open.*

The relationship between the two ideas is brought out more clearly by the (*compound, complex*) sentence.

916

---

a

1135

A pronoun such as *it, she,* or *they* can begin a new sentence even though its meaning depends on a previous sentence. (*True, False*)

1136

risen

Supply the correct form of the verb **rise:**

The price of gasoline has __________ again.

1355 1356

"Rudy *and* Vic are coming over tonight."

If someone made this remark to you, how many boys would you expect—*one* or *two*? ______

1575

---

a

In this and the following frames, underline the word which will not produce a **double negative.** (Some of the sentences require a negative word.)

The price doesn't make (*any, no*) **difference to him.**

1793 1794

---

ourselves

Why not let the guests serve (*themselves, theirselves*)**?**

2012 2013

---

b

a. **after Memorial day**
b. **after Memorial Day**

Which item is correctly capitalized? ___

2231 2232

---

boys

Since the answer to your question is **boys,** put the apostrophe after the word **boys.**

Several boys' lockers were left open.

Here the apostrophe goes after the letter ___.

2450 2451

None

36

One of the boys in our club graduated.

In this sentence, the last word of the subject is ______.

37

---

before

256

Besides showing *to whom* something is done, an **indirect object** can also show *for whom* something is done.

Uncle Frank cooked himself a big breakfast.

The indirect object that shows *for whom* Uncle Frank cooked the breakfast is the pronoun ______.

257

---

red

476

Joe spilled ______ red paint on himself.

Underline one of the following adjectives which could tell **how much** paint Joe spilled:

bright **some** **sticky** **that**

477

Yes

696

We talked to the jockey, and Bob learned a lot about horses.

Adding the name **Bob** makes this a **compound sentence,** and the comma after **jockey** is therefore (*right, wrong*).

697

---

complex

916

Grandfather has as much pep as a boy, and he is 75 years old.

To change the second statement to an adjective clause, drop the conjunction **and,** and put the clause signal **who** in place of the word ______.

917

True

1136

The adverb *then* or *therefore* (*can, cannot*) be the beginning of a new sentence.

1137

risen

1356

To raise means "to lift something."

PRESENT	SIMPLE PAST	PAST WITH HELPER
raise (lift)	**raised**	**have raised**

The two past forms of **raise** are (*alike, different*).

1357

Two

1575

Rudy *and* **Vic** (*is, are*) **coming over tonight.**
Two boys (*is, are*) **coming over tonight.**

The subjects of both these sentences are plural because both mean *two* boys.

Therefore, we choose the plural verb ______. 1576

---

any

1794

Don't say (*anything, nothing*) **about the party to Pat.**

1795

---

themselves

2013

I blamed (*my self, myself*) **for this quarrel.**

2014

---

b

2232

a. **our English test**
b. **our Biology test**

Which item is correctly capitalized? ____

2233

---

s

2451

If the answer to the question "Who is the owner?" is a word *without* an *s*, like **boy, dog,** or **children,** put the apostrophe after this word and before the *s*—**boy's, dog's, children's.**

Insert an apostrophe in the following sentence:

Where is your dads office? 2452

club 37	**The back wheels of our car skidded.** The last word of the subject is ______. 38
himself 257	**Uncle Frank cooked himself a big breakfast.** The indirect object ______________ comes before the direct object ______________. 258
some 477	**<u>Few</u> people enjoyed <u>this</u> movie.** The adjective that tells *which one* is ________. The adjective that tells *how many* is ________. 478
right 697	**Mr. Choy excused himself <u>and</u> he <u>and</u> his wife left the meeting.** This sentence contains two **and**'s. The **and** that connects the two parts of this compound sentence is the (*first, second*) **and.** 698
he 917	*who* **Grandfather has as much pep as a boy,** ~~*and he*~~ *is 75 years old.* Is the clause *who is 75 years old* where it should be—right after the word it is meant to modify? (*Yes, No*) 918
can 1137	Lesson **37** **When Does a Sentence End?** [Frames 1139–1159] *page 75*

alike

1357

The curtain . . . a half hour late.

In this sentence, do we want a verb that means *a* or *b*? ____

a. **to go up**
b. **to lift something**

1358

are

1576

Now suppose that the same person had said—

"Rudy *or* Vic is coming over tonight."

How many boys would you expect—*one* or *two*? ________

1577

anything

1795

We fished for several hours, but we caught (*anything, nothing*).

1796

myself

2014

Our cat spends most of the day washing (*its self, itself*).

2015

a

2233

a. **by umpire Todd**
b. **by Umpire Todd**

Which item is correctly capitalized? ____

2234

dad's

2452

If the answer to the question "Who is the owner?" is a word *with* an *s*, like **friends, students,** or **neighbors,** put the apostrophe after the entire word, including the *s*—**friends', students', neighbors'.**

Insert an apostrophe in this sentence:

Several neighbors trees were uprooted.

2453

car

38

The letter from Aunt Edna disappeared.

The last word of the subject is __________.

39

---

himself (indirect object)

breakfast (direct object)

258

PATTERN 3:

Subject—Action Verb→Indirect Object—Direct Object

Always look for an indirect object (*before, after*) the direct object.

259

---

this (which one)
Few (how many)

478

We have seen how **adjectives** give us a clearer picture or idea of **nouns** by telling *what kind, which one(s), how many,* or *how much.*

dark cloud **green hat** **ripe peach** **strong player**

Do the underlined adjectives answer the question "How many?" or "What kind?" ________ ________

479

---

first

698

Mr. Choy excused himself and he and his wife left the meeting.

A comma should be inserted before the (*first, second*) **and.**

699

No

918

Grandfather has as much pep as a boy, *who is 75 years old.*

To make this sentence sensible, the clause *who is 75 years old* should be put right after the noun __________, which it modifies.

919

We have seen that *it* (and other pronouns), *then,* and *therefore* may start a new sentence. However, they may also come in the middle of a sentence.

As I approached the bird, *it* **flew away.**

Can this sentence be divided into two separate and complete sentences? (*Yes, No*)

1139

a

1358

The speaker raised and lowered her voice.

We use **raised** rather than **rose** because the speaker **lifted** something – her ______________.

1359

One

1577

Rudy *or* **Vic** (*is, are*) **coming over tonight.**

Only *one* boy is coming. Rudy *is* coming, or Vic *is* coming—not both.

Since the subject of this sentence is singular, we choose the singular verb _______.

1578

---

nothing

1796

I couldn't reach (*either, neither*) **of the two doctors.**

1797

---

itself

2015

Lesson 66 Unit Review

[Frames 2017–2050]

---

b

2234

a. **with my Aunt Alma**
b. **with my aunt Alma**

Which item is correctly capitalized? ____

2235

---

neighbors'

2453

One students clothes were damaged.

Who is the owner of the clothes? The owner is one (*student, students*).

2454

Edna

39

Diego **graduated.**

Diego **graduated from our school.**

Diego **will graduate from our school in June.**

The parts of these sentences which in some cases have more than one word are the (*subjects, predicates*). 40

---

before

259

An indirect object tells *to whom* or *for whom* by its position alone—by coming *before* the direct object. A noun or pronoun used with *to* or *for* is never an indirect object.

a. **Pam told** *Helen* **a secret.**
b. **Pam told a secret** *to Helen.*

In which sentence is *Helen* an indirect object? ____ 260

What kind?

479

a. **clean dish** **sharp pencil** **fresh eggs** **juicy oranges**
b. **this dish** **that pencil** **these eggs** **those oranges**

Do the adjectives answer the question "Which one?" or "Which ones?" in group *a* or *b*? ____

480

---

first

699

Several boys and girls wrote and produced this program.

This sentence contains two **and**'s.

Is either **and** used to connect the two parts of a compound sentence? (*Yes, No*)

700

Grandfather

919

Grandfather, *who is 75 years old,* **has as much pep as a boy.**

The adjective clause is now correctly placed in this (*complex, compound*) sentence.

920

No

1139

As I approached the bird, *it* **flew away.**

As I approached the bird cannot stand by itself as a separate sentence.

Because it tells **when** about the verb **flew,** it is an *adverb* ____________.

1140

PRESENT	SIMPLE PAST	PAST WITH HELPER
raise (lift)	**raised**	**have raised**

voice

The roots raised the sidewalk several inches.

If we added the helper **have** to the verb, would we need to change the word **raised?** (*Yes, No*)

1359 1360

---

is

Neither means "not the one nor the other."

Neither **Rudy** *nor* **Vic . . . coming over tonight.**

Rudy *is* not coming—Vic *is* not coming. We are talking about two boys but only *one at a time.*
With **neither . . . nor,** we use a ______________ verb.

1578 1579

---

either

My dad hasn't (*never, ever*) **flown in a plane.**

1797 1798

---

a. **I** **he** **she** **we** **they**
b. **me** **him** **her** **us** **them**

Which pronouns can be used as the subjects of verbs—those in group *a* or *b*? ____

2017

---

a

In this and the following frames, underline only the words that now lack necessary capitals:

The people of Loomis county were genuinely impressed by the mexican ambassador.

2235 2236

---

student

One students clothes were damaged.

Since one **student** is the owner of the clothes, the apostrophe should go after the letter (*t, s*). ____

2454 2455

predicates

40

Diego **graduated.**
Diego **graduated from our school.**
Diego **will graduate from our school.**

About whom do all the predicates make statements?

______ 41

---

a

260

S V IO DO
Pam told *Helen* **a secret.**

S V DO
Pam told a secret *to Helen.*

When we change *Helen* to a position after the direct object **secret,** we are forced to say ______ *Helen.* 261

---

b

480

a. **five days** **most cars** **some schools** **no trees**
b. **warm days** **fast cars** **large schools** **tall trees**

Do the adjectives answer the question "How many?" in group *a* or *b*? ___

481

No

700

Several boys and girls wrote and produced this program.

This is not a compound sentence. Therefore a comma (*is, is not*) necessary.

701

---

complex

920

I know a child, *and* **his parents pay him to eat.**

Underline the pronoun you would use as a clause signal in changing this compound sentence to a complex sentence.

whose **which** **whom** **that**

921

---

clause

1140

a. **I approached the bird,** *it* **flew away.**
b. **As I approached the bird,** *it* **flew away.**

Which sentence is wrong because it is a run-on sentence—*a* or *b*? ___

1141

No 1360	**The roots raised the sidewalk several inches.** **The roots have raised the sidewalk several inches.** Both sentences are correct. (*True, False*) 1361
singular 1579	a. **Rudy** *and* **Vic . . . coming over tonight.** b. *Neither* **Rudy** *nor* **Vic . . . coming over tonight.** Which sentence requires the singular verb **is** because the subject is singular? ____ 1580
ever 1798	**I never trust** (*nobody, anybody*) **with secrets.** 1799
a 2017	a. **I he she we they** b. **me him her us them** Which pronouns can be used as the objects of verbs and prepositions—those in group *a* or *b*? ____ 2018
County, Mexican 2236	Underline the words that require capitals: **In her painting "Christmas at Home," grandma Moses recalls her girlhood memories of a country christmas.** 2237
t 2455	a. **One students' clothes were damaged.** b. **One student's clothes were damaged.** In which sentence is the apostrophe correctly placed—*a* or *b*? ____ 2456

Diego

Diego **graduated.**
Diego **graduated from our school.**
Diego **will graduate from our school in June.**

In how many of the above sentences does the predicate have more than one word? ________

41 | 42

---

to

a. **The trailer saved much money** *for the family.*
b. **The trailer saved** *the family* **much money.**

In which sentence is *family* an indirect object? ____

261 | 262

---

a

Lesson 17 More About Adjectives

[Frames 483–508]

481

---

is not

a. **Mr. Potter talks about democracy but he doesn't practice it.**
b. **Mr. Potter talks about democracy but doesn't practice it.**

Which sentence requires a comma because it is a compound sentence? ____

701 | 702

---

whose

a. **I know a child,** *and* **his parents pay him to eat.**
b. **I know a child** *whose parents pay him to eat.*

The relationship between the two ideas is brought out more clearly in sentence *b*, which is a (*compound, complex*) sentence.

921 | 922

---

a

a. **Because the price was reasonable,** *she* **bought the car.**
b. **The price was reasonable,** *she* **bought the car.**

In one of these sentences, the pronoun *she* should start a new sentence.

The run-on sentence is ____.

1141 | 1142

True

Be sure not to use **raise** unless the "something" that is lifted up is mentioned.

We raise the window, but the window rises.

You raise the price, but the price ________.

1361 | 1362

---

b

Two singular subjects that are connected by **and** are plural since one and one make two.

Two singular subjects that are connected by **or** or **nor** are ____________ since they mean one or the other—not both.

1580 | 1581

---

anybody

Mr. Armstrong would take (*no, any*) money for his help.

1799 | 1800

---

b

Write the object form of each of these subject pronouns:

she ________ **we** ________ **they** ________

2018 | 2019

Grandma, Christmas

Underline the words that require capitals:

The source of the Mississippi river is lake Itasca in minnesota.

2237 | 2238

---

b

Both students clothes were damaged.

To whom do the clothes belong? They belong to the (*student, students*).

2456 | 2457

Two

42

Shirley answered the phone.

The first word of the predicate is ______________.

43

---

b

262

S V IO DO

The trailer saved *the family* **much money.**

Now we shall put *the family* after the direct object:

S V DO

The trailer saved much money *for the family.*

When *the family* comes after the direct object, we are forced to say ______ *the family.* 263

We generally find adjectives right before the nouns they modify.

The new owner gave free samples to every customer.

The three underlined words in this sentence are all nouns.

Is each one of these three nouns modified by an adjective? (*Yes, No*)

483

---

a

702

a. **We can carry our lunch, or eat in the cafeteria.**
b. **The cap must be screwed on tight, or the perfume will evaporate.**

From which sentence should the comma be removed because it is not a compound sentence? ___

703

---

complex

922

Later in this lesson, you will find weak compound sentences in which two ideas are loosely connected by **and.**

You will improve each sentence by changing the italicized part to an adjective clause.

In other words, you are asked to change each weak compound sentence to a stronger ______________ sentence.

923

---

b

1142

a. **You should try your best,** *then* **no one can blame you.**
b. **If you try your best,** *then* **no one can blame you.**

Which sentence can be divided into two separate and complete sentences? ___

1143

rises	**The campers raised their tent, and the tent** (*raised, rose*).
1362	1363
singular	a. **Rain** *and* **snow . . . predicted for tonight.** b. **Rain** *or* **snow . . . predicted for tonight.** In which sentence is only one thing expected? ____
1581	1582
no	**Mother didn't order** (*any, no*) **supplies today.**
1800	1801
her, us, them	Write the subject form of each of these object pronouns: **me** ________ **him** ________ **us** ________
2019	2020
River, Lake, Minnesota	**The Hudson river runs along the Catskill mountains for many miles.**
2238	2239
students	**Both students clothes were damaged.** Since the answer to our question is **students,** the apostrophe should go after the letter (*t, s*). ____
2457	2458

answered 43	**Eddie Tolan won several gold medals at the Olympics.** The first word of the predicate is ______________. 44
for 263	To be an indirect object, a noun or pronoun must stand between the verb and its direct object. This is the position that means *to* or *for* without our using these words. a. **I wrote** *Dave* **a letter.** (DO over "letter") b. **I wrote a letter** *to Dave.* (DO over "letter") In which sentence is the noun *Dave* an indirect object? ____ 264
Yes 483	The normal position of an adjective is just before the noun it modifies. The main exception is adjectives that are used as subject complements. **The sky looks cloudy.** The adjective **cloudy** modifies the subject ________. 484
a 703	**The crowded bus stopped and took on still more people.** Should a comma be inserted before the conjunction **and?** (*Yes, No*) 704
complex 923	In changing a compound sentence to a complex sentence, you first need to (*drop, add*) the conjunction **and.** 924
a 1143	**You should try your best.** *Then* **no one can blame you.** These are two separate and complete sentences, each with a subject and predicate. We must either keep them apart or connect them with the ______________ **and.** 1144

rose 1363	**The men have raised an argument, and an argument has** (*rose, risen*). 1364
b 1582	a. **Rain** *and* **snow . . . predicted for tonight.** b. **Rain** *or* **snow . . . predicted for tonight.** In which sentence would the singular verb **is** be correct because the subject is singular? ___ 1583
any 1801	**We had plenty of sandwiches, but Ray didn't want** (*none, any*). 1802
I, he, we 2020	Pronoun errors occur mainly when pronouns are used in pairs or when a pronoun is paired with a noun. A good way to avoid such errors is to try each pronoun by itself. Then use the same pronouns when they are combined. *He* **was waiting for a bus.** *I* **was waiting for a bus.** Therefore: (*He, Him*) **and** (*I, me*) **were waiting for a bus.** 2021
River, Mountains 2239	**Dr. Akashi shares an office with another doctor over the Pickwick restaurant on Main street.** 2240
s 2458	a. **Both students' clothes were damaged.** b. **Both student's clothes were damaged.** In which sentence is the apostrophe correctly placed? ___ 2459

won

In many sentences, both the subject and the predicate consist of more than one word.

a. **My best friend graduated from our school.**

The subject of the above sentence consists of ________ words, and the predicate consists of ________ words.

44 | 45

---

a

To make sure that a word is an indirect object, see if the word *to* or *for* would make sense before it.

Natachee sold (   ) *me* **her stamps.**

Which word would make sense in the parentheses—*to* or *for*? ______

264 | 265

---

sky

The sky looks cloudy.

The adjective **cloudy** is used as a ________________ *complement.*

484 | 485

No

The train whistle woke me up and I couldn't fall asleep again.

Should a comma be inserted before the conjunction **and?** (*Yes, No*)

704 | 705

---

drop

After you drop the conjunction **and,** you will add an adjective clause signal to start your clause.

a. **who (whom, whose), which, that**
b. **if, as, when, because, after, although**

The words that can be used as adjective clause signals are those in group (*a, b*). ____

924 | 925

---

conjunction

a. **You should try your best,** *then* **no one can blame you.**
b. **You should try your best, and** *then* **no one can blame you.**

Which is the run-on sentence? ____

1144 | 1145

risen

1364

Let's compare the two verbs:

PRESENT	SIMPLE PAST	PAST WITH HELPER
rise (go up)	**rose**	**have risen**
raise (lift up)	**raised**	**have raised**

Which verb has two different past forms—**rise** or **raise?**

____

1365

---

b

1583

The teacher ***and*** **a student take the attendance.**

Since the job is done by *two* persons, we choose the plural verb __________.

1584

---

any

1802

The air was so stuffy that we (*couldn't, could*) **hardly breathe.**

1803

He, I

2021

Sandra can ride with the *Chens.* **Sandra can ride with** *us.*

Therefore: **Sandra can ride with the Chens and** (*we, us*).

2022

Restaurant, Street

2240

Aretha Franklin's version of "respect" was played on many european radio stations.

2241

---

a

2459

The word that comes before the apostrophe should indicate who the owner is.

a. **the boy's father**
b. **the boys' father**

Which means the father of *one* boy? ____

2460

three
four

45

The early bird catches the first worm.

The subject ends with the word ________, and the predicate begins with the word ____________.

46

---

to

265

Natachee sold (*to*) *me* **her stamps.**

Because the pronoun *me,* in this position, means *to me,* it is an ____________ ____________.

266

---

subject

485

a. **This bakery makes delicious pastries.**
b. **This bakery's pastries are delicious.**

Does the adjective **delicious** come after the noun it modifies in sentence *a* or *b*? ___

486

Yes

705

a. **We started on time but were delayed by a train.**
b. **We started on time but a train delayed us.**

Only one of these sentences could be split into two separate sentences.

Which sentence requires a comma because it is compound?
___

706

---

a

925

In making your adjective clause, never use the pronoun **which** as a clause signal to refer to persons.

Underline the correct adjective clause signal:

The driver (*which, who*) *rammed Dad's car* **was not insured.**

926

---

a

1145

a. **The meeting was very important,** *therefore* **most of the parents attended.**
b. **Most of the parents,** *therefore,* **attended this important meeting.**

Which can be divided into two separate and complete sentences? ___

1146

rise

In this and the following frames, underline the correct verb in each pair. Remember to choose **raise** only when the sentence mentions the "something" that is lifted.

Holidays always (*rise, raise*) **the accident rate.**

1365 | 1366

---

take

The teacher *and* **a student** (*takes, take*) **the attendance.**

If we changed the conjunction *and* to *or*, would we need to change the verb? (*Yes, No*)

1584 | 1585

---

could

There (*were, weren't*) **scarcely any people at the meeting.**

1803 | 1804

---

us

In this and the following frames, underline the correct pronouns. Always choose the same pronoun that you would choose if the pronoun were used alone.

Virginia and (*he, him*) **prepared the entire dinner.**

2022 | 2023

Respect, European

We don't study the French revolution until history (2).

2241 | 2242

---

a

the boy's father

This means the father of *one* boy because the apostrophe does not come after the plural noun **boys,** but after the singular noun ______.

2460 | 2461

bird,
catches

46

The fragrant pink blossoms attract the bees.

The subject ends with the word ________, and the predicate begins with the word ________.

47

---

indirect object

266

Karen made (   ) *the boys* **some fudge.**

Which word would make sense in the parentheses—*to* or *for*? ______

267

---

b

486

This bakery's pastries are delicious.

The adjective **delicious** is used as a *subject complement* and modifies the noun ________.

487

---

b

706

A sentence that can be divided into two separate sentences, each having its own subject and predicate, is a (*simple, compound*) sentence.

707

---

who

926

In this and the following frames, change the italicized part of each sentence to an adjective clause. Write the full sentence in the blank space.

Fred dreams up stories, *and they make him feel important.* ________________

____

927

---

a

1146

The meeting was very important. *Therefore* **most of the parents attended.**

These are two separate and complete sentences.

Can we connect them just with a comma without using the conjunction **and?** (*Yes, No*)

1147

raise 1366	**On holidays, the accident rate always** (*rises, raises*). 1367
Yes 1585	**The teacher** *or* **a student** (*takes, take*) **the attendance.** Since only *one* person does the job, we use the singular verb __________. 1586
were 1804	**The water was so shallow that we** (*couldn't, could*) **hardly swim.** 1805
he 2023	**The Owens and** (*we, us*) **share the same telephone line.** 2024
Revolution, History 2242	**My uncle Ted just won a new ford by writing a jingle telling why he likes krispie cornflakes.** 2243
boy 2461	a. **the boy's father** b. **the boys' father** Which means the father of *more than one* boy? ____ 2462

blossoms, attract 47	a. **the early train** b. **left his books on the bus** Which group of words could be the *subject* of a sentence—*a* or *b*? ____ 48
for 267	**Karen made** (*for*) *the boys* **some fudge.** Because *the boys,* in this position, means *for the boys,* it is an ____________ ____________. 268
pastries	**The soup was too salty for me.** The adjective **salty** comes (*before, after*) the noun it modifies.
compound 707	Lesson **24** **Building Good Compound Sentences** [Frames 709–743]
Fred dreams up stories that (which) make him feel important. 927	**We passed a car,** *and its door was partly open.* (Try *whose.*) ______________________________ ______________________________ 928
No 1147	a. **The meeting was very important, and** *therefore* **most of the parents attended.** b. **The meeting was very important,** *therefore* **most of the parents attended.** Which sentence is wrong because it is a run-on sentence? ____ 1148

rises 1367	**The passing cars** (*rise, raise*) **a lot of dust.** 1368
takes 1586	As you complete this lesson, don't trust your ear. What sounds right to you may be wrong. Reason out each problem, applying these rules: Two singular subjects that are connected by **and** are plural. Two singular subjects that are connected by **or** or **nor** are ________________. 1587
could 1805	**There** (*wasn't, was*) **scarcely any chicken in my salad.** 1806
we 2024	**What seems to be the trouble between Beverly and** (*she, her*)**?** 2025
Uncle, Ford, Krispie 2243	**I don't think that referee Grimes was fair to our pitcher in the game with Westover high.** 2244
b 2462	**the boys' father** This means the father of *more than one* boy because the apostrophe comes after the plural noun __________. 2463

a 48	a. **looked at his watch** b. **the driver of the truck** Which group of words could be the *predicate* of a sentence —*a* or *b*? ___ 49
indirect object 268	If a noun or pronoun is an indirect object, we can insert the word _____ or _______ before it. 269
after 488	**The soup was too salty for me.** The adjective **salty** is used as a *subject* _____________. 489
	A compound sentence can be made by joining two simple sentences with the conjunction **and, but,** or **or.** In a compound sentence, are there a subject and a predicate both before and after the conjunction? (*Yes, No*) 709
We passed a car whose door was partly open. 928	**A stranger helped me,** *and he happened to be a mechanic.* ______________________________ ______________________________ (Be sure to put the clause next to the noun it modifies.) 929
b 1148	In doing the remaining frames, remember that two separate sentences cannot be connected by a comma alone—without a conjunction to hold them together. a. **I checked all the tubes, then I put them back in the set.** b. **I checked all the tubes. Then I put them back in the set.** Which sentence is correct? ___ 1149

raise

Used car prices generally (*rise, raise*) **in the spring.**

1368 1369

singular

In this and the following frames, underline the verb that agrees with its subject. Remember that if a verb showing present time ends in *s*, it is singular, not plural.

The doctor or her assistant (*plan, plans*) **to see you tonight.**

1587 1588

was

Lesson 59 An *A–An* Checkup

[Frames 1808–1829]

1806

her

You can leave the key with the Wesbrooks or (*they, them*).

2025 2026

Referee, High

In her poem "I never saw a Moor," Emily Dickinson affirmed her belief in god.

2244 2245

boys

woman women

Which one of the above nouns is plural? ___________

2463 2464

a

49

a. **voted for María**
b. **bought a small farm**
c. **a piece of broken glass**

Which group of words could be the *subject* of a sentence?

___

50

---

to, for

269

S V DO
Gwendolyn Brooks read a poem *to us.*

As this sentence is printed, it contains no indirect object. Rewrite this sentence, changing the italicized words to an indirect object.

____

270

---

complement

489

The small and crowded room became very stuffy.

The adjective **stuffy** is used as a subject complement and modifies the subject ________.

490

Yes

709

He went his way, and I went mine.

In a compound sentence, the comma should be placed (*before, after*) the conjunction **and, but,** or **or.**

710

A stranger who (that) happened to be a mechanic helped me.

929

Her room was full of books, *and they showed her interest in science.*

____

____

930

---

b

1149

a. **Explorers do not look for danger. They try their best to avoid it.**
b. **Explorers do not look for danger, they try their best to avoid it.**

Which sentence is correct? ___

1150

Answer	Frame
rise 1369	a. **rose** b. **raised** One of these past forms means "went up" or "got up." The other means "lifted up something." Which word means "went up" or "got up"? ___ 1370
plans 1588	**The doctor and her assistant** (*plan, plans*) **to see you tonight.** 1589
	Whether we use **a** or **an** before a word depends on whether the word begins with a vowel or consonant *sound*. The vowels are **a, e, i, o, u.** **apple brick egg joke infant oven tree uncle** How many of the above words begin with vowels? ______ 1808
them 2026	**Either Diana Chang or** (*he, him*) **will read the poem.** 2027
Never, Saw, God 2245	Cross out each capital letter that is not correct: **My Mom brought my little Sister several guest-sized bars of Dermex Soap from the Madison Hotel.** 2246
women 2464	a. **the woman's advice** b. **the women's advice** Which means the advice of *more than one* woman? ___ 2465

c 50	a. **three airplanes** b. **improved the flavor of the cake** c. **the price of admission** Which group of words could be the *predicate* of a sentence? ____ 51
Gwendolyn Brooks read us a poem. 270	S V DO **Vic found a good job** *for himself.* Rewrite this sentence, changing the italicized words to an indirect object. ________________________________ 271
room 490	**The new model looks quite different from the old one.** The adjective ____________ is a subject complement and modifies the subject ________. 491
before 710	Only *similar* ideas of *equal importance* should be combined into a compound sentence. a. **The lightning flashed, and the thunder rumbled.** b. **The lightning flashed, and I was walking with Carl.** In which sentence do the ideas fit together better? ____ 711
Her room was full of books that (which) showed her interest in science. 930	**My uncle plays a violin,** *and he made it himself.* ________________________________ ________________________________ 931
a 1150	a. **Sunburn feels warm at first, then it begins to burn.** b. **Sunburn feels warm at first, and then it begins to burn.** Which sentence is correct? ____ 1151

a

1370

Our canoe drifted away when the tide (*rose, raised*).

1371

---

plan

1589

(Are you checking each sentence for **and, or,** and **nor** before choosing the verb?)

Neither the name nor the address (*was, were*) **legible**.

1590

---

five

1808

The vowels are **a, e, i, o, u.**

All the other letters of the alphabet are consonants.

a. **dollar**	**pencil**	**ball**	**flower**	**stamp**
b. **article**	**effect**	**inch**	**omelet**	**uncle**

In which group do the words begin with consonants? ____

1809

---

he

2027

The Montoyas invited Verna and (*I, me*) **to visit them.**

2028

Mom, Sister, Soap

2246

The Taos Glee Club will sing some Spanish Songs at our September meeting in the Church.

2247

---

b

2465

When writing a possessive noun, don't forget to ask yourself, "Who is the owner?" Then put the apostrophe right after your answer.

In the following sentence, place the apostrophe to show that *one girl* is the owner of the room:

Mom painted the girls room.

2466

a. **we won**
b. **won the opening game of the season**

b | Which group of words is a complete sentence? ____

(The capital letter and the period are omitted to avoid revealing the answer.)

51 | 52

Vic found himself a good job.

An indirect object is a noun or pronoun placed (*after*, *before*) the direct object to show *to whom* or *for whom*, or *to what* or *for what* something is done.

271 | 272

---

different, model

The words **a, an,** and **the** are special adjectives. They are usually called **articles.** We generally omit **articles** when identifying modifiers in sentences.

The special adjectives known as **articles** are **a, an,** and ________.

491 | 492

The lightning flashed, and the thunder rumbled.

a | Because both parts of this sentence are about weather conditions, this compound sentence is (*good, poor*).

711 | 712

My uncle plays a violin that (which) he made himself.

These masks are from Africa, *and they are on sale today.*

____

____

931 | 932

---

a. **While the young people danced, the older people visited.**
b. **The young people danced, the older people visited.**

b | Which sentence is correct? ____

1151 | 1152

rose

1371

At last our guests (*rose, raised*) **to go home.**

1372

was

1590

Mother or Dad (*do, does*) **the shopping.**

1591

a

1809

Use the word **a** before any word that begins with a consonant sound.

a.	**dollar**	**pencil**	**ball**	**flower**	**stamp**
b.	**article**	**effect**	**inch**	**omelet**	**uncle**

Would you use the word **a** before the words in group *a* or *b*? ____

1810

me

2028

Neither (*he, him*) **nor** (*I, me*) **could start the car.**

2029

$ongs, ¢hurch

2247

Cicely Tyson was the Actress who played the lead role in *The Autobiography Of Miss Jane Pittman.*

2248

girl's

2466

Now place the apostrophe to show that the room belongs to *two or more* girls.

Mom painted the girls room.

2467

a

52

a. **a heavy rain**
b. **a heavy rain spoiled our plans**

Which group of words is a complete sentence? ____

53

---

before

272

In this and the following frames, write in the missing words of the sentence framework. (S = Subject, V = Verb, IO = Indirect Object, DO = Direct Object)

The accident gave everyone a good scare.

S	V	IO	DO
________	gave	________	scare

273

---

the

492

A customer had dropped an egg on the floor.

The *articles* in this sentence are ____, ____, and ____.

493

---

good

712

I got an A in Spanish, and Steve is in my English class.

This is a poor compound sentence because the ideas are too (*alike, unlike*) to be combined.

713

These masks that (which) are on sale today are from Africa.

932

The witness made statements, *and he couldn't prove them* ________________

____

933

---

a

1152

a. **There was a convention in the city. Therefore all the hotels were full.**
b. **There was a convention in the city, therefore all the hotels were full.**

Which is correct—*a* or *b*? ____

1153

rose 1372	**The new manager** (*rose, raised*) **everyone's salary.** 1373
does 1591	**Neither mud nor snow** (*stop, stops*) **a tractor.** 1592
a 1810	Use **a** before every word that begins with a consonant *sound*, not necessarily with a consonant. Some words that begin with the vowel **u** sound as though they begin with the consonant **y**—like the word **unit** (pronounced *you-nit*). Does the word **uniform** begin with a **y** sound? (*Yes, No*) 1811
he, I 2029	**Miss Turner was sitting behind** (*she, her*) **and** (*me, I*). 2030
Of, Actress 2248	**Students who enter High School must take an Arithmetic test before they may enroll in Algebra (1).** 2249
girls' 2467	**lady** **ladies** When you write a possessive noun, be sure to have the correct spelling of the owner before the apostrophe. a. **a ladie's briefcase** b. **a lady's briefcase** Does the briefcase belong to a **ladie** or a **lady?** ________ 2468

b

53

a. **the bottle of red ink**
b. **squirrels bury nuts**

Which group of words is a complete sentence? ____

54

S
accident

IO
everyone

273

My sister made herself a good workbench.

S	V	IO	DO
sister	________	________	________

274

---

a, an, the

493

Young corn is tender.

The two adjectives in this sentence are ________ and ________.

494

---

unlike

713

a. **My mother was born in Ohio. She likes music.**
b. **My mother was born in Ohio. She grew up in Kentucky.**

Which sentences would make a better compound sentence—those labeled *a* or *b*? ____

714

The witness made statements that (which) he couldn't prove.

933

I have a friend, *and he helped me fix the motor.*

____

____

934

---

a

1153

a. **I searched through every pocket, my ticket was gone.**
b. **I searched through every pocket, but my ticket was gone.**

Which sentence is correct? ____

1154

raised

The temperature usually (*rose, raised*) **in the afternoon.**

1373 1374

stops

A sandwich and a glass of milk (*is, are*) **all I want.**

1592 1593

Yes

Although the word **uniform** begins with the vowel **u,** it is pronounced as though it begins with the consonant **y** (*you-ni-form*).

We therefore use the word (*a, an*) before **uniform.**

1811 1812

her, me

In making comparisons, you may be puzzled as to which pronoun to use after **than** or **as.** By supplying the omitted words, you will see which pronoun is needed.

I didn't walk as far as . . . (walked).

Underline two pronouns that would fit in the above sentence.

him he she her

2030 2031

~~H~~igh ~~S~~chool, ~~A~~rithmetic

2249

UNIT 11: **LEARNING TO USE COMMAS**

Lesson 73 Commas in Series

[Frames 2251-2285]

lady

a. **a ladie's briefcase**
b. **a lady's briefcase**

Which is correct—*a* or *b*? ____

2468 2469

b

54

a. **added a room to their house**
b. **the owner of the gas station**

Which group of words would be a sentence if a *subject* were added? ____

55

V IO
made herself
DO
workbench

274

Ali gave me his autograph at the arena.

S	V	IO	DO
Ali	________	________	autograph

275

Young, tender

494

Do both adjectives—**Young** and **tender**—modify the same noun? (*Yes, No*)

495

---

b

714

The food in our cafeteria is good. The prices are very reasonable.

Although each sentence has a different subject, both sentences are about the cafeteria's food—the first about its quality and the second about its ____________.

715

I have a friend who (that) helped me fix the motor.

934

who (whom, whose) **which** **that**

These words that are used as adjective clause signals are (*pronouns, adjectives*).

935

---

b

1154

a. **Gasoline is dangerous, it should never be used indoors.**
b. **Because gasoline is dangerous, it should never be used indoors.**

Which sentence is correct? ____

1155

rose

1374

a. **have risen** b. **have raised**

Which of these helper forms means "have gone up" or "have got up"? ____

1375

---

are

1593

Oil or wax (*protect, protects*) **the surface from rust.**

1594

---

a

1812

umpire **union**

Both the above words begin with the vowel **u.**

Before which of these words do we use **a** because the word sounds as though it begins with the consonant **y?**

____

1813

---

he, she

2031

The coach used Anne more often than (she used) . . . .

Underline two pronouns that would fit in the above sentence.

me **I** **her** **she**

2032

A **series** is a number of similar things in a row, like a series of games, a series of treatments, a series of explosions—one coming after another.

Men, women, **and** *children* **will enjoy this film.**

How many kinds of people does this sentence list? ____

2251

---

b

2469

Now suppose you want to write about the briefcases of *several* ladies.

a. **several ladies' briefcases**
b. **several ladys' briefcases**

Which is correct—*a* or *b*? ____

2470

a

55

a. **the heaviest boy on the team**
b. **needs a good pitcher**

Which group of words would be a sentence if a *predicate* were added? ____

56

V IO
gave me

275

The new lamp gives the room a cheerful look.

S	V	IO	DO
lamp	gives	________	________

276

Yes

495

Young corn is tender.

Because the adjective **tender** comes after the noun it modifies, it is a ____________ ________________.

496

---

prices

715

The food in our cafeteria is good. The prices are very reasonable.

Both these sentences are about food, and the ideas are of *(equal, unequal)* importance.

716

---

pronouns

935

Ordinarily, an adjective clause should be placed right (*after, before*) the noun or pronoun it modifies.

936

---

b

1155

a. **When the football season ended, the students turned to basketball.**
b. **The football season ended, the students turned to basketball.**

Which sentence is correct? ____

1156

a

1375

Underline the correct verb:

Taxes have (*rose, risen*) **again.**

1376

protects

1594

Neither Douglass nor Central High (*has, have*) **a pool.**

1595

union

1813

empty **useless** **awful**

All the above words begin with vowels.

Before which word would we use **a** because it begins with a consonant *sound*? ______________

1814

me, her

2032

I can't remember names as well as (*him, he*).

2033

Three

2251

In grammar, a series is a succession of three or more words, phrases, or clauses in a sentence—all used in the same way.

To form a series, there must be ____________ or more similar items in a row. (How many?)

2252

a

2470

a. **several ladies' briefcases**
b. **several ladys' briefcases**

The correct answer is *a* because the briefcases belong not to **ladys** but to ____________.

2471

a 56	**Ella sings.** If you added the word **beautifully** to this sentence, it would be a part of the (*subject, predicate*). 57
IO DO room look 276	**The graduates bought their school some new equipment.** S V IO DO graduates ______ ______ ______ 277
subject complement 496	Adjectives modify nouns and pronouns. However, we seldom use adjectives before pronouns, as we do before nouns. We are not likely to say *pretty she* or *delicious them.* a. ______ **<u>cities</u> have** ______ **<u>problems</u>.** (nouns) b. ______ **<u>she</u> bought** ______ **<u>them</u>.** (pronouns) It would be difficult to insert adjectives in sentence ___. 497
equal 716	**The food in our cafeteria is good, and the prices are very reasonable.** This is a (*good, poor*) compound sentence. 717
after 936	A sentence that consists of a main statement and an adjective clause is a (*compound, complex*) sentence. 937
a 1156	a. **Highways will be jammed, resorts will be overflowing.** b. **Highways will be jammed, and resorts will be overflowing.** Which sentence is correct? ___ 1157

Answer	Frame
risen 1376	**The accident rate has** (*risen, rose, raised*) **nearly every year.** 1377
has 1595	**The heat, the noise, and the crowd** (*was, were*) **too much for my nerves.** 1596
useless 1814	It is difficult to pronounce two vowels in a row. Notice how difficult it is to say **a apple, a egg, a Indian, a omelet, a uncle.** To make pronunciation easier, we use **an** before a word beginning with a vowel sound—**an egg, an Indian,** etc. We must use **an** before (*apple, banana*). 1815
he 2033	**Jo's report card pleased her mother more than** (*her, she*). 2034
three 2252	*Men, women,* **and** *children* **will enjoy this film.** All three italicized nouns in this sentence are used as subjects of the verb **will enjoy.** These three nouns, taken together, are called a ________. 2253
ladies 2471	**baby babies** The plural of **baby** is **babies.** How would you write that the doctor kept a record of the birthdays of *all* the babies under his care? **The doctor kept a record of all the ________ birthdays.** 2472

predicate

57

The box disappeared.

If you added the words **of candy,** they would be part of the (*subject, predicate*).

58

V IO
bought school
DO
equipment

277

Ms. Espinoza showed the women her beautiful painting.

S	V	IO	DO
______	______	______	______

278

b

497

To modify a pronoun, an adjective must generally be in the subject complement position.

It was beautiful. **He is very tall.**
They look expensive. **Some were green.**

In all these sentences, the adjectives come (*before, after*) the pronouns they modify.

498

good

717

Ella has a beautiful voice, and she attends law school.

Although both statements are about **Ella,** the two ideas have little to do with each other.

Therefore, this is a (*good, poor*) compound sentence.

718

complex

937

Lesson 31 Using *–ing* Word Groups to Combine Ideas

[Frames 939–978]

b

1157

a. **The next issue of our paper, therefore, will cost five cents more.**
b. **The two essays were judged to be equally good, therefore the prize was divided equally between us.**

Which sentence is correct? ____

1158

risen

The mayor's resignation has (*risen, raised*) much discussion.

1377 | 1378

were

Lesson 52 Sentences Beginning with *Here, There,* and *Where*

[Frames 1598–1617]

1596

apple

a. **athlete** **employer** **instant** **olive** **untruth**
b. **village** **shoulder** **family** **grape** **minute**

Would you use the word **an** before the words in group *a* or *b*? ____

1815 | 1816

her

My young sister knows as much about cars as (*I, me*)..

2034 | 2035

series

We can also have a series of three or more verbs.

This dealer *buys, sells,* **and** *trades* **used cars.**

The third verb in this series of verbs is ________.

2253 | 2254

babies'

baby **babies**

How would you write that the doctor kept a record of the birthday of only *one* baby?

The doctor kept a record of this ________ birthday.

2472 | 2473

subject 58	**The ball rolled.** If you added the words **into the street,** they would be a part of the (*subject, predicate*). 59
S V Ms. Espinoza showed IO DO women painting 278	**The store gave each customer a souvenir.** S ______ V ______ IO ______ DO ______ 279
after 498	Some words can be used as either **adjectives** or **nouns.** If the word modifies a noun or pronoun, it is an **adjective.** If the word is the name of a person, place, thing, or an idea, it is a ________. 499
poor 718	**Ella has a beautiful voice, and her songs are soothing.** Both statements in this compound sentence are about Ella's (*singing, job*). 719
938	*green* **leaves** *falling* **leaves** Both *green* and *falling* describe the noun ________. 939
a 1158	a. **Leslie arrived with her guitar, and then the fun began.** b. **Leslie arrived with her guitar, then the fun began.** Which sentence is correct? ____ 1159

raised 1378	**I have** (*risen, rose*) **early every day this week.** 1379
	We start many sentences with the words **There is** and **There are.** **There is no butter in this cake.** **(= No butter is in this cake.)** What noun is the subject of the verb **is?** ________ 1598
a 1816	a. **dollar** **theater** **raisin** **store** **minute** b. **action** **example** **Indian** **onion** **umpire** Would you use the word **an** before the words in group *a* or *b*? ___ 1817
I 2035	**Dad always feeds the dog, so it obeys him better than** (*she, her*). 2036
trades 2254	**Joan works** *after school, on Saturdays,* **and** *during the summer.* This series consists of three (*verbs, prepositional phrases*). 2255
baby's 2473	Copy the phrase in each frame. Then ask, "Who is the owner?" Underline the word that answers this question, and put an apostrophe after it; for example, **a <u>dog</u>'s life—the <u>girls</u>' voices.** **my uncles coat** 2474

predicate

59

A man came to the door.

If you added the words **tall and friendly,** they would be part of the (*subject, predicate*).

60

S V
store gave
IO
customer
DO
souvenir

279

Lesson 10 Completing the Linking Verb

[Frames 281-307]

---

noun

499

a. **Our paper came late.**
b. **We used paper spoons.**

Is **paper** used as an adjective in sentence *a* or *b*? ___

500

---

singing

719

a. **Ella has a beautiful voice, and she attends law school.**
b. **Ella has a beautiful voice, and her songs are soothing.**

Which compound sentence is better? ___

720

---

leaves

939

green **leaves**
falling **leaves**

Because both *green* and *falling* modify the noun **leaves,** both words are used as (*adjectives, adverbs*).

940

---

a

1159

Lesson 38 Unit Review

[Frames 1161-1193]

Answer		Frame	
risen	1379	**We went fishing before the sun had** (*risen, rose, raised*).	1380
butter	1598	**There are no eggs in this cake.** **(= No eggs are in this cake.)** What noun is the subject of the verb **are?** ________	1599
b	1817	**hour house** Both the above words begin with the consonant **h.** However, in one of these words the **h** is not sounded. The word that begins with a silent **h** is ________.	1818
her	2036	**The Tigers made two more hits than** (*them, they*).	2037
prepositional phrases	2255	a. **There are no telephones or electric lights on the island.** b. **There are no telephones, electric lights, or automobiles on the island.** Which sentence contains a series of nouns? ____	2256
my uncle's coat	2474	Copy the phrase, underline the word that answers the question "Who is the owner?" and put an apostrophe after it. **several doctors opinions** ________________________________	2475

subject

60

Most sentences have two parts. The naming part is called the ________________, and the telling part is called the ________________.

61

Up to now, we have been working only with *action* verbs. There is another type of verb that shows *no action* at all.

a. **My mother** ***hired*** **a nurse.**
b. **My mother** ***is*** **a nurse.**

In which sentence does the verb show *no action* of any kind? ____

281

---

b

500

We used paper spoons.

In this sentence, **paper** is an *adjective* because it modifies the noun ____________.

501

---

b

720

a. **Orlando Cepeda played for the Cardinals, and he was the National League's most valuable player.**
b. **Orlando Cepeda played for the Cardinals, and they have a big stadium.**

Are the ideas more *similar* and more *equal in importance* in sentence *a* or *b*? ____

721

---

adjectives

940

Leaves fall.

This is a complete sentence.

Leaves is the subject and __________ is the verb.

941

While I was feeding the dog.

Although this word group has a subject and a verb, it is not a (*sentence, clause*).

1161

risen

1380

Lesson 44 *Leave* and *Let*

[Frames 1382–1406]

eggs

1599

There is no butter in this cake.

There are no eggs in this cake.

In sentences that begin with **There is** and **There are,** the subjects come (*before, after*) the verbs.

1600

hour

1818

hour

The consonant **h** that starts this word is silent. The word **hour** is pronounced just like **our.**

Since **hour** sounds as though it begins with the vowel **o,** we say (*a, an*) *hour.*

1819

they

2037

Possessive pronouns show ownership without the use of apostrophes.

Underline the correct pronoun in each pair:

Does (*your's, yours*) **work the same as** (*our's, ours*)**?**

2038

b

2256

a. **I'll have to beg or borrow a formal for Saturday's party.**
b. **I'll have to beg, borrow, or steal a formal for Saturday's party.**

Which sentence contains a series of verbs? ____

2257

several doctors' opinions

2475

Copy the phrase, underline the word that answers the question "Who is the owner?" and put an apostrophe after it.

a childrens magazine

____

2476

(naming part) subject (telling part) predicate 61	The predicate makes a statement about the __________. 62
b 281	**My mother *is* a nurse.** The verb *is* shows no action. Instead, it is used to tie up or *link* the word **nurse** with the subject __________. 282
spoons 501	a. **Tommy has a tin airplane.** b. **Tin is a useful metal.** Is **tin** used as an adjective in sentence *a* or *b*? ____ 502
a 721	a. **Orlando Cepeda played for the Cardinals, and he was the National League's most valuable player.** b. **Orlando Cepeda played for the Cardinals, and they have a big stadium.** Which compound sentence is better? ____ 722
fall 941	a. **Leaves fall.** b. *falling* **leaves** In *a*, **fall** is a verb because it makes a statement about its subject, **Leaves.** In *b*, *falling* is an __________ because it describes the noun **leaves.** 942
sentence 1161	**While I was feeding the dog . . .** This word group is not a sentence because it leaves us wondering *"What happened?"* A word group that has a subject and verb but does not make sense by itself is a __________. 1162

To leave means (a) to go away from, (b) to place something and go away from it, (c) not to change or disturb something.

Which of the above meanings does the word **leave** have in the following sentence – *a*, *b*, or *c*? ____

Please take this note and leave it on Mr. Perez's desk.

1382

---

after

1600

a. **There is no butter in this cake.**
b. **There are no eggs in this cake.**

In sentence *a*, the singular verb **is** agrees with the singular subject **butter.**

In sentence *b*, the plural verb **are** agrees with the plural subject ________.

1601

---

an

1819

Before a word that begins with a vowel sound, use (*a, an*).

1820

---

yours, ours

2038

(*Its, It's*) **owner knows that** (*its, it's*) **vicious.**

2039

---

b

2257

Place commas *between* the items in a series—not before or after the series (unless they are needed for other reasons).

Punctuate this sentence:

His kindness patience and courtesy won him many friends.

2258

---

a <u>children</u>'s magazine

2476

Copy the phrase, underline the word that answers the question "Who is the owner?" and put an apostrophe after it.

both neighbors lawns

____

2477

subject

62

The subject of a sentence usually comes (*before, after*) the predicate.

63

---

mother

282

The weather *was* **cold.**

The verb *was* shows no action. It is used to tie up or *link* the word **cold** with the subject ______________.

283

---

a

502

a. **The candy spoiled my appetite.**
b. **The tree was decorated with candy canes.**

Is **candy** used as an *adjective* in sentence *a* or *b*? ___

503

---

a

722

a. **The car had no lights, and the accident occurred on our corner.**
b. **The car had no lights, and its brakes were bad.**

Are the ideas more *similar* and more *equal in importance* in sentence *a* or *b*? ___

723

---

adjective

942

a. **Leaves fall.**
b. *falling* **leaves**

To make an adjective of the verb **fall,** we add the letters ________ to the verb.

943

---

clause

1162

While I was feeding the dog . . .

Which word group could we add to make a complete sentence of this fragment? ___

a. **its evening meal**
b. **on the back porch**
c. **the telephone rang**

1163

b 1382	**To leave** means (a) to go away from, (b) to place something and go away from it, (c) not to change or disturb something. Which of the above meanings does the word **leave** have in the following sentence—*a*, *b*, or *c*? ____ **I leave school at three o'clock.** 1383
eggs 1601	**There was a dent in the fender.** The singular verb **was** agrees with the singular subject ________. 1602
an 1820	In this and the following frames, copy the word before which the word **an** is required, and write **an** before it: **picture** **request** **audience** _____ _______________ 1821
Its, it's 2039	(*Its, It's*) **collecting material for** (*it's, its*) **nest.** 2040
kindness, patience, 2258	Make a count to see how, in a series, the number of commas compares with the number of items: _______, _______, **and** _______ _______, _______, _______, **and** _______ The number of commas is always one (*more, less*) than the number of items in a series. 2259
both <u>neighbors'</u> lawns 2477	**a mans appearance** _______________________________ 2478

before

63

Every word in a sentence generally belongs to either the subject or the predicate. (*True, False*)

64

---

weather

283

Verbs like **is** and **was** are called **linking verbs** because they connect or *link* a word that follows them with the subject.

The tire *was* **flat.**

The linking verb *was* links the word **flat** with the subject ________, which it describes.

284

---

b

503

a. **Amy wore a pretty cotton dress.**
b. **Cotton grows in the South.**

Is **cotton** used as a *noun* in sentence *a* or *b*? ____

504

---

b

723

a. **The car had no lights, and the accident occurred on our corner.**
b. **The car had no lights, and its brakes were bad.**

Which compound sentence is better? ____

724

-ing

943

a. **Faucets leak.**
b. *leaking* **faucets**

In *a*, **leak** is a verb because it makes a statement about its subject, **Faucets.**

In *b*, *leaking* is an adjective because it describes the noun ________.

944

---

c

1163

While I was feeding the dog, the telephone rang.

The adverb clause **While I was feeding the dog** modifies the verb ________ in the main statement.

1164

a

1383

To leave means (a) to go away from, (b) to place something and go away from it, (c) not to change or disturb something.

Which of the above meanings does the word **leave** have in the following sentence—*a*, *b*, or *c*? ____

Leave the window open a little longer.

1384

---

dent

1602

There was a dent in the fender.

If we changed the subject **dent** to **dents,** would we need to change the verb **was?** (*Yes, No*)

1603

---

an audience

1821

Copy the word before which **an** is required, and write **an** before it:

foot   **inch**   **yard**

____ ________

1822

It's, its

2040

(*Hers, Her's*) **is right next to** (*theirs, their's*).

2041

---

less

2259

In a series of *three* items, we would use *two* commas.

In a series of *four* items, we would use ____________ commas.

2260

---

a <u>man</u>'s appearance

2478

the mens wages

____

2479

True

64

Lesson 3 The Simple Subject and the Verb

[Frames 66–95]

tire

Both **is** and **was** are forms of the linking verb **be.**

Be is by far the most common *linking verb.* It is important, therefore, to memorize its various forms.

FORMS OF *BE:* **is, am, are—was, were, been**

The verbs **is, am,** and **are** are (*present, past*) forms of the linking verb **be.**

284 285

b

Two or more adjectives can modify the same noun. (*True, False*)

504 505

b

a. **My grandparents are old, but they have modern ideas.**
b. **My grandparents are old, and they live on a farm.**

Which compound sentence is better? ____

724 725

faucets

a. **Faucets leak.**
b. *leaking* **faucets**

To make an adjective of the verb **leak,** we add the letters ______ to the verb.

944 945

rang

Grabbing the cat by its tail.

Does this **–ing** word group have a subject and a verb? (*Yes, No*)

1164 1165

c

1384

To let means "to permit" or "to allow."

In which of the following sentences does this definition fit—*a* or *b*? ____

a. **Bea . . . me use her book.**
b. **Bea . . . her book at home.**

1385

Yes

1603

There (*was, were*) **dents in the fender.**

The subject **dents** is plural.

Therefore, we choose the verb ________.

1604

---

an inch

1822

Copy the word before which **an** is required, and write **an** before it:

honor **hammer** **hotel**

______ ____________

1823

Hers, theirs

2041

When using expressions like "*We* boys" and "*Us* girls," select the same pronoun that you would use if you omitted the noun *boys* or *girls*.

Some of (*we, us*) ~~**boys**~~ **have after-school jobs.**

2042

---

three

2260

My collection of stamps, coins, and autographs is very large.

Do we use a comma before the first word or after the last word in a series? (*Yes, No*)

2261

---

the men's wages

2479

Marys speech

____

2480

A little black dog with big ears ran across our yard.

This sentence has two parts: first, it has a subject; second, it has a ________.

66

---

present

285

Keep repeating these six forms of the linking verb **be** until you remember them:

FORMS OF *BE*: **is, am, are—was, were, been**

The verbs **was, were,** and **been** are (*present, past*) forms of the linking verb **be.**

286

True

505

An adjective must always come *before* the noun it modifies. (*True, False*)

506

---

a

725

a. **I did the problem several times, and my friends were waiting for me.**
b. **I did the problem several times, and I always got the same answer.**

Which compound sentence is better? ____

726

–ing

945

We can turn any verb into an adjective by adding the letters *–ing* to it (sometimes making a slight change in the spelling); for example, **jump—jumping, lose—losing, bat—batting.**

The adjective form of the verb **boil** is ________.

946

No

1165

Grabbing the cat by its tail . . .

Does this **–ing** word group make sense by itself? (*Yes, No*)

1166

a 1385	This is the main point to remember: When you mean **permit,** always use **let,** not **leave.** (*Leave, Let*) **me carry your books.** This means: **Permit** me to carry your books. Therefore, the correct verb is ______. 1386
were 1604	In sentences that begin **Here is, Here are, Where is,** and **Where are,** we also find the subject after the verb. **Here is your ticket.** **(= Your ticket is here.)** What noun is the subject of the verb **is?** ______ 1605
an honor 1823	Copy the word before which **an** is required, and write **an** before it: **friend restaurant anecdote** ______ ______ 1824
us 2042	(*We, Us*) **girls have been waiting for nearly an hour.** 2043
No 2261	a. **Every train, bus, and airplane was jammed with people.** b. **Every train, bus, and airplane, was jammed with people.** Which sentence is correctly punctuated? ___ 2262
Mary's speech 2480	**both farmers corn** ______ 2481

predicate 66	**A little black dog with big ears ran across our yard.** Now let's look closely at just the *subject,* or *naming part,* of this sentence. The entire subject consists of __________ words. (How many?) 67
past 286	Supply the missing forms of the verb **be:** **is am** ________ **— was were** ________ 287
False 506	An adjective used as a subject complement usually comes (*before, after*) the noun or pronoun it modifies. 507
b 726	a. **My shoulder was lame. All my muscles ached.** b. **My shoulder was lame. Our next game was on Friday.** Which pair of sentences could be combined into a good compound sentence? ____ 727
boiling 946	The adjective form of the verb **win** is __________. 947
No 1166	**Grabbing the cat by its tail . . .** This **–ing** word group is a (*fragment, sentence*). 1167

Let

1386

(*Leave, Let*) **the water run until it's cold.**

This means: **Permit** the water to run until it's cold. Therefore, the correct verb is ________.

1387

---

ticket

1605

Here is your ticket.

If we changed the subject **ticket** to **tickets,** would we need to change the verb **is?** (*Yes, No*)

1606

---

an anecdote

1824

Copy the word before which **an** is required, and write **an** before it:

union **umbrella** **university**

____ ____________

1825

We

2043

Why don't you give (*we, us*) **fellows a chance to play?**

2044

---

a

2262

a. **Switzerland is bounded by, France, Germany, and Italy.**
b. **Switzerland is bounded by France, Germany, and Italy.**

Which sentence is correctly punctuated? ____

2263

---

both farmers' corn

2481

the womens meeting

____

2482

seven 67	**A little black dog with big ears . . .** These seven words are the **complete subject** of the sentence. There are no other words in the subject part of this sentence. These seven words are not just *part* of the subject. They are the entire or *com*__________ *subject.* 68
are, been 287	Supply the missing forms of the verb **be:** **is** ______ ______ — **was** ______ ______ 288
after 507	Some words can be used as either adjectives or nouns. (*True, False*) 508
a 727	**We won the football game, and my dad picked us up in his car.** This compound sentence is (*good, poor*). 728
winning 947	The adjective form of the verb **freeze** is ____________. 948
fragment 1167	**And wiped his muddy shoes on the mat.** Is this a complete sentence with both a subject and a predicate? (*Yes, No*) 1168

Let	Keep in mind that you always **let go**—never **leave go**—of an object like a rope, a hand, or a wheel. **Don't** (*leave, let*) **go of your end until I tell you.**
1387	1388
Yes	**Here** (*is, are*) **your tickets.** The subject **tickets** is plural. Therefore, we choose the plural verb ______.
1606	1607
an umbrella	Copy the word before which **an** is required, and write **an** before it: **hour** **harbor** **highway** ____ ____________
1825	1826
us	(*We, Us*) **students need to support our teams better.**
2044	2045
b	a. **My parents never coaxed, forced, or bribed, me to eat.** b. **My parents never coaxed, forced, or bribed me to eat.** Which sentence is correctly punctuated? ___
2263	2264
the <u>women</u>'s meeting	Copy the correct form: **a ladie's voice** **a lady's voice** ____________
2482	2483

(com)plete

68

A little black dog with big ears . . .

Now suppose that you were writing a telegram. You might have to reduce this **complete subject** to only one word.

Which word would you choose as the most important word in the complete subject—**little, black, dog,** or **ears?**

____

69

---

am, are, were, been

288

Supply the missing forms of the verb **be:**

________ ________ **are —** ________ ________ **been**

289

True

508

Lesson 18 And Now the Adverb

[Frames 510–544]

---

poor

728

I offered to help with the work, but Aunt May wouldn't let me.

This compound sentence is (*good, poor*).

729

---

freezing

948

An **-ing** word *by itself* cannot serve as a verb.

Our team winning.

This group of words (*is, is not*) a sentence.

949

No

1168

a. **and, but, or**
b. **then, therefore**

In which group are the words that do *not* have the power to connect two sentences into a compound sentence? ____

1169

let 1388	(*Leave, Let*) **go of my arm.** 1389
are 1607	a. **Where** (*was, were*) **her book?** b. **Where** (*was, were*) **her books?** Can we use the same verb in both sentences? (*Yes, No*) 1608
an hour 1826	Copy the word group before which **an** is required, and write **an** before it: **history course** **high tower** **honest man** _____ _____ _____ 1827
We 2045	Be careful not to use "*–self*" pronouns that do not exist. Write all "*–self*" pronouns as solid words without splitting them. Underline the correct word: **The sailors built** (*themselves, theirselves, their selves*) **a raft of logs.** 2046
b 2264	Supply the needed commas: **We made six hits three runs and two errors in the first inning.** 2265
a lady's voice 2483	Copy the correct form: **the ladies' voices** **the ladie's voices** _____ 2484

dog 69	**A little black dog with big ears . . .** It was not a **little** or **black** or **ears** that **ran across our yard.** It was a ______. 70
is, am, was, were 289	In a previous lesson, we saw that some *action verbs* can make complete statements about their subjects and that others cannot. a. **Sam awoke.** b. **Sam fixed . . .** In which sentence—*a* or *b*—does the *action verb* make a complete statement about its subject? ____ 290
	Adjectives can modify ________ and **pronouns,** but they cannot modify **verbs.** 510
good 729	Don't write two sentences together unless you use a **conjunction** to connect them. WRONG: **The lightning flashed, the thunder rumbled.** This sentence involves a serious error because there is no ________________ to hold the two sentences together. 730
is not 949	An **-ing** word cannot serve as a verb unless it is used with some form of the verb **be (is, am, are—was, were, been).** **Our team was winning.** **Winning** is not an adjective in this sentence. It is part of the verb **was** ____________. 950
b 1169	**The rug was rolled back,** *and* **then the dancing began.** If we removed the conjunction *and* from this sentence, this would be a (*correct, run-on*) sentence. 1170

Let 1389	PRESENT — SIMPLE PAST — PAST WITH HELPER **leave** — **left** — **have left** **let** — **let** — **have let** Which verb means "to go away from"—**leave** or **let?** ________ 1390
No 1608	a. **Where was her book?** b. **Where . . . her books?** In sentence *a*, the singular subject **book** requires the singular verb **was.** In sentence *b*, the plural subject **books** requires the plural verb ________. 1609
an honest man 1827	Copy the word before which **an** is required, and write **an** before it: **opportunity** **machine** **bakery** ____ ____________ 1828
themselves 2046	**I taught** (*myself, my self*) **to swim.** 2047
hits, runs, 2265	Supply the needed commas: **The scouts hiked through the woods over a mountain and across a stream.** 2266
the ladies' voices 2484	Lesson **80** **Using Apostrophes—A Few Don'ts** [Frames 2486–2527] *page 140*

dog

A little black dog with big ears . . .

The noun **dog** is the most important word in the *complete* (*subject, predicate*).

70

71

---

a

No linking verb, however, can ever make a complete statement about its subject.

If a verb does make a complete statement about its subject, it (*is, is not*) being used as a linking verb.

290

291

---

nouns

There is another *class of words* that answers questions about **verbs** in the same way that ______________ answer questions about **nouns** and **pronouns.**

510

511

---

conjunction

a. **I rang the doorbell, a child came to the door.**
b. **I rang the doorbell, and a child came to the door.**

Which sentence is wrong because the conjunction is missing—*a* or *b*? ____

730

731

---

winning

a. **Our team** *was winning.*
b. **The crowd cheered the** *winning* **team.**

In which sentence is *winning* used as an adjective to modify a noun? ____

950

951

---

run-on

a. **The rug was rolled back,** *then* **the dancing began.**
b. **The rug was rolled back.** *Then* **the dancing began.**

Which is correct—*a* or *b*? ____

1170

1171

leave

1390

Don't . . . a child play with matches.

In this sentence, do we want a verb that means *a* or *b*? ____

a. **to permit or allow**
b. **to go away from**

1391

---

were

1609

A word that is made by combining two words and omitting one or more letters is called a **contraction.**

There's = There is   Here's = Here is   Where's? = Where is?

There's is a short cut or contraction for two words: **There** and ______.

1610

---

an opportunity

1828

Copy the word group before which **an** is required, and write **an** before it:

useless part   unusual trip   useful tool

______ ______________ ______________

1829

---

myself

2047

The dog didn't recognize (*itself, it's self*) **in the mirror.**

2048

---

woods,
mountain,

2266

Supply the needed commas:

My father mother and I will pick up Betty and Ruth at the station.

2267

If you know **to whom** or **to what** something belongs, you know exactly where to place the apostrophe.

The owner is indicated by whatever comes before the ________________.

2486

subject

71

A little black dog with big ears . . .

We would have no idea of what **ran across our yard** if we dropped the word ________ from the complete subject.

72

---

is not

291

Skippy was . . . (What?)

This sentence is not complete. Any word that completes it might be thought of as a *completer*. The grammar term for *completer* is **complement.**

Any word that completes the meaning of this sentence would be a ________________. 292

---

adjectives

511

John swam recently.

Since the word **recently** tells **when** about **swam,** we say that it *mod*____________ the verb **swam.**

512

---

a

731

The car stopped, a police officer stepped out.

This sentence is (*right, wrong*).

732

---

b

951

a. **I did not disturb the** *sleeping* **child.**
b. **The child** *was sleeping* **on the sofa.**

In which sentence is *sleeping* used as an adjective to modify a noun? ____

952

---

b

1171

The roads were icy, therefore traffic moved slowly.

Adding the conjunction **and** after the comma would make this sentence (*right, wrong*).

1172

a

Don't . . . a child play with matches.

Because we want a verb that means "to permit" or "to allow," we should choose the verb ________.

1391 1392

is

a. **There's your friend.**
b. **There's your parents.**

Because **There's** means **There is,** which sentence is wrong—*a* or *b*? ____

1610 1611

an unusual trip

Lesson 60 Unit Review

[Frames 1831–1851]

1829

itself

My oldest brother put (*himself, his self*) **through college.**

2048 2049

father, mother,

Supply the needed commas:

The officer sounded her siren motioned me to the curb and asked to see my driver's license.

2267 2268

apostrophe

The boys room was untidy.

Until an apostrophe is inserted, we do not know whether the room belongs to one boy or to several.

If we put the apostrophe after the **y** in **boy,** we show that the room belongs to (*one, more than one*) boy.

2486 2487

dog

72

A little black dog with big ears . . .

Just as the trunk of a tree supports all the branches, the word **dog** supports all the other words in the complete subject—no matter how many there may be.

All the words in the **complete subject** are attached to the one word ______.

73

---

complement
(*or* completer)

292

Skippy was friendly.

The word **friendly** is a complement because it completes the meaning of the sentence.

The complement **friendly** describes the subject ________.

293

(mod)ifies

512

a. **John swam there.**
b. **John swam yesterday.**

In which sentence does the underlined word tell **where** John swam? ____

513

---

wrong

732

Don't use **and** where **but** would bring out the contrast more clearly.

We asked permission, ______ he refused.

Which conjunction makes better sense in this sentence—**and** or **but?** ______

733

---

a

952

a. **The car** *was speeding* **down the road.**
b. **The police stopped the** *speeding* **car.**

In which sentence is *speeding* used as an adjective? ____

953

---

right

1172

a. **The roads were icy, and** *therefore* **traffic moved slowly.**
b. **The roads were icy.** *Therefore* **traffic moved slowly.**

Both *a* and *b* are (*right, wrong*).

1173

let

1392

Don't . . . matches where a child can get at them.

In this sentence, do we want a verb that means *a* or *b*? ____

a. **to permit or to allow**
b. **to place something and go away from it**

1393

---

b

1611

There's (= There is) your parents.

This sentence is wrong because the subject **parents** is plural, and the contraction **There's** is ______________.

1612

---

a.	**frankly**	**regularly**	**efficiently**	**rapidly**
b.	**frank**	**regular**	**efficient**	**rapid**

Which group of words would you use to describe the action of a verb? ____

1831

---

himself

2049

We found (*our selfs, ourselves*) **on the bus without any money.**

2050

---

siren, curb,

2268

It is not wrong to omit the comma before the **and** that connects the last two items of a series. However, without this comma a sentence may be confusing.

These ties come in green, blue, red and gray.

This might mean *either* three or four kinds of ties. With a comma after **red,** the sentence would mean ________ kinds.

2269

---

one

2487

The boys room was untidy.

If we put the apostrophe after the **s** in **boys,** we show that the room belongs to (*one, more than one*) boy.

2488

dog

73

A little black dog with big ears . . .

In grammar, the word **dog** is called the **simple subject** of the sentence. We call it the simple subject because one word is simpler than three or five or ten words.

A little black dog with big ears is the *complete subject*, but the word **dog** is the __________ *subject*.

74

Skippy

293

The roads were . . . (What?)

The roads were muddy.

The complement **muddy** completes the meaning of the sentence and describes the subject __________.

294

---

a

513

a. **John swam away.**
b. **John swam fast.**

In which sentence does the underlined word tell **how** John swam? ____

514

---

but

733

We asked his permission, ______ he consented.

Which conjunction makes better sense in this sentence—**and** or **but?** ______

734

---

b

953

We can use **-ing** words to make word groups that are used like adjectives to modify nouns and pronouns.

A girl *carrying an umbrella* **was waiting for a bus.**

The word group *carrying an umbrella* describes or modifies the noun ________.

954

---

right

1173

The men pushed the truck. ***It*** **wouldn't move an inch.**

It and other pronouns can start a new sentence even though the meaning of the pronoun depends upon the previous sentence. (*True, False*)

1174

b

Don't . . . matches where a child can get at them.

We want a verb that means "to place something and go away from it."

Therefore, we should choose the verb ________.

1393 1394

singular

a. **Where's my keys?**
b. **Where's my key?**

Is the contraction **Where's** correct in *a* or *b*? ____

1612 1613

a

a. **Ward's apology was very . . . .**
b. **Ward apologized very . . . .**

The adverb **sincerely** should be used in sentence ____.

1831 1832

ourselves

UNIT 10: **HOW TO USE CAPITALS**

Lesson 67 Capitalizing Geographical and Group Names

[Frames 2052–2087]

2050

four

a. **We served soup, salad, chicken ‸ and biscuits.**
b. **We served soup, salad, cheese ‸ and egg sandwiches.**

In which sentence would inserting a comma at the point indicated prevent a misunderstanding? ____

2269 2270

more than one

a. **The <u>boy's</u> room was untidy.**
b. **The <u>boys'</u> room was untidy.**

Which sentence shows that more than one boy is the owner —*a* or *b*? ____

2488 2489

simple

74

A little black dog with big ears . . .

The *complete subject* consists of seven words, but the *simple subject* consists of only ______ word(s).

75

---

roads

294

Turtles are . . . (What?)
Turtles are reptiles.

The complement **reptiles** completes the meaning of the sentence and *explains* or *identifies* the subject ________.

295

---

b

514

a. **John swam frequently.**
b. **John swam backward.**

In which sentence does the underlined word tell **how much** or **how often** John swam? ___

515

---

and

734

There was a stop sign at the corner, ______ Dick didn't see it.

Which conjunction makes better sense here—**and** or **but?**

______

735

---

girl

954

A girl *carrying an umbrella* **was waiting for a bus.**

Because the word group *carrying an umbrella* modifies the noun **girl,** it is used as an (*adverb, adjective*).

955

True

1174

In this and the following frames, label each item according to the following key:

S=correct sentence: *F*=fragment; *R–S*=run-on sentence

During the five minutes between classes. ___

1175

leave

1394

. . . the door open.

Suppose that a door is open, and you want it to remain that way. Which one of the following definitions would express your meaning—*a* or *b*? ____

a. **To leave** means "not to change or disturb something."
b. **To let** means "to permit" or "to allow." 1395

---

b

1613

a. **Where's (= Where is) my keys?**
b. **Where are my keys?**

Sentence *b* is correct because the plural subject **keys** requires the plural verb ________.

1614

---

b

1832

Underline the correct word:

Raymond's reply to his dad's question seemed quite (*disrespectful, disrespectfully*) **to his friends.**

1833

---

man Moses

Which one of the above nouns means one *particular* man? ____________

2052

---

b

2270

When you connect all the items in a series with **and**'s, no commas should be used.

The way María Tallchief spins <u>and</u> leaps <u>and</u> dances always amazes her audience.

Does this sentence require any commas? (*Yes, No*)

2271

---

b

2489

Sometimes the thing owned is understood but not expressed.

Don's score was higher than Fred's.

We put an apostrophe in **Fred's** because it really means **Fred's** ____________.

2490

one

In our grammar work, we shall be more concerned with the simple subject than with the complete subject.

For convenience, therefore, we shall always refer to the simple subject as just the **subject.**

From here on, the word **subject** will mean not the *complete subject* but the ______________ subject.

75 | 76

Turtles

A complement that follows a linking verb and *describes* or *identifies* the subject is called a **subject complement.**

It is called a **subject complement** because it *describes* or *identifies* the ________________.

295 | 296

---

a

Words that tell **when, where, how, how much,** or **how often** about verbs are called **adverbs.**

Adjectives modify **nouns** and **pronouns,** but **adverbs** can modify ____________.

515 | 516

---

but

The sign was too small, ________ many people failed to see it.

Which conjunction makes better sense here—**and** or **but?**

____

735 | 736

---

adjective

A girl *carrying an umbrella* **was waiting for a bus.**
A girl **was waiting for a bus.**

When we omit the **-ing** word group from this sentence, do we have a complete sentence remaining? (*Yes, No*)

955 | 956

F

S = correct sentence; *F* = fragment; *R–S* = run-on sentence

The roads were poorly marked, we therefore lost our way.

____

1175 | 1176

a

1395

. . . the door open.

Suppose that someone is blocking a door so that it can't open. You want the person to **permit** or **allow** the door to open.

Which word would you choose—**leave** or **let?** ____________

1396

---

are

1614

a. **Here's my reason for refusing.**
b. **Here's my reasons for refusing.**

Is the contraction **Here's** correct in sentence *a* or *b*? ____

1615

---

disrespectful

1833

Underline the correct word:

The commission studied the causes of crime very (*scientific, scientifically*).

1834

Moses

2052

Boston city

Which noun means one *particular* city? ______________

2053

No

2271

The way María Tallchief spins and leaps and dances always amazes her audience.

If you omitted the **and** after **spins,** would the sentence require commas? (*Yes, No*)

2272

---

score

2490

Suppose that we are writing about Mom's car and say—

Moms would not start.

Place an apostrophe in the above sentence even though the thing owned is not expressed.

2491

simple

76

A little black dog with big ears ran across our yard.

To save words, we shall call the word **dog** not the *simple subject* of this sentence, but just the ______.

77

---

subject

296

The box was . . . (What?)

The box was empty.

Because the complement **empty** completes the meaning of the sentence and describes the subject **box,** it is a ______ *complement.*

297

---

verbs

516

Notice that the word **verb** occurs in the word **adverb.** This should help you to remember that there is a close connection between **adverbs** and ______.

517

---

and

736

Generally, it is not a good idea to begin a sentence with **and.**

a. **Ten years pass. And Suki is now a successful lawyer.**
b. **Ten years pass, and Suki is now a successful lawyer.**

Which is better—*a* or *b*? ____

737

Yes

956

A girl *carrying an umbrella* **was waiting for a bus.**

The verb that makes a statement about the subject **girl** is not *carrying,* but ______ ______. (two words)

957

R–S

1176

S = correct sentence; *F* = fragment; *R–S* = run-on sentence

Before one selects a vocation, he should consider his interests and abilities. ____

1177

let

1396

PRESENT	SIMPLE PAST	PAST WITH HELPER
leave	**left**	**have left**
let	**let**	**have let**

The two past forms of **leave** are (*alike, different*).
The two past forms of **let** are (*alike, different*).

1397

---

a

1615

The apostrophe **s ('s)** in **There's, Here's,** and **Where's** stands for the verb (*is, are*), which is singular.

1616

---

scientifically

1834

Use the adverb **well,** not the adjective **good,** to describe how an action is performed.

This electric heater is (*good, well*), **and it heats the room very** (*good, well*).

1835

Boston

2053

language **Spanish**

Which noun means one *particular* language? ________

2054

Yes

2272

The heat, the noise, and the crowd gave me a headache.

If you inserted an **and** after the word **heat,** how many commas would be necessary? ______

2273

Mom's

2491

You have seen apostrophes used in such expressions as **a day's work** and **a dollar's worth of gas. A day's work** means the work belonging to one day. **A dollar's worth of gas** means the amount that can be bought for one dollar.

Underline the two words that require apostrophes:

In five minutes time, it burns a dollars worth of gas. 2492

subject 77	**A little black dog with big ears ran across our yard.** Now let's look at just the *predicate,* or *telling part,* of our sentence. The *complete predicate* consists of _____ words. (How many?) 78
subject 297	Among other verbs that can be used as *linking verbs* are **seem, become, appear, look, feel,** and **get** (when it means **become**). **The room seems dark.** The verb **seems** is a _____________ *verb.* 298
verbs 517	**The dog ate greedily.** The adverb **greedily** tells (*how, when*) the dog **ate.** 518
b 737	a. **In those days people worked harder, and they needed more food.** b. **In those days people worked harder. And they needed more food.** Which is better—*a* or *b*? ___ 738
was waiting 957	**Bob,** *looking at the snow,* **saw rabbit tracks.** **Bob saw rabbit tracks.** The **-ing** word group *looking at the snow* modifies the noun **Bob.** The verb that makes a statement about **Bob** is not *looking,* but _______. 958
S 1177	*S, F,* or *R–S?* **Mr. Wetherby makes appointments, then he forgets to keep them.** ___ 1178

alike
alike

1397

In this and the following frames, underline the correct verb in each pair. Remember always to choose **let** when you mean **permit** or **allow.**

Don't (*leave, let*) **the toast burn.**

1398

is

1616

Do not use the contraction **There's, Here's,** or **Where's** unless you first look ahead in the sentence and see that a (*singular, plural*) subject is coming.

1617

good, well

1835

We paid the carpenter (*good, well*) **because her work was so** (*good, well*).

1836

Spanish

2054

A noun that names a *particular* person, place, or thing is called a **proper noun.**

Moses **Boston** **Spanish**

Each of the above nouns is a ____________ noun.

2055

None

2273

a. **My face, and neck, and arms were covered with mosquito bites.**
b. **My face and neck and arms were covered with mosquito bites.**

Which sentence is correctly punctuated? ____

2274

minutes, dollars

2492

We follow the usual rule for placing the apostrophe:

TIME: **an hour's delay, two days' pay, a week's vacation**
MONEY: **a nickel's worth, ten cents' worth, your money's worth**

Supply the missing apostrophe:

After an hours delay, the plane finally took off.

2493

four

. . . ran across our yard.

Here, too, we find a word that stands out from the others as the most important.

If you were writing a telegram, what one word in the *complete predicate* would you choose to tell what the dog did?

______

78 | 79

---

linking

The room became dark.

The verb ____________ is a linking verb.

298 | 299

---

how

The letter arrived today.

The adverb **today** tells (*where, when*) the letter **arrived.**

518 | 519

---

a

Two sentences should not be joined into a compound sentence unless their ideas are similar and are of (*equal, unequal*) importance.

738 | 739

---

saw

Sharon sat on the porch, *waiting for the letter-carrier.*

An **–ing** word group can be some distance away from the word it modifies.

The word group *waiting for the letter-carrier* modifies the noun (*Sharon, porch*).

958 | 959

R–S

S, F, or *R–S?*

We drove up and down the street, looking for a place to park.

_____

1178 | 1179

let 1398	**Don't** (*leave, let*) **your books on the stairs.** 1399
singular 1617	## Lesson 53 Unit Review [Frames 1619–1646]
well, good 1836	"Sense" words such as **look, taste,** and **feel** can be used as either action or linking verbs. a. **The bleachers** *looked* **empty.** b. **The golfers** *looked* **for the lost ball.** In which sentence is the verb *looked* used as a linking verb? ____ 1837
proper 2055	A noun that might be applied to *any* one of a class or group of persons, places, or things is called a **common noun.** **man city language** Each of the above nouns is a __________ noun. 2056
b 2274	In this and the following frames, insert the necessary commas. Several sentences require no commas at all. Remember that it takes at least three items to make a series. **Every hotel motel and tourist home was full.** (In the answer box, parentheses around a comma mean that the comma is a matter of choice.) 2275
hour's 2493	a. **The trip cost Alice one <u>weeks</u> pay.** b. **The trip cost Alice two <u>weeks</u> pay.** The word **weeks** requires an apostrophe in each sentence. In which sentence should the apostrophe come before the **s?** ____ 2494

ran

. . . ran across our yard.

The word **ran** is the most important word in the *complete* __________.

79 | 80

---

became

The room looked dark.

Because the word **dark** completes the sentence and describes the subject **room,** it is a __________ __________.

299 | 300

---

when

This pen leaks slightly.

The adverb **slightly** tells (*how much, where*) the pen **leaks.**

519 | 520

---

equal

Cathy works in Mrs. Daly's office. My mom bowls with Mrs. Daly.

Combining these two sentences would produce a (*good, poor*) compound sentence.

739 | 740

Sharon

Waiting for the letter-carrier, **Sharon sat on the porch.**
Sharon, *waiting for the letter-carrier,* **sat on the porch.**
Sharon sat on the porch, *waiting for the letter-carrier.*

In the above sentences, the word group *waiting for the letter-carrier* occupies __________ different positions. (How many?)

959 | 960

S

S, F, or *R–S?*

The map is helpful, it shows the location of every trailer camp. ____

1179 | 1180

leave

Please (*leave, let*) **me off at Twenty-first Street. (= Permit** me to get off.)

1399 1400

Use **don't** only when you can put the two words **do not** in its place.

Steve's father (*don't, doesn't*) **approve of his friends.**

1619

a

Underline the correct word:

The lights of the city looked (*beautiful, beautifully*) **from the plane.**

1837 1838

common

a. **month** **car** **country**
b. **April** **Buick** **Mexico**

Are the nouns in group *a* or *b* *proper* nouns? ____

2056 2057

hotel, motel(,)

Insert commas where needed:

Dolores speaks looks and acts just like her sister.

2275 2276

a

a. **I worked for two days.**
b. **I got two days pay.**

In which sentence does the word **days** require an apostrophe because it measures the noun that follows it? ____

2494 2495

predicate

80

↓ ↓

A little black dog with big ears ran across our yard.

The word **ran** makes a statement about **dog,** which is the

__________________.

81

---

subject complement

300

You can be sure that a verb is a *linking verb* if you can put some form of **be (is, am, are—was, were, been)** in its place.

The clothes feel (= are) **damp.**

In this sentence, **feel** is a *linking verb* because we can put

the verb ________ in its place.

301

---

how much

520

Tommy teases his brother continually.

The adverb **continually** tells (*how, how often*) Tommy teases.

521

---

poor

740

Can a comma without a conjunction be used to combine two separate sentences into a compound sentence? (*Yes, No*)

741

---

three

960

We can give interesting variety to our sentences if we learn to use **–ing** word groups.

An **–ing** word group is built upon an adjective made by adding the letters **–ing** to a __________.

961

R–S

1180

S, F, or *R–S?*

Sitting at his desk and doing nothing. ____

1181

let 1400	**The doctor won't (*leave, let*) me play for another month.** 1401
doesn't 1619	**"Rule of S":** When we add an *s* to the subject, we do not add an *s* to the verb. When we add an *s* to the verb, we do not add an *s* to the subject. Add one *s* to make this sentence singular: **The wheel____ squeak____.** 1620
beautiful 1838	**The customer smelled the new perfume very (*dubious, dubiously*) before buying it.** 1839
b 2057	a. **month car country** b. **April Buick Mexico** The nouns that begin with capital letters are (*common, proper*) nouns. 2058
speaks, looks(,) 2276	Insert commas where needed: **Children often don't realize that their slapping kicking and hair-pulling really hurt.** 2277
b 2495	a. **I had only <u>ten cents</u>.** b. **I bought <u>ten cents</u> worth of candy.** In which sentence does the word **cents** require an apostrophe because it measures the noun that follows it? ____ 2496

subject

A little black dog with big ears ran across our yard.

We saw that the word **dog** supports all the other words in the *complete subject.*

In the same way, the word **ran** supports all the other words in the *complete* ________________.

81 | 82

---

are

Arthur scolded his dog.

Try to put a form of the verb **be** in place of the verb **scolded.** The verb **scolded** (*is, is not*) a linking verb.

301 | 302

---

how often

When? Where? How? How much? How often?

Words that answer these questions about **verbs** are called ________________.

521 | 522

No

To bring out the contrast between two ideas, it is better to use the conjunction (*and, but*).

741 | 742

---

verb

To change a sentence to an **–ing** word group is simple.

~~We~~ *expected* **a storm. We closed all the windows.**

↓

Expecting a storm, **we closed all the windows.**

To change the first sentence to an **–ing** word group, drop the **We,** and change the verb *expected* to ________________.

961 | 962

F

S, F, or *R–S?*

A plastic pen which shows the supply of ink. ____

1181 | 1182

let

1401

We (*left, let*) **everything just as we found it.**

1402

(squeak)s

1620

Whenever a prepositional phrase follows the subject, select the verb that agrees with the subject, not with a noun in the prepositional phrase.

The spelling . . . very tricky.
The spelling of some words . . . very tricky.

Would the verb **is** be correct in both sentences? (*Yes, No*)

1621

dubiously

1839

This bread tastes so (*fresh, freshly*)**!**

1840

proper

2058

a. **month** **car** **country**
b. **April** **Buick** **Mexico**

The nouns that begin with small letters are (*common, proper*) nouns.

2059

slapping, kicking(,)

2277

Insert commas where needed:

Casals, King and the team's coach organized the exhibition match for the handicapped students.

2278

b

2496

Supply one missing apostrophe:

For just nineteen cents, I got fifty cents worth of cookies.

2497

predicate 82	**. . . ran across our yard.** The *complete predicate* consists of four words, but the *simple predicate* is only _____ word(s). 83
is not 302	**The engine became noisy.** Can we substitute **was** for the verb **became** in this sentence? The verb **became** (*is, is not*) a linking verb. 303
adverbs 522	**Betty drove the car** ____________________. (How?) Underline the **adverb** that would fit in this sentence and answer the question printed in parentheses: **back** **cautiously** **regularly** **sometimes** 523
but 742	Starting sentences with the conjunction **and** (*is, is not*) a good idea generally. 743
Expecting 962	**He drove around the block. ~~He~~** *looked* **for a place to park.** ↓ **He drove around the block,** *looking* **for a place to park.** To change the second sentence to an **–ing** word group, we must drop the subject **He** and change the verb *looked* to ____________________. 963
F 1182	*S, F,* or *R–S?* **Tickets to the telecast are free, they may be obtained by writing to the sponsor.** ____ 1183

left 1402	**Greg** (*left, let*) **go of the ladder too soon.** 1403
Yes 1621	**Each, every, either,** and **neither** are either singular themselves or modify singular nouns or pronouns. In either case, they require singular verbs. **Each one of these sets** (*is, are*) **guaranteed.** 1622
fresh 1840	Form the second and third degree of short words such as **fast, high,** and **cold** by adding **-er** and **-est,** not by using the adverbs **more** and **most.** **It was the** (*most strong, strongest*) **coffee I have ever drunk.** 1841
common 2059	A capital letter is required at the beginning of every ____________ noun. 2060
King (,) 2278	**Many people have been killed because they didn't stop look and listen before crossing railroad tracks.** 2279
fifty cents' worth 2497	Supply two missing apostrophes: **Miss Young spent two years savings on a months travel in Europe.** 2498

one

83

A word that can be used as the *simple predicate* of a sentence is called a **verb.** A *simple predicate* and a *verb* are the same thing.

. . . ran across our yard.

The verb in this complete predicate is ______.

84

---

is

303

The lettuce looks fresh.

See if you can put a form of **be** in place of the verb **looks.**

If you can, **looks** is a linking verb.

Is the verb **looks** a linking verb? (*Yes, No*)

304

---

cautiously

523

Betty drove the car ______________. (How often?)

Underline the adverb that answers this question.

skillfully **away** **frequently** **yesterday**

524

---

is not

743

Lesson 25 Understanding the Adverb Clause

[Frames 745–777]

---

looking

963

Rice *changed* **his mind. He ran back to third base.**

↓

Changing his mind, **he ran back to third base.**

In changing the first sentence to an **–ing** word group, we lost the subject of this sentence, which was ______.

964

R–S

1183

S, F, or *R–S?*

The driver tried to save a few minutes, but he lost his life.

1184

let

1403

Joyce had (*left, let*) **the light on all night.**

1404

---

is

1622

Two singular nouns connected by **and** require a plural verb.

Two singular nouns connected by **or** or **nor** require a singular verb.

The principal or her assistant (*attends, attend*) **each game.**

1623

---

strongest

1841

Each burst of fireworks seemed to be (*wonderfuller, more wonderful*) **than the last.**

1842

---

proper

2060

a. **asia** **robert** **harvard**
b. **hotel** **pupil** **kitchen**

Which words require capital letters because they are *proper* nouns—those in group *a* or *b*?

2061

---

stop, look(,)

2279

Dogs rats guinea pigs and other animals are used for medical experiments.

2280

---

years', month's

2498

Don't insert an apostrophe wherever you see a final **s.** Some careless writers put apostrophes in ordinary plural nouns that don't show ownership at all.

a. **Rita bought some apple's and pear's.**
b. **Rita bought some apples and pears.**

Which sentence is correct—*a* or *b*? ____

2499

ran

84

A little black dog with big ears ran across our yard.

The verb tells us what the dog *did*. It didn't *bark* or *walk* or *jump*. The verb tells that the dog ______.

85

Yes

304

A few verbs can be used as either action or linking verbs.

a. **The coach** *felt* **my ankle.**
b. **The coach** *felt* **sorry for me.**

In one sentence, *felt* is used as an *action* verb; in the other, as a *linking* verb.

In which sentence can we substitute **was** for **felt?** ____ 305

---

frequently

524

Myra looked ____________________ **for her bat.** (Where?)

Underline the adverb that answers this question.

everywhere **again** **carefully** **quickly**

525

Do you remember how adverbs answer such questions as **"When?"** and **"Where?"** and **"How?"** about verbs?

WHEN? **Pete awoke** *early.*

Early is an adverb because it modifies the ________ **awoke.**

745

Rice

964

Rice changed his mind. **He ran back to third base.**

↓ **Rice**

Changing his mind, ~~**he**~~ **ran back to third base.**

To let the reader know who the sentence is about, we substitute **Rice** for the pronoun _____ in the main statement of the sentence. 965

S

1184

F, *S*, or *R–S*?

The preface is important, it explains how the author collected his facts. ____

1185

left 1404	**You should have** (*left, let*) **the glue harden longer.** 1405
attends 1623	Before you choose between **There is** or **There are, Here is** or **Here are,** and so forth, look ahead in the sentence to see whether a singular or a plural subject is coming. **There** (*was, were*) **no electric lights in those days.** 1624
more wonderful 1842	Is it correct to use **more** with the adjective **taller,** and **most** with the adjective **cheapest?** (*Yes, No*) 1843
a 2061	Any ordinary noun becomes a proper noun when it is used as part of a particular name. a. **The river was rising.** b. **The Ohio River was rising.** In which sentence is **river** used as part of the name of a particular river? ____ 2062
Dogs, rats, guinea pigs (,) 2280	**I washed windows and dusted furniture and cleaned floors most of the day.** 2281
b 2499	Several nouns in the following sentence end in **s,** but only one shows ownership. Place the apostrophe in this word. **The dog always barks at and jumps on the familys visitors.** 2500

ran

85

A little black dog with big ears ran across our yard.

Suppose that you were asked to reduce this sentence to only two words. Underline the two words which best "tell the story" of this sentence.

little dog **big ears** **our yard** **dog ran**

86

---

b

305

a. **The coach** *felt* **my ankle.**
b. **The coach** *felt* **sorry for me.**

In which sentence is *felt* used as a linking verb? ____

306

---

everywhere

525

Miss Ming read the story __________. (How?)

Underline the adverb that answers this question.

often **aloud** **again** **here**

526

---

verb

745

Prepositional phrases, too, can be used as adverbs.

a. **Pete awoke** *early.*
b. **Pete awoke** *in the morning.*

The adverb phrase *in the morning* in sentence *b* does the same job as the adverb __________ in sentence *a.*

746

---

he

965

George *hoped* **to meet Bill Cosby. He went backstage.**

↓

Hoping to meet Bill Cosby, **he went backstage.**

In changing the first sentence to an **–ing** word group, we lost the subject **George.** The reader won't know whom we are talking about unless we substitute __________ for the pronoun **he** in the new sentence.

966

R–S

1185

F, S, or *R–S?*

Which was not included in the price of the trip. ____

1186

Answer	Frame
let 1405	**Ray's parents should have** (*left, let*) **him bring his friends home.** 1406
were 1624	From here on, the various types of subject-verb problems will be mixed. Don't put down your answer until you can give an exact reason for it. Underline the one subject among the three in parentheses that could be used as the subject of the verb: (*My shoes, The pails, The canoe*) **was full of water.** 1625
No 1843	**The water is** (*deeper, more deeper*) **on the other side of the raft.** 1844
b 2062	a. **Judy attends a small college.** b. **Judy attends Albion college.** In which sentence should **college** be capitalized because it is part of the name of a particular college? ____ 2063
None 2281	**Cocker spaniels make lively friendly intelligent and obedient pets.** 2282
family's 2500	Supply any needed apostrophes: **The missing nuts and bolts were in my brothers drawer.** 2501

dog ran

A little black dog with big ears ran across our yard.

The two words **dog ran** do not give every detail of the sentence. However, they tell more about what happened than any other two words that you might choose.

Dog is the *subject*, and **ran** is the *simple predicate* or ________.

86 | 87

---

b

The coach felt my *ankle.*
The coach felt *sorry* **for me.**

Only a linking verb can be followed by a subject complement.

Which word is a subject complement—*ankle* or *sorry*?

____

306 | 307

---

aloud

I did my homework ________ **last night.** (When?)

Underline the adverb that answers this question.

eagerly **quickly** **carelessly** **early**

526 | 527

---

early

WHEN? **Pete awoke** *in the morning.*

The prepositional phrase *in the morning* modifies the verb by telling *when* Pete **awoke.**

It is therefore called an (*adjective, adverb*) phrase.

746 | 747

George

We went from door to door. We reminded people to vote.

We went from door to door, ________ *people to vote.*

After combining the two sentences by using an **-ing** word group, what word will we have on the blank line?

____

966 | 967

F

F, S, or *R–S?*

The manager blamed Rinehart, who should have tested his brakes. ___

1186 | 1187

let

1406

Lesson 45 Bring and Take

[Frames 1408–1432]

The canoe

1625

Underline the one subject that could be used as the subject of the verb:

(*Our town, Schools, Cars*) **was much smaller in those days.**

1626

deeper

1844

Velvet is the most (*gentle, gentlest*) **horse that I have ever ridden.**

1845

b

2063

a. **The Crosby high school was completed last year.**
b. **The high school was completed last year.**

In which sentence should the words **high school** be capitalized because they are part of a proper noun? ____

2064

lively, friendly, intelligent (,)

2282

Two or three coyotes will team together to hunt rabbits antelope and other game.

2283

brother's

2501

Another careless mistake is to put apostrophes in verbs that end in **s.** A verb, of course, cannot possibly show ownership.

a. **Martha sings while she plays the piano.**
b. **Martha sing's while she play's the piano.**

Which sentence is correct—*a* or *b*? ____

2502

verb

A little black dog with big ears ran across our yard.

The framework upon which this entire sentence is built is the subject ______ and the verb ______.

87 | 88

sorry

307

Lesson 11 The Subject Complement Pattern

[Frames 309–328]

early

Don pushed the car ______________. (Where?)

Underline the adverb that answers this question.

forward **easily** **often** **slightly**

527 | 528

adverb

WHEN? **Pete awoke** *when I called him.*

The word group *when I called him* is not an adverb phrase. It is a different kind of word group.

Because the word group *when I called him* also tells *when* Pete **awoke,** it does the same job as an (*adjective, adverb*).

747 | 748

reminding

In this and the following frames, combine each pair of sentences by changing the italicized sentence to an **–ing** word group. Write the full sentence.

We heard a crash. **We rushed to the window.**

____

967 | 968

S

F, S, or *R–S?*

The sky was cloudy, therefore the eclipse was not visible.

1187 | 1188

Bring, like **come,** is a movement **toward** the person speaking.

Come over tonight and bring your accordion with you.

The movement in this sentence is (*toward, away from*) the person speaking.

1408

Our town

1626

(*The sandwiches, Two boys, My coat*) **was in the other car.**

1627

gentle

1845

Use only a single negative word to make a negative statement.

Our family didn't go (*anywhere, nowhere*) **last summer.**

1846

a

2064

Capitalize all geographical names, such as the names of particular countries, states, and cities.

Japan **North Carolina** **New York**

Write the name of the country in which you live.

____

2065

rabbits, antelope(,)

2283

Our beds and our clothes and our food were full of sand.

2284

a

2502

Five words in the following sentence end in **s,** but only one shows ownership. Place the apostrophe in this word.

My friends mother collects and repairs antique clocks which she often exhibits at fairs.

2503

(subject) dog (verb) ran 88	**The car ahead of us skidded on the ice.** The framework upon which this sentence is built is the subject ______ and the verb ______________. 89
	A **linking verb** (*does, does not*) show action. 309
forward 528	Many **adverbs**—especially those that tell **how** about the verb—end in **-ly.** **Lasorda argued firmly but politely with the umpire.** Does this sentence contain one or two adverbs? ________ 529
adverb 748	Now let's remove this word group from the sentence and look at it more closely: *when I called him* Unlike a prepositional phrase, this word group has both a subject, ____, and a verb, ______________. 749
Hearing a crash, we rushed to the window. 968	**Sandra took the wrong coat.** *She thought it was hers.* ____ ____ 969
R–S 1188	*F*, *S*, or *R–S*? **The tornado, destroying everything in its path.** ____ 1189

toward 1408	**Take,** like **go,** is a movement **away from** the person speaking. **Go to the game and take your camera along.** The movement in this sentence is (*toward, away from*) the person speaking. 1409
My coat 1627	(*My sisters, He, Rosemary*) **don't like movies.** 1628
anywhere 1846	**If I were you, I wouldn't buy** (*neither, either*) **of these two suits.** 1847
the United States 2065	Write the name of the state in which **Chicago** is located. ________________ 2066
None 2284	**Eggs may be used as a substitute for meat fish or cheese in planning meals.** 2285
friend's *or* friends' 2503	Supply any needed apostrophes: **The way Stanley teases his younger sisters and brothers gets on his fathers nerves.** 2504

(subject) car
(verb) skidded

89

A small fire often spreads to a large area.

Fire is the ____________ of the sentence, and **spreads** is the ____________.

90

---

does not

309

A **linking verb** with its subject *(can, cannot)* form a complete sentence.

310

Two

529

Many words have two forms—the **adjective** form without **-ly** and the **adverb** form with **-ly.**

EXAMPLES: **eager—eagerly** **polite—politely**
simple—simply **serious—seriously**

Write the *adverb* form of the *adjective* **prompt.** ____________

530

(subject) I
(verb) called

749

when I called him

Although this word group has both a subject and a verb, does it form a complete sentence by itself? (*Yes, No*)

750

Sandra took the wrong coat, thinking it was hers.

969

The planes fly low. **They drop emergency supplies.**

____

____

(Remember to put back the lost subject *planes.*)

970

F

1189

F, S, or *R–S?*

They made a down payment, then they discovered that they couldn't keep up the monthly payments. ____

1190

away from

1409

The difference between **bring** and **take** is a difference in the direction of the movement.

If you mean *come with,* use ____________.

If you mean *go with,* use ____________.

1410

My sisters

1628

(*The bread, The pie, The cookies*) **don't taste fresh.**

1629

---

either

1847

The fog was so thick that we (*could, couldn't*) **hardly see ten feet ahead of the car.**

1848

Illinois

2066

Write the name of the **capital** of the United States.

____

2067

---

meat, fish (,)

2285

Lesson 74 Commas in Compound Sentences

[Frames 2287–2320]

---

father's

2504

Be careful when you use apostrophes with people's names that end in **s,** like **Jones** and **Burns.**

First, you need to know how to form the ordinary plurals of these names.

Mr. Jones (one person) the **Joneses** (the whole family)

What is the plural of the name **Burns?** ____________

2505

(fire) subject
(spreads) verb

90

In this and the following frames, underline the simple subject with one line and the verb with two lines. These are the two words that "tell the story" of the sentence better than any other two words.

Some people worry about very silly things.

91

---

cannot

310

To complete the meaning of the sentence, every **linking verb** must be followed by a ____________ *complement.*

311

---

promptly

530

Write the adverb form of these two adjectives:

frequent ____________ **courteous** ____________

531

Nc

750

when I called him

Word groups like this are called **clauses.**

A **clause** is a group of words which has a subject and a verb but (*does, does not*) form a complete sentence by itself.

751

Flying low, the planes drop emergency supplies.

970

He explained the problem. *He made each step clear.*

____

____

971

R–S

1190

F, S, or *R–S?*

If the weather is good, a dog team can cover eleven miles in an hour. ____

1191

(come with)
bring

(go with)
take

1410

When you are puzzled, try to fit in the words *come with* or *go with.*

My sister often . . . a friend home from college. (= *comes with* a friend)

The correct word is (*brings, takes*). 1411

The cookies

1629

Don't (*Mr. Kwan, Shirley, the Carters*) **live on your street?** 1630

---

could

1848

Use the word **an** before any word that begins with a (*vowel, vowel sound*). 1849

Washington

2067

Capitalize, too, the complete names of oceans, rivers, lakes, mountains, parks, etc.

Arctic Ocean **Ohio River** **Duck Lake** **Hyde Park**

Write the capital letters you would need to use in writing

zion national park. ___________ 2068

A sentence that consists of two (or more) sentences joined by the conjunction **and, but,** or **or** is called a **compound sentence.**

In a compound sentence, there is a complete sentence both before and after the ____________________. 2287

Burnses

2505

Mr. Jones (one person) **the Joneses** (the whole family)

a. **Our dog was in Mr. Jone's car.**
b. **Our dog was in Mr. Jones's car.**

Which is correct because the apostrophe comes after the full name of the owner—*a* or *b*? ____ 2506

people worry 91	Underline the simple subject with one line and the verb with two lines: **Heavy black smoke blew back over the deck.** 92
subject 311	A **subject complement** is a word that describes or identifies the ______________ of the sentence. 312
frequently courteously 531	A final **-ly** is often, though not always, the sign of an ______________. 532
does not 751	a. **Pete awoke** *early.* b. **Pete awoke** *when I called him.* Both the clause *when I called him* and the adverb *early* tell *when* Pete **awoke.** Because the clause modifies the verb **awoke**—just like any adverb—we call it an (*adverb, adjective*) clause. 752
He explained the problem, making each step clear. 971	In this and the following frames, eliminate the *and* in each sentence by changing the italicized part to an **-ing** word group. Write the full sentence. *I thought the envelope was empty,* **and I threw it away.** ______________________________ ______________________________ 972
S 1191	*F, S,* or *R–S?* **Although Frances has many admirable qualities.** ____ 1192

brings

1411

We usually . . . our car to Miller's garage. (= *go with* our car)

The correct word is (*bring, take*).

1412

---

the Carters

1630

In this and the following frames, underline the correct verb:

Either of these roads (*leads, lead*) **to the park.**

1631

---

vowel sound

1849

Write **a** or **an** in each blank:

I spent _____ hour looking over _____ history book.

1850

Z N P

2068

In this and the following frames, copy the words that require capitals. If no capitals are required, write *None*. (Do not copy the first word of the sentence, which must always be capitalized.)

The family moved from sweden to this country. __________

2069

---

conjunction

2287

a. **The judge rapped on the table and waited for order.**

b. **The judge rapped on the table, and the court quieted down.**

Which sentence is compound? ____

2288

---

b

2506

a. **Our dog was in Mr. Jone's car.**
b. **Our dog was in Mr. Jones's car.**

Sentence *a* is wrong because the man's name is not **Mr. Jone,** but **Mr.** __________.

2507

smoke blew

92

Underline the simple subject with one line and the verb with two lines:

The bright headlights blinded the approaching driver.

93

---

subject

312

Underline the *three* words that are forms of the linking verb **be:**

is can seems are was will

313

---

adverb

532

The rain started suddenly.

Because the word **suddenly** modifies the verb **started,** it is an ____________.

533

---

adverb

752

Think of an **adverb clause** as a "stretched-out" adverb of several words that modifies a verb, like any ordinary ____________.

753

Thinking the envelope was empty, I threw it away.

972

We sauntered down the street *and looked in the shop windows.*

____

____

973

F

1192

F, *S*, or *R–S*?

There were very few flies or mosquitoes, the swamp had been recently drained. ____

1193

take 1412	**I asked my brother to . . . in the newspaper.** If you are outside and want your brother "to *go* in with the paper," use ________. 1413
leads 1631	**Mrs. Sevenstar or another instructor** (*give, gives*) **lectures at the Indian Art Center.** 1632
an (hour) a (history) 1850	Write **a** or **an** in each blank: **Dad belongs to _____ union that has _____ unusual record.** 1851
Sweden 2069	Copy and capitalize the words that require capitals: **The park is on pine lake.** ____________________ 2070
b 2288	**The judge rapped on the table, and the court quieted down.** This is a **compound sentence** because there is a complete sentence both before and after the conjunction **and.** What punctuation mark comes after the first statement and before the conjunction? __________ 2289
Jones 2507	Now suppose that we want to write about the car of the whole family, the **Joneses.** a. **Our dog was in the Joneses' car.** b. **Our dog was in the Jones's car.** Which is correct because the apostrophe comes after the name of the whole family—*a* or *b*? ___ 2508

headlights
blinded

93

Underline the simple subject with one line and the verb with two lines:

Two big salty tears streamed down the little boy's face.

94

---

is, are, was

313

Underline the *three* words that are forms of the linking verb **be:**

were shall might am do been

314

---

adverb

533

Suddenly the rain started.
The rain suddenly started.
The rain started suddenly.

These sentences consist of the same words. However, one word occupies a different position in each sentence. This word is the adverb ____________. 534

---

adverb

753

Now let's look at modifiers that answer the question **"Where?"** about the action of the verb.

WHERE? **Connie works** *there.*
WHERE? **Connie works** *on the third floor.*

Both the adverb *there* and the adverb phrase *on the third floor* modify the verb ____________.

754

We sauntered down the street, looking in the shop windows.

973

The lady turned around **and asked us not to talk.**

____

____

(Be sure to put back the lost subject *lady.*)

974

R–S

1193

UNIT 6: **USING VERBS CORRECTLY**

Lesson 39 Overcoming the Dangerous Six

[Frames 1195–1236]

page 187

take

1413

I asked my brother to . . . in the newspaper.

If you are inside and want your brother "to *come* in with the paper," use ______.

1414

gives

1632

Here (*are, is*) **the essays by Maxine Hong Kingston.**

1633

a (union)
an (unusual)

1851

UNIT 9: **USING PRONOUNS CORRECTLY**

Lesson 61 The Subject Form of Pronouns

[Frames 1853–1891]

Pine Lake

2070

Copy and capitalize the words that require capitals:

Sibley park is on a lake. ______

2071

comma

2289

In a compound sentence, the comma is placed at the point where you would pause if you were speaking the sentence.

Put a comma where you would naturally pause in saying this sentence:

We didn't want the picture but Mom couldn't refuse it.

2290

a

2508

a. **Our dog was in the Joneses' car.**
b. **Our dog was in the Jones's car.**

Sentence *a* is correct because the car belongs not to the **Jones,** but to the ______.

2509

tears streamed

94

Underline the simple subject with one line and the verb with two lines:

The director of the company resigned because of the criticism.

95

---

were, am, been

314

If we can substitute **is, was,** or some other form of **be** for a verb, this verb (*is, is not*) used as a linking verb.

315

---

suddenly

534

Now let's return, for one frame, to **adjectives.**

The wet pavement caused a serious accident.

Can either adjective—**wet** or **serious**—be moved from its present position before the noun it modifies to any other position in the sentence? (*Yes, No*)

535

---

works

754

WHERE? **Connie works** *where our family shops.*

Because *where our family shops* has a subject and a verb but does not form a complete sentence by itself, it is a (*phrase, clause*).

755

Turning around, the lady asked us not to talk.

974

Mom went on a vacation *and left me in charge of the shop.*

____

____

975

PRESENT: **I collect stamps.**
PAST: **I collected stamps.**

What letters do we add to change the verb **collect** from present to past time? ______

1195

bring 1414	PRESENT — SIMPLE PAST — PAST WITH HELPER **bring** — **brought** — **have brought** **take** — **took** — **have taken** Both past forms of the verb ________ are alike. 1415
are 1633	**The hinges of the door** (*needs, need*) **oiling.** 1634
	Jerry wants Jerry's friends to go with Jerry. This sentence sounds very monotonous because of the repetition of the noun ________. 1853
Park 2071	**It is the largest island in the pacific ocean.** ________________________ 2072
picture, 2290	Without a comma to indicate the pause, the reader might get the wrong idea. In the sentence below, suppose the reader were to pause at the vertical line: **Jane painted the porch and her parents | paid her for the job.** To prevent misreading, put a comma after ________. 2291
Joneses 2509	a. **Charle's story won a prize.** b. **Charles's story won a prize.** Which is correct because the apostrophe comes after the full name of the owner—*a* or *b*? ____ 2510

director
resigned

95

Lesson 4 Finding the Verb

[Frames 97–128]

---

is

315

a. **The driver looked angry.**

b. **The driver looked at his speedometer.**

In which sentence can we substitute **was** for **looked?**

The verb **looked** is used as a linking verb in sentence ____.

316

No

535

Adjectives can seldom be moved to another position in the sentence. **Adverbs,** on the contrary, can sometimes be shifted from one position to another.

Adverbs are (*more, less*) movable than **adjectives.**

536

---

clause

755

WHERE? **Connie works** *where our family shops.*

Because the clause *where our family shops* modifies the verb **works,** it is an *(adverb, adjective)* clause.

756

Mom went on a vacation, leaving me in charge of the shop.

975

We can form an adjective from any verb by adding the letters________ to it.

976

–ed

1195

The simple past form of most verbs ends in **–ed.**

The simple past form of the verb **collect** is **collected.**

The simple past form of the verb **jump** is ____________.

1196

bring

1415

Mother said, "You forgot to . . . your books to school this morning." (= *go* to school with)

The movement of the books would be (*toward, away from*) the mother, who is speaking.

1416

---

need

1634

Any one of these boys (*know, knows*) **where the office is.**

1635

Jerry

1853

Once we make it clear that we are talking about **Jerry,** we can avoid repetition and save time by using *pronouns* in place of the noun **Jerry.**

a. **Jerry wants Jerry's friends to go with Jerry.**
b. **Jerry wants his friends to go with him.**

In sentence *b,* **his** and **him** are (*nouns, pronouns*).

1854

Pacific Ocean

2072

There is not a single large city on this river.

2073

---

porch,

2291

Put a comma at the end of the first statement in a compound sentence—that is, just before the conjunction **and, but,** or **or.**

Supply the necessary comma:

The gate must be kept closed or the dog will run away.

2292

---

b

2510

In an earlier lesson, you learned that pronouns have special forms that show ownership **without** apostrophes. Don't put an apostrophe before the final **s** in any possessive pronoun.

Underline the two possessive pronouns in this sentence:

Yours are better than theirs.

2511

The verb is the most important word in the (*subject, predicate*).

97

---

a

316

The sky . . . cloudy.

Underline *two* of the following verbs that could be used as linking verbs in the above sentence to show that **cloudy** describes **sky.**

looked believed grew lived

317

---

more

536

The new pitcher stepped confidently to the mound.

The adjective **new** cannot be moved, but the adverb ________________ can be moved to another position.

537

---

adverb

756

Adverb clauses, just like adverbs, can also answer the question **"How?"** about the action of the verb.

HOW? **Tom ate** *greedily.*
HOW? **Tom ate** *as though he were starved.*

Both the adverb *greedily* and the adverb clause *as though he were starved* modify the verb ________.

757

–ing

976

An **–ing** word by itself (*can, cannot*) serve as a verb.

977

---

jumped

1196

a. **I collected stamps.**
b. **I have collected stamps.**

The verbs in both of these sentences show past time. In *a*, the verb that shows past time consists of one word.

In *b*, the verb that shows past time consists of ____ word(s).

1197

away from 1416	**Mother said, "You forgot to** *(bring, take)* **your books to school this morning."** The movement of the books would be **away from** the speaker. Therefore, the correct verb is ________. 1417
knows 1635	**The speed and power of Jim Thorpe** *(were, was)* **remarkable.** 1636
pronouns 1854	**Pronouns** are words used in place of nouns. Pronouns can do the same work in a sentence that ________ do. 1855
None 2073	**Chesapeake bay divides maryland into two parts.** ________________ 2074
closed, 2292	The comma makes a compound sentence easier to read. The reader can take it in two small bites instead of one big bite. a. **Urban areas are constantly growing in population and rural areas are diminishing.** b. **They won and we lost.** In which sentence would a comma be more helpful? ____ 2293
Yours, theirs 2511	POSSESSIVE PRONOUNS: **his, hers, yours** **its** (belonging to **it**), **ours, theirs** **Hers was parked behind Joans.** The above sentence contains a possessive noun and a possessive pronoun. How many apostrophes are needed? ____ 2512

predicate

Most verbs are *action words.* Verbs like **break, swim, build,** and **write** represent actions that we see going on around us.

apple stumbled shirt

Which one of these words is an *action verb?* ____________

97 98

looked, grew

Washington . . . our first President.

Underline *two* verbs that could be used as linking verbs to show that **President** identifies **Washington.**

chose was became has

317 318

confidently

A serious accident occurred there.

An adverb in this sentence tells **where** the accident occurred. This *adverb* is __________.

537 538

ate

Although single adverbs cannot answer the question **"Why?"** about verbs, **adverb clauses** can.

WHY? **Bobby cried** *because he bumped his head.*

In the clause *because he bumped his head,* the subject is *he,* and the verb is ____________.

757 758

cannot

An **-ing** word is useful for forming word groups that are used as (*adjectives, adverbs*).

977 978

two

a. **I collected stamps.**
b. **I have collected stamps.**

In *b,* the past form of the verb consists of two words: the main verb **collected** and the helping verb __________.

1197 1198

take 1417	**The teacher asked, "Why didn't you . . . your books to school today?"** (= *come* to school with) The movement of the books would be (*toward, away from*) the teacher, who is speaking. 1418
were 1636	(*Was, Were*) **the refreshments as good as usual?** 1637
nouns 1855	a. **Joe liked Sue.** b. **Sue liked Joe.** In sentence *a*, **Joe** is the subject, and **Sue** is the direct object. In sentence *b*, **Sue** is the subject, and **Joe** is the ________ ________. 1856
Bay, Maryland 2074	**The most densely populated country in europe is belgium.** ________________________ 2075
a 2293	**They won and we lost.** This sentence is so short and simple that it doesn't need a comma. The reader can take it comfortably in a single bite. A comma is not necessary and is usually omitted in a (*long, short*) compound sentence. 2294
one (Joan's) 2512	**Hers was parked behind Joan's.** Only one apostrophe is needed because an apostrophe should not be used in a possessive (*noun, pronoun*). 2513

stumbled

98

painted grass teacher

Which one of these words is an *action verb*? ________

99

---

was, became

318

A word that completes a linking verb and *describes* or *identifies* the subject is called a ________________ ________________.

319

---

there

538

The children soon spent all their money.

An adverb in this sentence tells **when** about the verb **spent.**

This *adverb* is ________.

539

---

bumped

758

An adverb clause can also tell **on what condition** an action will occur.

ON WHAT CONDITION? **Jim will go** *if he can get a ticket.*

The adverb clause *if he can get a ticket* explains **on what condition** Jim ________ ________.

759

---

adjectives

978

Lesson 32 Using Appositives to Combine Ideas

[Frames 980–1012]

---

have

1198

Joy has collected stamps for a long time.

In this sentence, the past form of the verb consists of two words: the main verb **collected** and the helping verb ________.

1199

toward 1418	**The teacher asked, "Why didn't you** (*bring, take*) **your books to school today?"** The movement of the books would be **toward** the speaker. Therefore, the correct verb is ________. 1419
Were 1637	**One of my front teeth** (*is, are*) **loose.** 1638
direct object 1856	a. **Joe liked Sue.** b. **Sue liked Joe.** Do the nouns **Joe** and **Sue** change in form or spelling when their use in the sentence changes? (*Yes, No*) 1857
Europe, Belgium 2075	**Our town is in cook county.** ____________________ 2076
short 2294	a. **Hot air rises but cold air falls.** b. **You can lead a horse to water but you cannot make him drink.** Which compound sentence does not require a comma? ___ 2295
pronoun 2513	In this and the following frames, insert the necessary apostrophes, remembering the various don'ts in this lesson. Several frames require no apostrophes. **This girls job is to check the ladies wraps.** 2514

painted

Some verbs like **decide, remember, think, hope,** and **understand** represent *actions of the mind.* These actions can't be seen by an outsider.

planted **planned**

Which verb represents an action of the mind? ________

99

100

---

subject complement

PATTERN 4:
Subject—Linking Verb ← Subject Complement

This is another common sentence pattern.

The three other patterns we studied contained action verbs.

The verb in this pattern is always a ____________ verb.

319

320

---

soon

Carla reads well for her age.

The word ________ is an *adverb* because it tells **how** Carla **reads.**

539

540

---

will go

Learn to recognize the **clause signals** that tell us that an adverb clause is beginning. They are grouped according to the kind of information that the clauses supply.

WHEN? **while** **when** **whenever** **as**
before **after** **since** **until**

The clause signals (*begin, end*) adverb clauses.

759

760

Suppose that someone should say to us—

"Archibald bit me."

We wouldn't know whether **Archibald** is a dog, a turtle, or a neighbor's child. To be clear, this sentence needs some words to explain *who* or *what* ____________ is.

980

---

has

Joy had collected many stamps.

Here the main verb is **collected,** and the helping verb is ________.

1199

1200

Answer	Frame
bring 1419	**Take these flowers to Mrs. Smith, but bring back the vase.** Which verb shows a movement **away from** the speaker—**take** or **bring?** ________. 1420
is 1638	(*Doesn't, Don't*) **this knob turn on the radio?** 1639
No 1857	Now let's change the nouns **Joe** and **Sue** to pronouns: a. **He liked her.** b. **She liked him.** Although these sentences concern only two persons, **Joe** and **Sue,** how many different pronouns are used? ______ 1858
Cook County 2076	**Denver is situated at the very foot of the rocky mountains.** ______________________________ 2077
a 2295	Don't mistake a sentence with two (compound) *predicates* for a compound sentence. Their punctuation is different. a. ______ ____________ , **and** ______ ____________ . b. ______ ____________ **and** ______________ . One diagram represents a compound sentence. Which diagram represents a compound predicate? ___ 2296
girl's, ladies' 2514	Insert any necessary apostrophes: **Bobby complains about his headaches only on school days.** 2515

planned

100

In each line, underline *one* verb that represents an action of the mind:

regretted **pushed** **departed**
crossed **erased** **disliked**

101

---

linking

320

In this and the following frames, write in the missing words of the sentence framework. (S = Subject, V = Verb, SC = Subject Complement)

The road through the woods is much shorter.

S V SC
road is ______________

321

---

well

540

Dad never eats between meals.

The word ______________ is an *adverb* because it modifies the verb **eats.**

541

---

begin

760

There are only two **clause signals** which can start adverb clauses that answer the question **"Where?"**

WHERE? **where, wherever**

a. **The days get longer** *as the summer advances.*
b. **Gloria was sitting** *where we couldn't see her.*

In which sentence does the clause tell **where?** ___

761

Archibald

980

"Archibald, *our* <u>*cat*</u>*,* **bit me."**

Now we know that **Archibald** is a *cat.*

The noun *cat* comes (*before, after*) the noun **Archibald,** which it explains.

981

---

had

1200

Most verbs show past time in these two ways:

1. By the simple past form that ends in **–ed.**
2. By this same simple past form combined with the ______________*ing* verb **have, has,** or **had.**

1201

take

1420

←brought →took

Mom brought home a visitor and took her to the airport after dinner.

Which verb shows a movement **toward** the speaker—**brought** or **took?** ____________

1421

Doesn't

1639

Each of these girls (*have, has*) **a part in the play.**

1640

---

four

1858

a. **He liked her.**
b. **She liked him.**

The two pronouns that refer to **Joe** are **He** and **him.**

The two pronouns that refer to **Sue** are **She** and ______.

1859

Rocky Mountains

2077

Capitalize the words **street, avenue, road, boulevard,** etc., when they are parts of particular names.

Beacon Street Fifth Avenue Salem Road

Continue to copy the words that require capitals:

This avenue crosses jackson boulevard.

____________________________________ 2078

---

b

2296

a. ______ ____________, **and** ______ ____________.
b. ______ ____________ **and** ________________.

Diagram *b* represents a compound predicate since only a predicate—not a subject and a predicate—follows the **and.**

Does a sentence with a compound predicate require a comma? (*Yes, No*)

2297

None

2515

Insert any necessary apostrophes:

Joyce made hers with only ten cents worth of materials.

2516

regretted, disliked 101	Verbs are the only words that can show by a change in spelling whether they mean *present* or *past* time; for example, **shout—shouted, play—played, take—took, give—gave.** **washes** **washed** Which verb means *past* time? ____________ 102
SC shorter 321	**Jimmy Walker became a star on television.** S V SC ____________ became ____________ 322
never 541	**Dad does not eat between meals.** The word ______ is an *adverb* because it modifies the verb **does eat,** which it interrupts, as adverbs often do. 542
b 761	Several clause signals can start adverb clauses that answer the question **"Why?"** WHY? **because, since, as, so that** a. **The bag tore** *when I picked it up.* b. **The bag tore** *because it was wet.* Which sentence explains **why** the bag tore? ___ 762
after 981	**"Archibald,** *our cat,* **bit me."** A noun or pronoun that is set *after* another noun or pronoun to explain it is called an **appositive.** In the above sentence, the noun ______ is an **appositive.** 982
help(ing) 1201	With most verbs, we use the same form with **have, has,** or **had** that we use for the simple past. SIMPLE PAST — PAST WITH HELPER looked — have looked walked — have walked played — have ____________ 1202

brought 1421	In this and the following frames, underline the correct verb in each pair. Remember always to choose **take** when the movement is **away from** the speaker. **Why don't you** (*bring, take*) **this souvenir home to your children?** (= *go* home with this souvenir) 1422
has 1640	**Either Harry or his brother** (*has, have*) **a pocket radio.** 1641
her 1859	a. **He liked Sue.** b. **Sue liked him.** When the pronoun takes the place of the subject **Joe,** we use **He.** When the pronoun takes the place of the direct object **Joe,** we use ______. 1860
Jackson Boulevard 2078	**We live three streets beyond miller road.** ________________________ 2079
No 2297	a. **Nancy Lopez sank the final putt, and she won the tournament.** b. **Nancy Lopez sank the final putt and won the tournament.** Which sentence requires a comma because it is a compound sentence with both a subject and a predicate after the conjunction **and?** ___ 2298
cents' 2516	**All the pupils parents met in the schools auditorium.** 2517

washed

102

writes **wrote**

Which verb means *present* time? ______________

103

S
Jimmy Walker

SC
star

322

Sarah Winnemucca was a prominent advocate of American Indian rights.

S V SC

______________ was ______________

323

---

not

542

The river often overflows in the spring.

The adverb in this sentence is ____________.

543

---

b

762

Ellen's parents bought her ice skates . . . *she would learn to skate.*

Underline the clause signal you would add to explain **why** Ellen's parents bought the ice skates.

while **as if** **so that** **although**

763

---

cat

982

The word **appositive** has four syllables.

ap-pos-i-tive

You will spell it correctly if you will write the letters **ap** in front of the word ______________.

983

---

played

1202

SIMPLE PAST	PAST WITH HELPER
earned	have earned
painted	have painted
changed	have changed

The form of the verb used with the helper and the form used without the helper are (*different, alike*).

1203

take

1422

Dad often (*brought, took*) **us foreign stamps from the office.** (=*came* home with foreign stamps)

1423

---

has

1641

There (*was, were*) **no zeroes in the Roman numbering system.**

1642

---

him

1860

a. **She liked Joe.**
b. **Joe liked her.**

When the pronoun takes the place of the subject **Sue,** we use **She.**

When the pronoun takes the place of the direct object **Sue,** we use ________.

1861

Miller Road

2079

Woodward avenue is our main business street.

____

2080

---

a

2298

Nancy Lopez sank the final putt, and she won the tournament.

If we omitted the underlined **she** from this sentence, would we still keep the comma? (*Yes, No*)

2299

---

pupils', school's

2517

Theirs always runs and barks after passing cars.

2518

writes

103

What is the *past* form of the verb **walks?** ________

104

S
Sarah
Winnemucca

SC
advocate

323

My friend seemed very unhappy about something.

S	V	SC
friend	________	________

324

---

often

543

Adverbs are a class of words that can tell **when, where, how much,** and **how often** about ________.

544

---

so that

763

There are only two clause signals which can start adverb clauses that answer the question **"How?"**

HOW? **as if, as though**

a. **Bobby cried** *when his toy balloon broke.*
b. **Bobby cried** *as if his heart would break.*

Which sentence tells **how** Bobby cried? ____

764

---

positive

983

Jerry, *my locker partner,* **lost his key.**

The appositive is the noun ________.

984

---

alike

1203

When we use the same **–ed** form of a verb with **have, has,** or **had** that we use for the simple past, the verb is said to be **regular.**

a. **We talked to the principal.**
b. **We have talked to the principal.**

The verb **talk** is a(n) (*regular, irregular*) verb.

1204

brought

1423

Whenever I went to the hospital, I (*brought, took*) **candy along for Donnie.** (= *went* with candy)

1424

---

were

1642

Neither of these coats (*seem, seems*) **warm enough for winter.**

1643

---

her

1861

a. **He liked her.**
b. **She liked him.**

Do the pronouns change when their use in the sentence changes? (*Yes, No*)

1862

Avenue

2080

Capitalize the names of particular nationalities, languages, races, and religions.

Italian	**Black**	**Chinese**	**Catholic**
American	**Indian**	**Jewish**	**Protestant**

Supply the missing letter:

A citizen of Canada is called a ____anadian.

2081

No

2299

Paul drove to the side of the road and ‸ let the other car pass.

If we added **he** at the point indicated, would we need to insert a comma after the word **road?** (*Yes, No*)

2300

None

2518

The boys gym holds more people than our girls study hall.

2519

walked

104

What is the *present* form of the verb **took?** ________

105

V SC
seemed unhappy

324

A good driver is always ready for emergencies.

S	V	SC
________	________	ready

325

---

verbs

544

Lesson 19 A Special Kind of Adverb

[Frames 546–579]

---

b

764

The dog was limping . . . *it had been hurt.*

Underline the clause signal you would add to explain **how** the dog was limping.

unless   **as though**   **since**   **although**

765

---

partner

984

Jerry, *my locker* *<u>partner</u>*, **lost his key.**

The noun *partner* is an appositive because it is set *after* another noun, ________, to explain it.

985

---

regular

1204

Most verbs, fortunately, are regular. However, there are a number of verbs that do not follow the usual pattern.

PRESENT: **I see Donna every day.**
PAST: **I saw Donna every day.**

The past form of **see** does not end in ______, as all regular verbs do.

1205

Answer	Frame
took 1424	**The milkman** (*brought, took*) **us our milk too late for breakfast.** 1425
seems 1643	**The air and the water** (*were, was*) **perfect for swimming.** 1644
Yes 1862	a. **I he she we they** b. **me him her us them** **. . . drove the car.** Which pronouns could be used as the subject of the little sentence above—those in group *a* or *b*? ____ 1863
C (capital) 2081	**A citizen of Japan speaks ____apanese.** 2082
Yes 2300	a. **We must raise the price of our paper, or we shall have to reduce its size.** b. **We must raise the price of our paper, or reduce its size.** From which sentence should the comma be omitted? ____ 2301
boys', girls' 2519	**Childrens haircuts cost less than mens.** 2520

take *or* takes 105	When you change a sentence from *present* to *past* or from *past* to *present*, only one word changes—the verb. PRESENT: **The girls manage the shop.** PAST: **The girls managed the shop.** The word **manage** is a verb because it is the only word that ________________. 106
S V driver is 325	**They were the only Americans in this little town.** S V SC They ________________ ________________ 326
	We have studied two classes of words that modify other words: (1) **adjectives** and (2) **adverbs.** **Adjectives** modify ___________ and **pronouns.** 546
as though 765	Four signal words can start adverb clauses that answer the question **"On what condition?"** ON WHAT CONDITION? **if, unless, though, although** **Jerry will play** *if he can be the pitcher.* This clause explains **on what condition** Jerry ___________ ___________. 766
Jerry 985	Although an appositive is usually a single noun or pronoun, we generally add other words to modify it. a. **Jerry,** *my locker partner,* **lost his key.** b. **Jerry,** *my careless locker partner with the red hair,* **lost his key.** Does the appositive have more modifiers in *a* or *b*? ___ 986
–ed 1205	Underline one of the following verbs whose past form does not end in **–ed:** **follow** **bring** **cook** 1206

brought 1425	**Henry must have** (*brought, taken*) **his blue suit to the cleaner.** 1426
were 1644	**One of us** (*have, has*) **to stay home with the baby.** 1645
a 1863	**her he him** Which pronoun can be used as the subject of a sentence and is, therefore, in the subject form? ______ 1864
J (capital) 2082	**The Pope is the spiritual leader of the ___atholics.** 2083
b 2301	a. **This is a powerful engine but runs very quietly.** b. **This is a powerful engine but it runs very quietly.** In which sentence should a comma be inserted after **engine?** ___ 2302
Children's, men's 2520	**I got twenty-five cents worth of cookies for only ten cents.** 2521

changes
or changed

106

PRESENT: **I often see my uncle.**
PAST: **I often saw my uncle.**

The word ____ is a verb because it is the only word that changes.

107

V	SC
were	Americans

326

The tires on the car looked quite new.

S	V	SC
__________	looked	__________

327

---

nouns

546

The **adverbs** that we studied in the previous lesson modified only __________.

547

---

will play

766

a. **This chair will collapse** *if you sit on it.*
b. **This chair will collapse** *because it is broken.*

Which sentence explains **on what condition** the chair will collapse? ____

767

---

b

986

Ms. Wade, *our new coach,* **is very good.**

The noun *coach* comes after the noun **Ms. Wade** and explains it.

The noun **coach,** therefore, is an ______________.

987

---

bring

1206

Verbs like **bring, see,** and **go** whose past forms do not end in **–ed** are called **irregular verbs.**

I saw Donna every day.

See is an **irregular** verb because its past form, **saw,** does not end in _____.

1207

taken 1426	**We** (*brought, took*) **our dog to the vet last week.** 1427
has 1645	**Only two customers** (*were, was*) **in the store at the time.** 1646
he 1864	**they us me I them her** Which two pronouns are in the subject form? ________ and ________ 1865
C (capital) 2083	**Martina Aroya is a great ____merican singer.** 2084
b 2302	This sentence has two **and**'s. Only one of them, however, is used to connect the two parts of this compound sentence. **Larry has worked after school and on Saturdays and he has saved up nearly $500.** A comma is needed before the (*first, second*) **and.** 2303
cents' worth 2521	**This post shows where theirs leaves off and ours begins.** 2522

see *or* saw

107

Now let's change a sentence from *past* to *present* time and see which word changes.

PAST: **This job took too much time.**
PRESENT: **This job takes too much time.**

The word __________ is a verb because it is the only word that changes.

108

S SC
tires new

327

A warm sweater feels cozy on a chilly day.

S	V	SC
__________	__________	__________

328

verbs

547

Both **adjectives** and **adverbs** modify or change the pictures or ideas we get from words by making their meaning (*more, less*) clear and exact.

548

a

767

We placed the notice *so that everyone would see it.*

The clause signal consists of two words: ______ ________.

768

appositive

987

Ms. Wade, *our new coach,* **is very good.**

Ms. Wade is the *coach*, and the *coach* is **Ms. Wade.**

An appositive and the noun it explains are always the ________ person, place, or thing.

988

–ed

1207

a. **I saw Donna every day.**
b. **I have seen Donna every day.**

Compare the past form of the verb **see** in *a* with the form used in *b*.

The simple past form and the form used with the helper **have** are (*alike, different*).

1208

took

1427

We (*brought, took*) our dog home from the vet's today.

1428

were

1646

UNIT 8: **CHOOSING THE RIGHT MODIFIER**

Lesson 54 Words That Describe Actions

[Frames 1648–1682]

they, I

1865

a. **You like it.**
b. **It likes you.**

Do the pronouns **you** and **it** change in form when their use in the sentence changes? (*Yes, No*)

1866

A (capital)

2084

Adjectives that are formed from proper nouns should also be capitalized.

French bread **Russian dressing** **Asiatic flu**

Julius Caesar was a ___oman general.

2085

second

2303

The three conjunctions that can connect the two parts of a compound sentence are ______, ______, ______.

2304

None

2522

Gail did a weeks work in three days time.

2523

took *or* takes 108	**The temperature usually dropped in the evening.** Which word would change if you changed this sentence from *past* to *present*? ________ 109
S V sweater feels SC cozy 328	Lesson **12** **Recognizing Basic Sentence Patterns** [Frames 330–363]
more 548	**The weather is cold.** **The weather is very cold.** In both sentences, the adjective **cold** modifies the noun ________. 549
so that 768	**The fire wouldn't start because our wood was wet.** The adverb clause starts with the clause signal ________ and ends with the word ________. 769
same 988	An appositive with its modifiers should be set off from the rest of the sentence by commas. The commas are missing below. **Ms. Wade** *our new coach* **is very strict.** One comma is needed after **Ms. Wade,** and another after ________. 989
different 1208	Most irregular verbs have two different past forms: one for the simple past and one to be used with **have, has,** or **had.** Underline one of the following verbs that is irregular because it has two different past forms: **escape return take** 1209

brought 1428	**Would you please** *(bring, take)* **this report to Mrs. Brown.** 1429
	There are hundreds of words that have two forms: an adjective form without **–ly** and an adverb form with **–ly.** a. **bad** **lazy** **polite** **careful** **foolish** b. **badly** **lazily** **politely** **carefully** **foolishly** Which group of words consists of adverbs? ____ 1648
No 1866	**she you we I it they** Which two pronouns could be used as either a subject or an object without changing their form? ________ and ________ 1867
R (capital) 2085	**The styles from Paris are called ____arisian styles.** 2086
and, but, or 2304	In this and the following frames, supply the necessary commas. Several sentences do not require commas because they are not compound. **We talked to the animal trainer and we asked her many questions.** 2305
week's, days' 2523	**Mothers car was not in its parking space.** 2524

dropped 109	**All my friends go to church.** Which word would change if you changed this sentence from *present* to *past*? ________ 110
	We have now studied *four* basic sentence patterns. PATTERN I: *Subject—Action Verb* EXAMPLES: **His grades improved.** **The lake freezes in the winter.** The verbs in these sentences make (*complete, incomplete*) statements about their subjects. 330
weather 549	a. **The weather is cold.** b. **The weather is very cold.** Which sentence gives you the idea of greater coldness? ___ 550
because, wet 769	**Ralph jumped from the bus before it came to a stop.** The adverb clause starts with the clause signal ________ and ends with the word ________. 770
coach 989	**Ms. Wade** *the basketball coach at Delta State* **is very good.** One comma is needed after **Ms. Wade,** and another after ________. 990
take 1209	PRESENT: **see** — SIMPLE PAST: **saw** — PAST WITH HELPER: **have seen** **We** ‸ *saw* **several porpoises.** If you added the helping verb *have* at the point marked by the caret, you would need to change the verb *saw* to ________. 1210

take 1429	**The manager urged us to** (*bring, take*) **the set home for a free trial.** 1430
b 1648	To modify a noun or a pronoun, we use an (*adjective, adverb*). 1649
you, it 1867	When a single pronoun is the subject of a sentence, it is almost impossible to make a mistake. Only a small child would say, "*Us* want a drink" or "*Her* took a cookie." (*Her, She*) **saw the accident.** Which is the correct pronoun? ____ 1868
P (capital) 2086	**Tom-toms are a kind of ____frican drum.** 2087
trainer, 2305	Insert any necessary commas: **The product must be advertised or the public will never ask for it.** 2306
Mother's 2524	**After Phil borrowed yours, he borrowed Elmers.** 2525

go

110

The milk in our refrigerator sometimes freezes.

The verb in this sentence is ______________.

111

---

complete

330

a. **The other team always wins.**
b. **The other team always wins the game.**

In which sentence does the verb complete the meaning of the sentence without requiring an additional word? ____

331

---

b

550

a. **The weather is cold.**
b. **The weather is very cold.**

The added word which gives you the idea of greater coldness in sentence *b* is __________.

551

---

before, stop

770

Don't drink the water unless it has been boiled.

The adverb clause starts with the clause signal ____________ and ends with the word ______________.

771

State

990

Yosemite, *the famous national park,* **is in California.**
We spent a week at Yosemite, *the famous national park.*

An appositive word group that comes in the middle of a sentence requires two commas.

How many commas does an appositive word group require when it comes at the end of a sentence? ________

991

---

seen

1210

PRESENT	SIMPLE PAST	PAST WITH HELPER
take	**took**	**have taken**

The simple past form of this verb is **took.**

The form that must be used with **have, has,** or **had** is (*took, taken*).

1211

take

The librarian said, "You should have (*brought, taken*) this book back yesterday."

1430 | 1431

---

adjective

To describe the action of a verb, we use an (*adjective, adverb*).

1649 | 1650

She

When a sentence has a compound subject—either two pronouns or a noun and a pronoun—mistakes sometimes occur.

a. **She saw the accident.**
b. **Ken and (*her, she*) saw the accident.**

In sentence *b*, which pronoun is correct? ______

1868 | 1869

A (capital)

2087

Lesson 68 Using Capitals for Organizations and Institutions

[Frames 2089–2123]

---

advertised,

Insert any necessary commas:

The sailor looked out over the water and pointed to a small speck in the distance.

2306 | 2307

Elmer's

Copy the correct words in this sentence:

(*Charles's, Charle's*) **dog was in the** (*Jones's, Joneses'*) **yard.**

______ ______

2525 | 2526

freezes

An empty bottle rolled down the basement stairs.

The verb in this sentence is ________.

111 | 112

---

a

PATTERN 2: *Subject—Action Verb → Direct Object*

EXAMPLES: **Jan changed the tire.**

The baby swallowed the button.

In these sentences, the action passes from the *subjects* to the *direct* ________, as the arrows show.

331 | 332

---

very

The weather is very cold.

The word **very** modifies the adjective ________.

551 | 552

---

unless, boiled

Sarah Lincoln treated Abe as though he were her own son.

The adverb clause starts with the two-word clause signal ______ ________ and ends with the word ______.

771 | 772

One

Juan, *the best hitter on the team,* **sprained his wrist.**
Juan sprained his wrist.

If we omit the appositive word group from this sentence, do we have a complete sentence remaining? (*Yes, No*)

991 | 992

---

taken

Irregular verbs cause many errors because people sometimes confuse the two past forms.

PRESENT	SIMPLE PAST	PAST WITH HELPER
do	**did**	**have done**

Which past form is required in the following sentence?

I should have ________ better on the test.

1211 | 1212

brought 1431	**Walter should have** (*brought, taken*) **his problem to the principal.** 1432
adverb 1650	**Pete's report was accurate.** **Accurate** modifies the noun **report.** It is, therefore, an ________________. 1651
she 1869	**Ken and she saw the accident.** The subject form **she** is correct because **she,** as well as **Ken,** is the subject of the verb ________. 1870
	A noun that names a *particular* person, place, or thing is a (*common, proper*) noun. 2089
None 2307	**The coat was a bargain but I had spent all my money.** 2308
Charles's, Joneses' 2526	Copy the correct words in this sentence: (*Mrs. Jone's, Mrs. Jones's*) **plans are better than** (*hers, her's*). ________________ ________________ 2527

rolled

112

When looking for the *subject* and *verb* in a sentence, always find the *verb* first.

Look for the verb (*before, after*) you find the subject.

113

---

objects

332

PATTERN 3:

Subject—Action Verb→Indirect Object—Direct Object

EXAMPLES: **The company sent us a sample.** (to us)
Dad built us a workshop. (for us)

Before the *direct object* we find an ________ *object.*

333

---

cold

552

very cold **so cold** **rather cold**
extremely cold **quite cold** **slightly cold**
terribly cold **too cold** **somewhat cold**

All the underlined words give a more exact idea of *how* **cold** something is. We say, therefore, that these words *mod*________ the adjective **cold.**

553

---

as though, son

772

To be a clause, a word group must have both a ________ and a **verb.**

773

Yes

992

a. **Juan the best hitter on the team made a home run.**
b. **A home run was made by Juan the best hitter on the team.**

Which sentence requires only one comma because the appositive word group comes at the end of the sentence—*a* or *b*? ____

993

---

done

1212

PRESENT	SIMPLE PAST	PAST WITH HELPER
do	**did**	**have done**

Which past form is required in the following sentence?

George ________ the problem twice.

1213

taken

1432

Lesson 46 Unit Review

[Frames 1434–1456]

adjective

1651

Pete reported the game accurately.

Accurately describes *how* Pete **reported** the game.

Because **accurately** modifies the verb **reported,** it is an

______________.

1652

saw

1870

When two pronouns (or a noun and a pronoun) are used as subjects, choose the same form of each pronoun that you would choose if the pronoun were used alone.

a. **He missed the bus. I missed the bus.**
b. **He and** (*I, me*) **missed the bus.**

In sentence *b,* which pronoun is correct? ____

1871

proper

2089

Every proper noun and adjective should begin with a (*capital, small*) letter.

2090

bargain,

2308

Columbus had expected to make a fortune but died a pauper.

2309

Mrs. Jones's, hers

2527

Lesson 81 Pronouns and Contractions —Avoiding Confusion

[Frames 2529–2567]

before 113	After you find the verb, find the subject in this way: If, for example, the verb is **ran,** ask yourself, "Who or what **ran?"** The answer to this question always tells you the subject. **The plane from Nashville arrives at six.** What **arrives?** The __________ arrives. 114
indirect 333	a. **They gave the winner a car.** b. **They gave a car to the winner.** Which sentence contains an indirect object? ___ 334
(mod)ify 553	**The car was going fast.** **The car was going extremely fast.** In both sentences, the adverb **fast** modifies the ________ **was going.** 554
subject 773	a. **We postponed the picnic** *because of bad weather.* b. **We postponed the picnic** *because the weather was bad.* Although both italicized word groups begin with *because,* only one has a subject and a verb. Which sentence contains an adverb clause? ___ 774
b 993	**St. Augustine the oldest city in the United States is in Florida.** (Commas are missing.) This sentence contains an appositive word group. One comma is needed after **St. Augustine,** and another after the word __________. 994
did 1213	a. **Dad done all the painting himself.** b. **Dad did all the painting himself.** Which sentence is wrong because the helper form of the verb is used without a helper? ___ 1214

PRESENT	SIMPLE PAST	PAST WITH HELPER
call	**called**	**have called**
take	**took**	**have taken**

Which verb is irregular—**call** or **take?** ________

1434

Pete reported the game (*accurate, accurately*).

adverb — To describe *how* Pete **reported,** we should choose the adverb ________________.

1652 — 1653

I — You would never say, "*Him* missed the bus" or "*Me* missed the bus"; so don't make the same mistake by saying, "*Him* and *me* missed the bus."

(*He, Him*) **and I share the same locker.**

1871 — 1872

Capitalize the names of companies, organizations, buildings, hotels, theaters, etc.

Logan Drug Company	**Red Cross**	**Bayview Hotel**
Union Bank Building	**Curtis Garage**	**Hollywood Theater**

capital — Write the capital letters you would need to use in writing **empire state building.** ____________

2090 — 2091

None — **The weather was cold and rainy or we would have walked to the library.**

2309 — 2310

Apostrophes are also used to show where letters have been omitted from words.

EXAMPLE: **We've** (= *We have*) **won the game.**

The apostrophe in **We've** takes the place of the missing letters ______.

2529

plane

The plane from Nashville arrives at six.

The subject of the verb **arrives** is ________.

114 | 115

---

a

PATTERN 4: *Subject—Linking Verb ← Subject Complement*

EXAMPLES: **The apples are ripe.** (describes subject)

Bea became a judge. (identifies subject)

In these sentences, the subject complements *describe* or *identify* the ____________, as the arrows show.

334 | 335

---

verb

a. **The car was going fast.**
b. **The car was going extremely fast.**

Sentence *b* gives an idea of greater speed than sentence *a*. The added word which gives the idea of greater speed in sentence *b* is ____________.

554 | 555

---

b

Unlike a sentence, a clause (*does, does not*) form a complete sentence by itself.

774 | 775

States

Learn the difference between an **appositive word group** and an **adjective clause.**

An adjective clause has both a subject and a verb.

An appositive is just a ________, often with modifiers.

994 | 995

---

a

a. **Dad did all the painting himself.**
b. **Dad has did all the painting himself.**

Which sentence is wrong because the simple past form of the verb, instead of the helper form, is used with the helper **has?** ____

1214 | 1215

take

1434

Walter wrote a letter of apology.

If you added *should have* to the verb, you would need to change **wrote** to ______________.

1435

---

accurately

1653

Ellen's voice is very pleasant.

Pleasant is an adjective because it modifies the noun ____________.

1654

He

1872

They are at the top of the league.
We are at the top of the league.

Underline the correct pronouns.

(*They, Them*) **and** (*we, us*) **are at the top of the league.**

1873

E S B

2091

a. **a fence company**
b. **the Master Fence Company**

Which item could mean *any* fence company at all? ___

2092

---

rainy,

2310

He went his way and I went mine.

2311

---

ha

2529

I'll (= *I will*) **tell you a secret.**

In this sentence, the apostrophe takes the place of the two letters ______.

2530

plane

The man at the desk refused.

Who **refused?** The answer to this question is not **desk** but ________.

115 | 116

---

subjects

It is easy to see the difference between a direct object and a subject complement.

A direct object can follow only an *action verb,* but a subject complement always follows a ____________ *verb.*

335 | 336

---

extremely

The car was going extremely fast.

The word **extremely** modifies the adverb ________.

555 | 556

---

does not

An adverb clause does the work of a single (*adjective, adverb*).

775 | 776

---

noun

a. **Tom,** *our talented pianist,* **got us a radio engagement.**
b. **Tom,** *who is our talented pianist,* **got us a radio engagement.**

One sentence contains an adjective clause and the other an appositive.

Which sentence contains the appositive? ___

995 | 996

---

b

PRESENT	SIMPLE PAST	PAST WITH HELPER
give	**gave**	**have given**

Which past form of the verb is required in the following sentence?

Joan Baez has __________ **concerts in many towns.**

1215 | 1216

written

1435

The verb in one of the following sentences is wrong:

a. **I saw Don yesterday.**
b. **Their dog ran away.**
c. **The mail come late today.**
d. **The painter did a good job.**

The incorrect verb is in sentence ____.

1436

---

voice

1654

Ellen speaks very pleasantly over the phone.

Pleasantly describes *how* Ellen **speaks.**

Because **pleasantly** modifies the verb **speaks,** it is an ____________.

1655

They, we

1873

Be just as careful to choose the correct pronoun when the pronoun is paired with a noun. Use the same pronoun that you would choose if the pronoun were used alone.

Rosa and (*her, she*) **reported on the same book.**

1874

---

a

2092

a. **a fence company**
b. **the Master Fence Company**

Which item names a particular company? ____

2093

None

2311

We had no use for the old picture but my brother couldn't refuse it.

2312

---

wi

2530

They're going to New York.

The apostrophe takes the place of the letter ____.

2531

man

116

The man at the desk refused.

The subject of the verb **refused** is ______.

117

---

linking

336

If a verb is a linking verb, we can always put **is, was,** or some other form of **be** in its place.

The teacher *corrected* **the papers.**
The teacher *seemed* **happy.**

For which verb can we substitute **was**—*corrected* or *seemed?* ______________

337

---

fast

556

very fast	**so fast**	**rather fast**
extremely fast	**quite fast**	**slightly fast**
terribly fast	**too fast**	**somewhat fast**

All the underlined words increase or decrease the "power" of the adverb ________.

557

---

adverb

776

The first word of an adverb clause is generally the (*clause signal, subject*).

777

---

a

996

a. **Rayon, which is an artificial silk, is made from wood.**
b. **Rayon, an artificial silk, is made from wood.**

Which sentence contains an appositive? ____

997

---

given

1216

PRESENT	SIMPLE PAST	PAST WITH HELPER
give	**gave**	**have given**

Joan Baez has given concerts in many towns.

The helper form **given** is correct because it is used after the helping verb ________.

1217

c

1436

Our landlord had given us notice.

If you omitted the helper **had,** you would need to change **given** to ________.

1437

---

adverb

1655

Ellen speaks very (*pleasant, pleasantly*) **over the phone.**

To describe *how* Ellen **speaks,** we need to use the adverb ________________.

1656

---

she

1874

Rosa and she reported on the same book.

This sentence is correct because if we used each subject separately, we would say:

Rosa reported on the same book.
(*Her, She*) **reported on the same book.**

1875

---

b

2093

a. **The Keystone lumber company owns the property.**
b. **A lumber company owns the property.**

In which sentence should the words **lumber company** be capitalized because they are part of a particular company's name? ____

2094

---

picture,

2312

You must be completely satisfied or your money will be cheerfully refunded.

2313

---

a

2531

To contract means *to shorten*. The shortening of words by omitting letters is called **contraction.**

The word **doesn't** is a contraction of ________ ________.

2532

man

117

The keys to our car disappeared last night.

The subject of the verb **disappeared** is ________.

118

---

seemed

337

The teacher *corrected* **the papers.**
The teacher *seemed* (*was*) **happy.**

Because we can put *was* in its place, *seemed* is a ________ *verb.*

338

---

fast

557

very fast	**so fast**	**rather fast**
extremely fast	**quite fast**	**slightly fast**
terribly fast	**too fast**	**somewhat fast**

All the underlined words give a more exact idea of the adverb **fast.** We say, therefore, that these words ________ the adverb **fast.**

558

---

clause signal

777

Lesson 26 How to Make Adverb Clauses

[Frames 779–813]

---

b

997

When one sentence explains something mentioned in the previous sentence, we can sometimes use an appositive to combine the two sentences.

I welcomed Dick. He was the only boy in the class.

The second sentence explains something about ________ in the first sentence.

998

---

has

1217

PRESENT	SIMPLE PAST	PAST WITH HELPER
go	**went**	**have gone**

Which past form of the verb is required?

The Johnsons had ________ to their cottage.

1218

gave 1437	The "past with helper" form of many irregular verbs ends with **-en** or **-n.** This form should be used after all forms of **be** and ______. 1438
pleasantly 1656	a. **Your solution of this problem was . . . .** b. **You solved this problem . . . .** The adverb **differently** should be used in sentence ___. 1657
She 1875	(*They, Them*) **were on the same plane.** **The Seeleys and** (*they, them*) **were on the same plane.** Would you choose the same pronoun in both the above sentences? (*Yes, No*) 1876
a 2094	a. **Paul works at a garage.** b. **Paul works at the Fuller garage.** In which sentence should **garage** be capitalized because it is part of the name of a particular business? ___ 2095
satisfied, 2313	**Ada had heard about the Dodgers and the White Sox and wanted to see them play.** (Look at this sentence carefully before you make your decision.) 2314
does not 2532	The use of the apostrophe to take the place of missing letters has nothing to do with ownership. a. **We'll call for you at seven.** b. **You can use anyone's ticket.** Is the apostrophe used for a contraction in sentence *a* or *b*? ___ 2533

keys 118	In this and the following frames, find the verb first and underline it with two lines. Then find the subject and underline it with one line. **The lock on our back door often sticks.** 119
linking 338	**The teacher seemed (was) happy.** **Seemed** is a *linking verb.* Therefore the word **happy,** which follows it and completes the meaning of the sentence, is a (*direct object, subject complement*). 339
modify 558	MODIFY ADJECTIVES: **very sudden**, **quite steady**, **more convenient** MODIFY ADVERBS: **very suddenly**, **quite steadily**, **more conveniently** The same special words that modify adjectives can also modify ________. 559
	In one way, a **clause** is like a sentence because it has both a ________ and a verb. 779
Dick 998	**I welcomed Dick. (He was)** *the only boy in the class.* By omitting the words **He was,** we change the second sentence into an appositive phrase. **I welcomed Dick,** *the only boy in the class.* The noun *boy* has now become an ________. 999
gone 1218	**The Johnsons had gone to their cottage.** If you omitted the helper **had,** what word would you need to put in place of **gone?** ________ 1219

have

1438

a. **break** c. **sell** e. **fly**
b. **drive** d. **fall** f. **cry**

Two of the above verbs do not have an **-en** or **-n** form.

They are ____ and ____.

1439

---

b

1657

a.	**prompt**	**skillful**	**careless**	**courteous**
b.	**promptly**	**skillfully**	**carelessly**	**courteously**

Which group of words would you use to describe how an action was performed? ____

1658

Yes

1876

In this and the following frames, select the correct pronouns. Always choose the same form of the pronoun that you would use if the pronoun were used by itself.

My mom and (*I*, *me*) **are learning how to sail.**

1877

---

b

2095

a. **The bank was closed.**
b. **The Wabash bank was closed.**

In which sentence should **bank** be capitalized? ____

2096

None

2314

Ross must make up this test or lose credit for the entire course.

2315

---

a

2533

In contractions, the apostrophe always goes in where the letters come out.

it ~~i~~s = it's	**we ~~wi~~ll = we'll**	**I ~~ha~~ve = I've**
who ~~i~~s = who's	**you ~~a~~re = you're**	**I ~~woul~~d = I'd**

The contraction of **they are** would be ____________.

2534

lock sticks

119

First find and underline the verb; then find and underline the subject:

The huge trailer swayed along behind the car.

120

---

subject complement

339

The teacher seemed (was) happy.
The teacher corrected the papers.

Seemed is a *linking verb,* but **corrected** is an __________ *verb.*

340

---

adverbs

559

We have been working with special words that control the "power" of other modifiers. These words are **adverbs.**

These special adverbs can modify both __________

and other __________.

560

---

subject

779

In another way, a clause is **not** like a sentence because it (*does, does not*) form a complete sentence by itself.

780

---

appositive

999

In combining sentences, put the appositive word group next to the noun it explains.

a. **Dick was absent,** *the only boy in the class.*
b. **Dick,** *the only boy in the class,* **was absent.**

Which sentence is correct because the appositive word group comes right after the noun it explains? ____

1000

---

went

1219

PRESENT	SIMPLE PAST	PAST WITH HELPER
come	**came**	**have come**

The simple past form of **come** is not **come** but __________.

1220

c, f

The verb in one of the following sentences is wrong:

a. **Dave give me his ticket.**
b. **The gale had broken many windows.**
c. **The driver was thrown through the windshield.**

The incorrect verb is in sentence ____.

1439 | 1440

---

b

In the case of a few words, the adjective form without **–ly** can also serve as an adverb. Here are several examples:

Drive slow or **slowly.** **He works steady** or **steadily.**
Don't talk so loud or **loudly.** **He plays fair** or **fairly.**

The words **slow, loud, fair,** and **steady** are both adjectives and adverbs. (*True, False*)

1658 | 1659

I

The Potters and (*us, we*) shop at the same market.

1877 | 1878

---

b

The ‸ company has opened several branches.

If you inserted the name **C. K. Jensen** before the word **company,** would you need to capitalize the noun **company?** (*Yes, No*)

2096 | 2097

None

The train had started to move and we couldn't find Jimmie anywhere in the station.

2315 | 2316

---

they're

Many contractions end with **n't,** which is a shortened form of the adverb **not.**

doesn't **isn't** **shouldn't** **wasn't**

The apostrophe in **n't** takes the place of the missing ____.

2534 | 2535

2535

trailer
swayed

120

First find and underline the verb; then find and underline the subject:

Gloria's friends often phoned at inconvenient times.

121

---

action

340

The teacher corrected the papers.

The noun **papers** shows what *received the action* of the verb **corrected.**

Papers, therefore, is a (*direct object, subject complement*).

341

---

adjectives, adverbs

560

Although certain adverbs like **very, quite,** and **extremely** modify adjectives and other adverbs, most adverbs modify

__________.

561

---

does not

780

a. **The store closed.**
b. *When the store closed*

Which word group does not form a complete sentence by itself? ____

781

---

b

1000

The dessert was the big treat of the meal. (It was) *a fluffy lemon pie.*

To change the second sentence to an appositive word group, drop the subject _____ and the verb ______.

1001

---

came

1220

Select the correct form of the verb **come:**

The package (*come, came*) **by express.**

1221

a

The verb in one of the following sentences is wrong:

a. **These tomatoes were grown under glass.**
b. **Ripe figs are eaten raw.**
c. **Much English is spoke in Japan.**

The incorrect verb is in sentence ____.

1440 1441

True

a. **Frank doesn't play** (*fair, fairly*).
b. **Frank doesn't play** (*honest, honestly*).

In which sentence are both forms of the word correct—*a* or *b*? ____

1659 1660

---

we

Either you or (*her, she*) must **write the review.**

1878 1879

Yes

The Lennox Hotel was full.

If you dropped the name **Lennox** from this sentence, would you still write **Hotel** with a capital letter? (*Yes, No*)

2097 2098

---

move,

In a compound sentence, the comma comes *after* the conjunction **and, but,** or **or.** (*True, False*)

2316 2317

---

o

People sometimes misplace the apostrophe in writing words that end with **n't.** The apostrophe is not used to separate **nt** from the verb, but to take the place of the missing **o.**

a. **was'nt, should'nt, have'nt, does'nt**
b. **wasn't, shouldn't, haven't, doesn't**

Which group of words is correct—*a* or *b*? ____

2535 2536

friends
phoned

121

First find and underline the verb; then find and underline the subject:

The drugstore on our corner never closes before midnight.

122

direct object

341

The *subject* and the *direct object* are usually two *different*. things, and the action passes from the first to the second.

1 ⟶ 2
Eileen raises cats.

Eileen and **cats** are (*one, two*) thing(s).

342

verbs

561

Adjectives can modify only *two* different classes of words—nouns and pronouns, but adverbs can modify (*two, three*) different classes of words.

562

b

781

a. **The store closed.**
b. *When the store closed*

Which word group is a clause? ____

782

It, was

1001

a. **The dessert was the big treat of the meal,** *a fluffy lemon pie.*
b. **The dessert,** *a fluffy lemon pie,* **was the big treat of the meal.**

In which sentence is the appositive word group correctly placed right after the noun it explains? ____

1002

came

1221

The package came by express.

If you added the helper **has** to the verb, what word would you need to put in place of **came?** ________

1222

c

1441

The verb in one of the following sentences is wrong:

a. **The Hills have gone back to Pasadena.**
b. **A light snow had fell during the night.**
c. **Eleanor has written a humorous poem.**

The incorrect verb is in sentence ____.

1442

a

1660

Frank doesn't play (*fair, fairly*).

Although both **fair** and **fairly** are correct in this sentence, we should, as a general rule, choose the adverb form (*with, without*) **–ly** to modify a verb.

1661

she

1879

My cousins and (*he, him*) **are going to Silver Lake.**

1880

No

2098

Capitalize the complete names of particular schools, colleges, churches, clubs, libraries, hospitals, etc.

King High School **Trinity Church** **Parkman Library**
Oberlin College **Rotary Club** **Cardozo Hospital**

Write the capital letters you would need to use in writing **stevens memorial hospital.** ________

2099

False

2317

In a compound sentence, there are *both* a subject and a predicate *after* the conjunction. (*True, False*)

2318

b

2536

Write out the two words for which each contraction stands:

I'll (________________) **go if you're** (________________) **willing.**

2537

drugstore closes	Many sentences are built upon the framework of a *subject* and a ________.
122	123
two	A subject complement refers back to the subject, which it *describes* or *identifies*. When the subject complement *identifies* the subject, both words mean the *same* person or thing. 1 ←—— 2 **Ms. Jones is our attorney.** **Ms. Jones** and the **attorney** are (*one, two*) person(s).
342	343
three	We can now define **adverbs** as words that modify ________, **adjectives,** and **other adverbs.**
562	563
b	a. **The store closed.** b. *When the store closed* One of these word groups is one word longer than the other. The word group with the added word is the (*sentence, clause*).
782	783
b	**Dr. Gomez calls her farm "Tooth Acres." Dr. Gomez is a dentist.** The second sentence can be changed to an appositive word group of (*one, two, three*) word(s).
1002	1003
come	The form of **come** that should be used after **have, has,** or **had** is ________.
1222	1223

b

1442

The verb in one of the following sentences is wrong:

a. **Someone had drove a nail into the tree.**
b. **We must have known half the people in town.**
c. **Our neighbors have flown to Miami.**

The incorrect verb is in sentence ____.

1443

---

with

1661

a. **Colette's dresses are very** (*stylish, stylishly*).
b. **Colette dresses very** (*stylish, stylishly*).

In which sentence shall we use the adjective **stylish** because it modifies the *noun* **dresses?** ____

1662

---

he

1880

The Angelos and (*they, them*) **organized a neighborhood club for teenagers.**

1881

S M H

2099

a. **A new high school is needed.**
b. **Sierra high school won the cup.**

In which sentence should the words **high school** be capitalized because they are part of the name of a particular school—*a* or *b*? ____

2100

True

2318

A sentence with a *compound predicate* requires a comma just like a compound sentence. (*True, False*)

2319

I will *or* I shall, you are

2537

Write out the two words for which each contraction stands:

He's (____________) **sure that we've** (______________) **taken it.**

2538

verb 123	The verb is the most important word in the (*subject, predicate*). 124
one 343	a. **Ralph called the usher.** b. **Ralph is an usher.** In which sentence are the **usher** and **Ralph** two different persons? ____ 344
verbs 563	Since adjectives and adverbs are **modifiers,** we can simplify our definition in this way: **Adverbs** modify **verbs** and **other modifiers.** By **"other modifiers"** we mean adjectives and ________. 564
clause 783	a. **The store closed.** b. *When the store closed* When we put a signal word before a sentence, it is no longer a sentence. The added word changes the sentence to a ________. 784
two 1003	**Dr. Gomez calls her farm "Tooth Acres." (Dr. Gomez is)** *a dentist.* The words *a dentist* should be placed in the first sentence right after (*Dr. Gomez, Acres*). 1004
come 1223	PRESENT SIMPLE PAST PAST WITH HELPER **run** **ran** **have run** The simple past form of **run** is not **run** but ______. 1224

a

1443

Be careful not to write **of** when you mean **have.**

a. **Most of the food was left over.**
b. **We should of started earlier.**
c. **They printed a picture of our team.**

In which sentence should **of** be changed to **have?** ____

1444

---

a

1662

a. **Colette's dresses are very** (*stylish, stylishly*).
b. **Colette dresses very** (*stylish, stylishly*).

In which sentence shall we use the adverb **stylishly** because it modifies the *verb* **dresses?** ____

1663

---

they

1881

You and (*me, I*) **can't do this alone.**

1882

---

b

2100

a. **The meeting will be held in our High School.**
b. **The meeting will be held in Truman High School.**

Which sentence contains errors in capitalization? ____

2101

False

2319

Commas are generally omitted in short compound sentences. (*True, False*)

2320

---

he is, we have

2538

Write the contraction of each pair of underlined words. Remember that the apostrophe goes in where the letters come out.

Where is (________________) **the pen that does not** (____________) **write?**

2539

predicate

124

The verb makes a statement about the ______.

125

---

a

344

1 ⟶ 2

Ralph called the usher.

Because the **usher** and **Ralph** are two different persons, **usher** is a (*direct object, subject complement*).

345

---

adverbs

564

an extremely hot day

Hot is an adjective because it modifies the noun **day.**

Does **extremely** modify the adjective **hot** or the noun **day?**

565

---

clause

784

SENTENCE: **Kim needed the car.**
CLAUSE: *Because Kim needed the car*

The clause has one more word than the sentence.

The added word is a (*preposition, clause signal*).

785

Dr. Gomez

1004

Edison's next invention astonished the world, *and* **it was the phonograph.**

To eliminate the *and*, which noun in the second part of the sentence could be used as an appositive to explain **invention?** ______

1005

---

ran

1224

PRESENT	SIMPLE PAST	PAST WITH HELPER
run	**ran**	**have run**

a. **Yesterday I run into an old friend.**
b. **Yesterday I ran into an old friend.**

Which sentence is wrong because the helper form of the verb *run* is used without a helper? ___

1225

b 1444	a. **lie, sit, rise** b. **lay, set, raise** Which verbs would you use to state that you put, place, or change the position of something—those in *a* or *b*? ____ 1445
b 1663	In this and the following frames, choose the **–ly** word (adverb) when there is action in the sentence, and the word describes this action. Choose the word *without* **–ly** (adjective) where there is no action in the sentence, and the word describes the subject. Underline the correct choice. **Peggy does everything** (*perfect, perfectly*). 1664
I 1882	(*She, Her*) **and her mother look alike.** 1883
a 2101	a. **I plan to attend Colby College.** b. **I must get good grades for College.** Which sentence contains an error in capitalization? ____ 2102
True 2320	Lesson **75** **Commas After Introductory Phrases and Clauses** [Frames 2322–2356]
Where's, doesn't 2539	Write the contraction of each pair of underlined words: **I am** (________) **sure that we** **must not** (______________) **sign in pencil.** 2540

subject

125

When you change a sentence from present to past or from past to present time, the only word that changes is the

________.

126

---

direct object

345

$1 \longleftarrow 1$

Ralph is an usher.

Because, in this sentence, the **usher** and **Ralph** are the same person, **usher** is a (*direct object, subject complement*).

346

---

hot

565

an <u>extremely</u> hot day

Because **extremely** modifies the adjective **hot,** it is an

________.

566

---

clause signal

785

In this and the following frames, capitals and periods are omitted to avoid revealing the answers.

a. **the ice is melting**
b. **if the ice is melting**

Which of the above word groups is a clause? ____

786

---

phonograph

1005

Edison's next invention astonished the world, *and* **(it was)** *the phonograph.*

The words *the phonograph* should be placed right after the word ________________, which it explains.

1006

---

a

1225

Underline the correct verb in each of the two pairs:

I (*ran, run*) **to see who had** (*ran, run*) **through the corridor.**

1226

b

1445

Write in the missing forms:

PRESENT	SIMPLE PAST	PAST WITH HELPER
lie (in bed)	________	**have lain**
lay (put)	________	**have laid**

1446

---

perfectly

1664

Miss Dean usually treats her customers very (*courteous, courteously*).

1665

She

1883

The Moodys and (*we, us*) **took turns in driving the children to school.**

1884

---

b

2102

a. **a Baptist church**
b. **Calvary Baptist Church**

Which item could mean *any* Baptist church at all? ____

2103

I wanted to be a cowboy when I was five years old.

One of these word groups makes the *main statement* of the sentence; the other is an *adverb clause* that does not make complete sense by itself.

The main statement in this sentence comes (*first, last*).

2322

I'm, mustn't

2540

Write the contraction of each pair of underlined words:

It is (________) **not too late if you are** (__________) **ready now.**

2541

verb

126

Most, but not all, verbs show actions that one can see.

a. **threw, walked, pushed, arrived, laughed, turned**
b. **thought, hoped, expected, decided, remembered**

Which group of verbs represents actions that one might *not* be able to see? ____

127

---

subject complement

346

a. **The lemon improved the punch.**
b. **The lemon was sour.**

Which sentence concerns only one thing? ____

347

---

adverb

566

a very sharp pain

Does **very** modify the adjective **sharp** or the noun **pain?**

567

---

b

786

a. **after the sun went down**
b. **the sun went down**

Which word group is a clause? ____

787

---

invention

1006

a. **Edison's next invention astonished the world, and it was the phonograph.**
b. **Edison's next invention, the phonograph, astonished the world.**

Which sentence is more direct and better organized? ____

1007

---

ran, run

1226

Underline the correct verb in each of the two pairs:

This explorer (*saw, seen*) **something that few people ever have** (*saw, seen*).

1227

(lie) lay
(lay) laid

1446

Underline the correct verb in each pair:

I (*laid, lay*) **my book aside and** (*laid, lay*) **down for a nap.**

1447

---

courteously

1665

Miss Dean is usually very (*courteous, courteously*) **to her customers.**

1666

---

we

1884

Neither the Webbs nor (*them, they*) **own a dog.**

1885

---

a

2103

a. **a Baptist church**
b. **Calvary Baptist Church**

Which item names a *particular* church? ____

2104

---

first

2322

a. **I wanted to be a cowboy when I was five years old.**
b. **When I was five years old, I wanted to be a cowboy.**

In which sentence does the main statement of the sentence come ahead of the adverb clause? ____

2323

It's, you're

2541

There are several pairs of words that sound alike but have entirely different meanings.

your **you're**

Copy the contraction that means **you are.** ________

2542

b 127	In analyzing a sentence, always look for the verb first. If the verb is **fell,** find its subject by asking yourself, "________ or ________ **fell?"** 128
b 347	1 ← **The lemon was sour.** **Sour** is not a different thing, apart from the **lemon.** **Sour** describes the subject **lemon.** **Sour,** therefore, is a __________ ____________. 348
sharp 567	**a very sharp pain** The word **very** is an (*adjective, adverb*). 568
a 787	a. **although West High lost the game** b. **West High lost the game** Which word group is a clause? ____ 788
b 1007	In this and the following frames, change the italicized part of each sentence to an appositive word group. Then put it after the word it explains in the other sentence. **We visited the Grand Canyon.** *It is one of the great sights of the world.* ____________________ ______________________________ 1008
saw, seen 1227	Underline the correct verb in each of the two pairs: **This morning I** (*done, did*) **the work that I should have** (*done, did*) **last night.** 1228

laid, lay 1447	Underline the correct verb in each pair: **Uncle Ray had** (*lain, laid*) **some newspapers on the grass and had** (*lain, laid*) **down to relax.** 1448
courteous 1666	**The mechanic fixed the car** (*satisfactory, satisfactorily*). 1667
they 1885	**Peggy and** (*she, her*) **are always together.** 1886
b 2104	a. **a Baptist Church** b. **Calvary Baptist Church** Which item contains an error in capitalization? ____ 2105
a 2323	a. **I wanted to be a cowboy when I was five years old.** b. **When I was five years old, I wanted to be a cowboy.** Only one of the above sentences contains a comma. The comma is used when the main statement comes (*first, last*). 2324
you're 2542	**your** **you're** Copy the possessive pronoun that means **belonging to you.** ________ 2543

who *or* what

128

Lesson 5 Here Comes the Noun!

[Frames 130–163]

subject complement

348

1 ←

The water felt cold.

Cold is not a different thing, apart from the **water.**

Cold describes the subject **water.**

Cold, therefore, is a (*direct object, subject complement*).

349

adverb

568

an unusually hard test

The word **unusually** is an (*adjective, adverb*).

569

a

788

although West High lost the game

The adverb clause signal that starts this clause is ________________.

789

We visited the Grand Canyon, one of the great sights of the world.

1008

Mrs. Hill made many changes. *She is the new principal.*

____

____

1009

did, done

1228

Underline the correct verb in each of the two pairs:

Mother (*give, gave*) **me the ring which her father had** (*gave, given*) **her.**

1229

laid, lain	**Why would anyone want to** (*sit, set*) **where he** (*sat, set*).
1448	1449
satisfactorily	**Diane takes her work quite** (*serious, seriously*).
1667	1668
she	In this and the following frames, underline the two correct pronouns in each sentence: (*They, Them*) **and** (*we, us*) **are tied for first place.**
1886	1887
a	**The ‸ Lutheran church has been completed.** If you inserted the name **Hillside** at the point indicated, would you need to capitalize the noun **church?** (*Yes, No*)
2105	2106
last	**At the end of the game the fans swarmed over the field.** One of these word groups makes the *main statement;* the other consists of two *prepositional phrases.* The main statement of this sentence comes (*first, last*).
2324	2325
your	**your you're** Write the word that fits in the following sentence: **I know that __________ joking.**
2543	2544

Words—just like tools—can be grouped according to the jobs they do. There are *eight* different kinds, or classes, of words. Each kind does a different job in the sentence.

We have already met one class of words—the words that make statements about subjects. These words are called

________.

130

---

subject complement

349

1 ⟶ 2

Ann purchased a house.

Ann and **house** are two different things. **House,** therefore, is a (*direct object, subject complement*).

350

---

adverb

569

The lake suddenly grew extremely rough.

One adverb modifies the verb; the other modifies an adjective.

Which adverb modifies an adjective? ________

570

---

although

789

a. **he knew everything about planes**
b. **as though he knew everything about planes**

Which word group is a clause? ____

790

Mrs. Hill, the new principal, made many changes.

1009

Ellen was walking with her dog. *It is a frisky French poodle.*

____

____

1010

---

gave, given

1229

If you had (*gone, went*), **I would have** (*gone, went*), **too.**

1230

sit, sat 1449	**The young man** (*sat, set*) **his suitcase in the aisle of the bus and** (*set, sat*) **down on it.** 1450
seriously 1668	**The company's answer to my letter was very** (*prompt, promptly*). 1669
They, we 1887	(*Him, He*) **and** (*me, I*) **caught most of the fish.** 1888
Yes 2106	a. **I joined the Woodlawn camera club.** b. **I joined a camera club.** In which sentence should the words **camera club** be capitalized? ____ 2107
last 2325	a. **At the end of the game, the crowd swarmed over the field.** b. **The crowd swarmed over the field at the end of the game.** The comma is used when the main statement of the sentence comes (*first, last*). 2326
you're 2544	Here is another confusing pair: **their** **they're** Copy the word that means **they are.** ____________ 2545

verbs

130

We can't talk about anything unless it has a name, can we? We therefore need a class of words to name the persons, places, and things we talk about.

These words are called **nouns.**

A **noun** is the ________ of a person, place, or thing.

131

---

direct object

350

1 ———————→ 2

________ **sold his** ________.

If you were to complete this sentence, the word in the space that follows the verb would be a (*direct object, subject complement*).

351

---

extremely

570

Jade Snow Wong spoke quite frankly about writing as a career.

Which of the two underlined adverbs modifies the verb **spoke?** ________

571

---

b

790

a. **while we were waiting impatiently for the bus**
b. **we were waiting impatiently for the bus**

Only one of these word groups could be used by itself as a complete sentence.

The sentence contains one (*more, less*) word than the clause.

791

Ellen was walking with her dog, a frisky French poodle.

1010

Sam struck out. *He was the first boy at bat.*

____

____

1011

---

gone, gone

1230

Earl (*came, come*) **home early, but Vic hasn't** (*came, come*) **home yet.**

1231

set, sat 1450	**The company's prices** (*raised, rose*) **soon after it** (*raised, rose*) **the workers' wages.** 1451
prompt 1669	**The company answered my letter very** (*prompt, promptly*). 1670
He, I 1888	(*She, Her*) **and** (*he, him*) **attended the same college.** 1889
a 2107	Do not capitalize the word **the** or any short preposition **(of, in, for, to)** when it is part of a name. **Boy Scouts of America** **Daughters of the American Revolution** Underline the words you would capitalize in this name: **society for the preservation of democracy** 2108
last 2326	A group of words that comes ahead of the main statement is called an **introductory word group.** Just as a speaker's introductory remarks lead into his main speech, an introductory word group leads into the main statement. Underline the introductory word group: **Sitting down on a log, Jeff took off his shoes.** 2327
they're 2545	**their** **they're** Copy the word that fits in this sentence: **Don't walk on ____________ grass.** 2546

name

131

Miami office Mexico restaurant

These nouns are the names of (*persons, places, things*).

132

---

direct object

351

1 ⟵ 1

Manhattan is an island.

Island and **Manhattan** are one and the same thing.

Island, therefore, is a (*direct object, subject complement*).

352

---

frankly

571

Jade Snow Wong spoke quite frankly about writing as a career.

Which of the two underlined adverbs modifies another adverb? ________________

572

---

less

791

Adverb clauses are useful for combining sentences. They can make the relationship between two facts much clearer.

a. **The game was close. We finally won.**
b. *Although the game was close,* **we finally won.**

Which arrangement shows more clearly how the two facts are related? ____

792

Sam, the first boy at bat, struck out.

1011

Get rid of the *and* by changing the italicized part of this sentence to an appositive phrase.

Archie was the next batter, *and he was a strong hitter.*

____

____

1012

---

came, come

1231

Claire (*ran, run*) **for the same office for which her father had** (*ran, run*).

1232

rose, raised 1451	**The cost of automobile insurance is** (*raising, rising*) **because the accident rate has** (*rose, risen*). 1452
promptly 1670	**Ann reads more** (*rapid, rapidly*) **than Mark.** 1671
She, he 1889	**Neither** (*them, they*) **nor** (*us, we*) **made a touchdown in the first quarter.** 1890
Society for the Preservation of Democracy 2108	**The injured fire fighter was taken to the ^ hospital.** If you inserted the name **Lexington** at the point indicated, would you need to capitalize the noun **hospital?** (*Yes, No*) 2109
Sitting down on a log, 2327	An introductory word group is generally an *adverb clause*, an *-ing word group*, or one or two *prepositional phrases*. An introductory word group always modifies something in the main statement of the sentence. Could an introductory word group make sense by itself—apart from the sentence? (*Yes, No*) 2328
their 2546	**their** **they're** Copy the word that fits in this sentence: **Tell me when ______________ ready to eat.** 2547

places

132

Henry **doctor** **uncle** **Mr. Smith**

These nouns are the names of (*persons, places, things*).

133

---

subject complement

352

1 ⟵ 1

__________ **was a** __________.

If you were to complete this sentence, the word in the space that follows the verb would be a (*direct object, subject complement*).

353

---

quite

572

I had a <u>very</u> strange experience <u>today</u>.

Which of the two underlined adverbs modifies an adjective?

____

573

---

b

792

a. **We didn't hear the doorbell** *<u>because</u> the radio was turned on.*

b. **We didn't hear the doorbell. The radio was turned on.**

Which arrangement shows more clearly how the two facts are related? ____

793

Archie, a strong hitter, was the next batter.

1012

Lesson 33 Unit Review

[Frames 1014–1041]

---

ran, run

1232

The past forms of most verbs end in **-ed.**

These verbs are called (*regular, irregular*) verbs.

1233

rising, risen

1452

This is the main point to remember about the use of **leave** and **let:**

Always use (*let, leave*) when you mean "to permit" or "to allow."

1453

---

rapidly

1671

The wooden bridge is only (*temporary, temporarily*).

1672

---

they, we

1890

(*Her, She*) **and** (*me, I*) **can make the posters.**

1891

Yes

2109

Our club meets weekly in the Schomburg library.

The noun that needs to be capitalized in this sentence is (*club, library*).

2110

No

2328

Use a comma after an introductory word group—especially if it is more than a few words in length.

a. **When something disappears they always blame Ralph.**
b. **When some article disappears around the house they always blame Ralph.**

Which sentence requires a comma? ____

2329

---

they're

2547

whose who's

Copy the contraction that means **who is.** ________

2548

persons

133

peach pencil automobile book

These nouns are the names of (*persons, places, things*).

134

---

subject complement

353

a. **The other team always wins the game.**
b. **The other team is much heavier.**

Which sentence contains a *subject complement* which describes the subject **team?** ____

354

---

very

573

Too many cooks spoil the broth.

One of the underlined modifiers is an adjective because it modifies a noun; the other is an adverb because it modifies an adjective.

Which word is the adverb? __________

574

---

a

793

Now let's look in this frame at a single adverb:

Finally Bert got the right answer.
Bert **finally** got the right answer.
Bert got the right answer **finally.**

The adverb **finally**—like many adverbs—(*can, cannot*) be moved from one position to another in a sentence.

794

In a compound sentence, there are a subject and a verb before (*and also, but not*) after the conjunction.

1014

---

regular

1233

The simple past form and the helper form of regular verbs such as **look** and **open** are (*the same, different*).

1234

Answer	Frame
let 1453	**The Burdicks** (*leave, let*) **their friends use their pool.** 1454
temporary 1672	**How do you comb your hair so** (*neat, neatly*)? 1673
She, I 1891	**Lesson 62 The Object Form of Pronouns** [Frames 1893–1933]
library 2110	**Our club meets weekly in the Schomburg Library.** If you dropped the name **Schomburg** from this sentence, would you still write **Library** with a capital letter? (*Yes, No*) 2111
b 2329	a. **In some schools, several grades are taught in the same classroom.** b. **In some of the country schools of our state, several grades are taught in the same classroom.** In which sentence might we omit the comma after the introductory word group? ____ 2330
who's 2548	**whose** **who's** Copy the possessive pronoun that means **belonging to whom.** __________ 2549

things

134

Underline the noun that is the name of a *person:*

money **church** **teacher** **kitchen**

135

---

b

354

In one sentence, the verb **broke** is complete; in the other, it requires a word to show what *receives the action.*

a. **The strain broke the chain.**
b. **The chain between the two cars broke.**

Which sentence contains a *direct object?* ____

355

Too

574

I eat a fairly big breakfast.

Which one of the two modifiers is an adverb? ________

575

---

can

794

a. **A dog walked on the cement** *before it had hardened.*
b. *Before it had hardened,* **a dog walked on the cement.**

In which sentence has the adverb clause been moved from the end to the beginning of the sentence? ____

795

---

and also

1014

a. **Brandy was my own horse, and I felt very proud of my possession.**
b. **I had my own horse and felt very proud of my possession.**

Which sentence is compound? ____

1015

---

the same

1234

Verbs whose past forms do not end in **-ed** are called (*regular, irregular*) verbs.

1235

let	**When Marlene came over last night, she** (*took, brought*) **her guitar along.**
1454	1455
neatly	**Uncle Will eats rather** (*hearty, heartily*) **for a sick person.**
1673	1674
	a. **Joe liked Sue.** b. **Sue liked Joe.** In sentence *a,* **Joe** is the subject, and **Sue** is the direct object. In sentence *b,* **Sue** is the subject, and **Joe** is the ________ ________.
	1893
No	**lake** **club** **church** **hotel** **river** **company** **school** **college** Words like these should not be capitalized unless they are part of a proper noun. (*True, False*)
2111	2112
a	Use a comma even after a short introductory word group if there is any danger that your sentence might be confusing. a. **Whenever I eat my dog begs for food.** b. **Whenever I eat I use a napkin.** In which sentence would a comma help to prevent confusion? ____
2330	2331
whose	**whose** **who's** Don't use the word **who's** unless the words **who is** would fit in. a. **. . . bike is on our sidewalk?** b. **. . . ringing our doorbell?** In which sentence would **Who's** be correct? ____
2549	2550

teacher 135	Underline the noun that is the name of a *place:* **soldier piano Paul hospital** 136
a 355	a. **The band played** *poorly.* b. **The band played a** *march.* In which sentence is the italicized word a direct object? ____ 356
fairly 575	**Miss Hagerty sometimes becomes impatient with us.** Which one of the two modifiers is an adverb? ________ 576
b 795	An adverb clause can frequently be moved from one position to another, just like an (*adjective, adverb*). 796
a 1015	**I had my own horse and felt very proud of my possession.** This is *not* a compound sentence because a (*subject, verb*) is missing after the conjunction **and.** 1016
irregular 1235	When an irregular verb is used with **have, has,** or **had,** the (*simple past, helper*) form of the verb should be used. 1236

brought

1455

Everyone who goes to Mexico should (*take, bring*) **his camera with him.**

1456

heartily

1674

This tie will go (*nice, nicely*) **with your blue suit.**

1675

direct object

1893

He liked Sue.
Sue liked him.

Which form of the pronoun is used for the direct object—**he** or **him?** ______

1894

True

2112

Capitalize all nouns and pronouns that refer to God.

God Almighty Lord His mercy

Copy each word that requires capitals, adding the needed capitals:

We thanked the lord for his many blessings.

____

2113

a

2331

a. **As she slipped she grabbed the railing.**
b. **As she turned the car got out of control.**

After which of the short introductory word groups is a comma necessary for clearness? ____

2332

b

2550

Underline the correct word:

Where's the man (*whose, who's*) **car was wrecked?**

2551

hospital	Underline the noun that is the name of a *thing:* **onion Europe farmer Ohio**
136	137
b	**The bright headlights blinded the approaching driver.** The noun **driver** is a (*direct object, subject complement*).
356	357
sometimes	Any word that modifies a noun or a pronoun is an ________.
576	577
adverb	**Our sales increased** *when we lowered our price.* Can the adverb clause *when we lowered our price* be moved to the beginning of the sentence? (*Yes, No*)
796	797
subject	The conjunctions commonly used to connect the two parts of a compound sentence are **and,** ______, and ______.
1016	1017
helper	Lesson **40** **Thirteen Irregular Verbs** [Frames 1238–1277]
1236	*page 273*

take

1456

UNIT 7: **AGREEMENT OF SUBJECT AND VERB**

Lesson 47 *Was* and *Were*; *Don't* and *Doesn't*

[Frames 1458–1495]

nicely

1675

The patient's temperature is now (*normal, normally*) **again.**

1676

him

1894

a. **I** **he** **she** **we** **they**
b. **me** **him** **her** **us** **them**

Joe liked . . . .

Which pronouns could be used as the direct object of the verb **liked** in the little sentence above—those in group *a* or *b*? ____

1895

Lord, His

2113

In this and the following frames, cross out each capital letter that is not correct; for example, **a Catholic ~~S~~chool.**

The new High School will be on Fuller Avenue.

2114

b

2332

To Ellen Stuart was very attentive.

Would you recommend a comma after the name **Ellen?** (*Yes, No*)

2333

whose

2551

its (= *belonging to it*) **it's** (= *it is*)

No two words cause more trouble than these. Try hard not to confuse them.

Write the word that fits in this sentence:

________ **your turn to play.**

2552

onion

137

A noun is the name of a person, __________, or __________.

138

---

direct object

357

Some of us felt dizzy after the ride.

The word **dizzy** is a (*direct object, subject complement*).

358

---

adjective

577

To explain **how** sweet an apple is or **how** quietly a motor runs, we would need to use an __________.

578

Yes

797

a. **Our sales increased** *when we lowered our price.*
b. *When we lowered our price,* **our sales increased.**

A comma is needed when the adverb clause comes (*before, after*) the main statement of the sentence.

798

---

but, or

1017

a. **My grandmother doesn't care for housework, and her years of experience have taught her many short cuts.**
b. **Whales reach their full size in about 12 years, and live for about 40 years.**

Because it is not a compound sentence, the comma should be omitted from sentence ____.

1018

Most verbs are **regular.** They have only a single past form that ends in **–ed.** We use the same **–ed** form with **have, has,** or **had** that we use for the simple past.

a. **Tony** *pitched* **as he never** *had pitched* **before.**
b. **Leo** *gave* **me the ticket that the coach** *had given* **him.**

Which sentence contains a regular verb? ____

1238

Singular means **one; plural** means **more than one.**

apple **apples**

To change a noun from singular to plural, we usually add the letter ____.

1458

---

normal

1676

The patient was breathing (*normal, normally*) **again.**

1677

---

b

1895

The form of a pronoun that can be used as the object of a verb or a preposition is called the **object form.**

a. **I** **he** **she** **we** **they**
b. **me** **him** **her** **us** **them**

Which pronouns are in the object form—those in group *a* or *b*? ____

1896

~~H~~igh ~~S~~chool

2114

Continue to cross out each capital letter that is not correct:

The Stanford Inn is the best Hotel in our City.

2115

Yes

2333

It began to rain at the very beginning of the game.

Is a comma needed after the word **rain?** (*Yes, No*)

2334

It's

2552

Its (no apostrophe) is a possessive pronoun—just like **ours, yours, theirs.** Apostrophes are needed to make nouns possessive. Pronouns show ownership *without* apostrophes.

The violin is in ______ case.

2553

place, thing

138

Most of the things that we talk about can be *seen* or *touched*—just like the things in this room. But we sometimes talk about something that we can't *see* or *touch.*

Underline the word that names something we can't see or touch:

grass **freedom** **brother**

139

---

subject complement

358

The explosion shook the entire neighborhood.

In this sentence, the *direct object* is ________________.

359

---

adverb

578

A word that modifies a verb, an ________________ or another ______________ is an adverb.

579

---

before

798

A salesperson will call *if you leave your name.*

No comma is needed in this sentence because the adverb clause comes (*before, after*) the main statement.

799

---

b

1018

Only *similar* ideas *of equal importance* should be combined into a compound sentence.

a. **The lake was rough, and our boat was very small.**
b. **The lake was rough, and my two cousins were in the boat with me.**

Which is the better sentence? ____

1019

---

a

1238

PRESENT	SIMPLE PAST	PAST WITH HELPER
take	**took**	**have taken**

This job has taken too much time.

Because **has** is part of the verb, we use the (*simple past, helper*) form of the verb **take.**

1239

s 1458	Although we form the plural of most nouns by adding **s** to the singular, there are some exceptions: **man** **men** **woman** **women** **tooth** **teeth** **child** ________ 1459
normally 1677	**Students often write** (*bad, badly*) **when they are not interested in their subject.** 1678
b 1896	**Joe liked . . . .** The pronouns like **I, we,** and **she** that do *not* fit after the verb are in the (*subject, object*) form. 1897
Hotel, City 2115	**The Carson Insurance Company has an Office in the Scott Building.** 2116
No 2334	**It began to rain at the very beginning of the game.** If the underlined word group were moved to the beginning of the sentence, would a comma be needed? (*Yes, No*) 2335
its 2553	Do not use the contraction **it's** unless you can put the two words _____ _____ in its place. 2554

freedom

139

Words like **freedom, strength, truth,** and **imagination** are also nouns because they are the names of *ideas* that we have in our minds.

Underline the noun that is the name of an *idea:*

wallet **actor** **honesty**

140

neighborhood

359

Mother felt ________ about Bob's grades.

The missing word in this sentence would be a (*direct object, subject complement*).

360

adjective, adverb

579

Lesson 20 Learning to Recognize Prepositions

[Frames 581–614]

after

799

If you leave your name, **a salesperson will call.**

Now a comma is needed because the adverb clause comes at the (*beginning, end*) of the sentence.

800

a

1019

As a general rule, it is not a good idea to begin a sentence with the conjunction **and.**

a. **It was a hot July day, and all the windows were open.**
b. **It was a hot July day. And all the windows were open.**

Which is better—*a* or *b*? ____

1020

helper

1239

When an irregular verb has two past forms, one form is used for the simple past, and the other with a helping verb.

The job . . . too much time.
The job has . . . too much time.

Can the same past form of the verb **take** be used in both sentences? (*Yes, No*)

1240

children 1459	Underline the one noun that is plural: **boy** **doctor** **women** **student** 1460
badly 1678	**The management of the hospital seemed quite** (*bad, badly*) **to me.** 1679
subject 1897	We use one set of pronouns *before* verbs as their subjects and another set of pronouns *after* verbs as their ________. 1898
ɸffice 2116	**You will pass a new Methodist Church on the way to the Library.** (This sentence does not give the name of a particular church building.) 2117
Yes 2335	**Although they spoke different languages the children played well together.** Is a comma needed after the word **languages?** (*Yes*, *No*) 2336
it is 2554	a. **It's time to eat.** b. **It's meal is ready.** Which sentence is wrong because you cannot substitute **it is** for **it's?** ____ 2555

honesty 140	Underline the noun that is the name of an *idea:* **friendship** **theater** **airplane** 141
subject complement 360	**Dorothy peeled the ___________ for dinner.** The missing word in this sentence would be a (*direct object, subject complement*). 361
	Look at these two unrelated nouns: **man** **car** No word stands between them to tell us whether the man is **in, by, under, behind, beside,** or **near** the _____. 581
beginning 800	a. *Unless you have good grades* **a college will not accept you.** b. **A college will not accept you** *unless you have good grades.* In which sentence should a comma be added? ___ 801
a 1020	A clause that tells *when, where, how,* and so forth, about the action of the verb is an (*adjective, adverb*) clause. 1021
No 1240	You have seen that the helper form of the verb is used with **have, has,** and **had.** It is also used with all forms of the verb **be (is, am, are—was, were, been).** Besides being used after **have, has,** and **had,** the helper form is also used after all forms of the verb _____. 1241

women

1460

The noun **women** is plural even though it does not end in ___.

1461

---

bad

1679

a. **angry** **loose** **strict** **thorough**
b. **angrily** **loosely** **strictly** **thoroughly**

Which group of words would you use to describe the action of a verb? ___

1680

---

objects

1898

she **him** **he**

Which one of these pronouns can be used after a verb as its object and is, therefore, in the object form? ______

1899

Church, Library

2117

The Knights Of Columbus is a Society for men of the Catholic faith.

2118

Yes

2336

Although they spoke different languages, the children played well together.

If the underlined word group were moved to the end of the sentence, would the comma still be needed? (*Yes, No*)

2337

---

b

2555

a. **It's time to eat.**
b. **It's meal is ready.**

Which sentence is right because you can substitute **it is** for **it's?** ___

2556

friendship

141

The noun **truth** is not the name of a *person, place,* or *thing.*

It is the name of an ________ that exists in people's minds.

142

---

direct object

361

The coat looked too ______________ for me.

The missing word in this sentence would be a ____________

________________.

362

---

car

581

man **car**

There is no word to tell us the **relationship** between the

_______ and the _______.

582

---

a

801

Unless you have good grades, **a college will not accept you.**

Because the adverb clause comes at the beginning of this sentence, the comma is (*right, wrong*).

802

---

adverb

1021

a. **who (whom, whose), which, that**
b. **because, when, if, unless, although**

In which group can the words be used as signals for adverb clauses? ____

1022

---

be

1241

PRESENT	SIMPLE PAST	PAST WITH HELPER
take	**took**	**have taken**

These pictures were (*took, taken*) **last year.**

Which past form of the verb is right?

1242

s

1461

In grammar, we speak of **singular** and **plural** as **number.** The number of a noun tells us whether it means *one* or *more than one.*

The noun **tree** is singular in number; the noun **trees** is plural in ____________. 1462

---

b

1680

Does a student study his lesson **thorough** or **thoroughly?**

____________________ 1681

---

him

1899

them **we** **I** **they** **me**

Which two pronouns are in the object form? ________ and ________ 1900

ϕf, $ociety

2118

In this and the following frames, copy only the words that now lack required capitals, adding the needed capitals:

The Ferndale stamp club has a display of rare american stamps in the Wilson library. 2119

No

2337

In most of our writing, we generally put our main statements first, not last.

a. **Our dog begins to howl whenever it hears a siren.**
b. **Whenever it hears a siren, our dog begins to howl.**

Which sentence begins with the main statement, not with the adverb clause? ____ 2338

---

a

2556

The contraction **Let's** (= *Let us*) combines a verb and a pronoun. **Lets**—without an apostrophe—is just an ordinary verb like **talks** or **runs.**

a. **. . . go to the game.**
b. **Dad . . . Peggy drive the car.**

In which sentence would **let's** (= *let us*) fit? ____ 2557

idea 142	We have now become acquainted with two kinds or *classes* of words: **verbs** and **nouns.** The class of words that makes, or helps to make, statements about subjects is called ________. 143
subject complement 362	**We carried the ____________ to the attic.** The missing word in this sentence would be a ____________ ____________. 363
man, car 582	**man** {*in* / *by* / *with*} **car** **man** {*near* / *behind* / *under*} **car** Each italicized word standing between **man** and **car** shows (*the same, a different*) **relationship** between the two nouns. 583
right 802	*Whenever I pass their home,* **their dog barks at me.** If we move the adverb clause *whenever I pass their home* to the end of the sentence, the sentence will require no comma. (*True, False*) 803
b 1022	**All members approve this change.** To change this sentence to an adverb clause, we would need to (*add, drop*) a word. 1023
taken 1242	**These pictures were taken last year.** We use **taken,** rather than **took,** because the verb is used with the helper ________. 1243

number

1462

car pen room shoe

These nouns are all of the same number because they are all (*singular, plural*).

1463

---

thoroughly

1681

fair—fairly **loud—loudly**
slow—slowly **cheap—cheaply**
quick—quickly **steady—steadily**

These are examples of a small number of words that can be used either with or without **-ly** to modify verbs. (*True, False*)

1682

---

them, me

1900

she you we I it they

Which two pronouns could be used as either subjects or objects without changing their forms? ________ and ________

1901

Stamp Club, American, Library

2119

Copy the words that require capitals:

Catholics, protestants, and jews all worship the same god.

2120

---

a

2338

For the sake of variety, it's a good idea now and then to begin a sentence with an introductory word group.

a. **The job will take all day if I have to do it alone.**
b. **If I have to do it alone, the job will take all day.**

If you had written several sentences beginning with the main statement, which sentence would add more variety? ___

2339

---

a

2557

In the next sentences, choose the correct word from the two words printed in parentheses, and write this word on the blank line. Don't choose a contraction unless the two words for which it stands would make sense in the sentence.

________ **color changes when** ________ **ripe.**
(It's, Its) (it's, its)

2558

verbs

The class of words that names persons, places, things, and ideas is called ________.

143 | 144

---

direct object

363

Lesson **13** Sentences with Compound Parts

[Frames 365–392]

---

a different

man {*in* / *by* / *with*} **car** **man** {*near* / *behind* / *under*} **car**

Each time we change the word between **man** and **car,** we change the *rela*________ between the two nouns.

583 | 584

True

It is important to select the right clause signal.

We placed the sign ________ *passers-by would be sure to see it.*

Underline the adverb clause signal that shows the relationship between the two ideas most clearly:

if **because** **while** **where**

803 | 804

---

add

If all members approve this change, we should make it.

In this sentence, the adverb clause begins with the clause signal ____ and ends with the word ________.

1023 | 1024

---

were

In this lesson, we shall study the two past forms of thirteen irregular verbs that we use constantly. Here are the helper forms of eight of these verbs:

have broken	**have eaten**	**have given**	**have taken**
have driven	**have fallen**	**have spoken**	**have written**

The last two letters of each helper form are ____.

1243 | 1244

singular 1463	**streets cloud cookies window** Because two of these nouns are singular and two are plural, we say that they are not alike in *n*__________. 1464
True 1682	Lesson **55** **Choosing Between *Good* and *Well*** [Frames 1684–1704]
you, it 1901	**You liked it.** **It liked you.** The subject and object forms of the pronouns **you** and **it** are (*alike, different*). 1902
Protestants, Jews, God 2120	**Members of St. Andrew's church may use the parking lot of the Studio theater.** 2121
b 2339	In this and the following frames, supply the necessary commas. Some of the sentences do not require commas. **Ever since Lois was a little girl she has wanted to be a doctor.** 2340
its, it's 2558	__________ **the girl** __________ **story won first prize?** (Who's, Whose) (who's, whose) 2559

nouns

144

It is hard to talk about anything unless it has a name. For this reason, the subject of a sentence is very often a **noun.**

The rain stopped.

In this sentence, the subject **rain** is a ________.

145

We can talk about more than one thing at a time. A sentence, therefore, can have more than one subject.

EXAMPLE: **The smoke and water caused much damage.**

This sentence has two subjects—**smoke** and ________.

365

(rela)tionship

584

Here we have the verb **rushed** and the noun **hospital:**

rushed hospital

There is no word between them to tell us whether someone **rushed** *to, from, past* or *around* the ________.

585

---

where

804

________ *it was a sunny day,* **Uncle Pete was wearing a raincoat.**

Underline the adverb clause signal that shows the relationship between the two ideas most clearly:

although because until wherever

805

If, change

1024

A comma is needed in a sentence when the adverb clause comes (*first, last*).

1025

–en

1244

Here are the helper forms of five more irregular verbs:

have flown have known have thrown
have grown have seen

Each one of these helper forms ends with the letter ___.

1245

(n)umber

1464

Verbs, too, sometimes—though not always—show number. Some verb forms are singular, and other verb forms are plural.

The house *is* **new.** **The houses** *are* **new.**

Which verb is plural—*is* or *are*? ______

1465

The aim of this lesson is to teach you not to use the *adjective* **good** in place of the *adverb* **well.**

These pens are good.

Good is an adjective because it modifies the noun ______.

1684

---

alike

1902

a. **I** **he** **she** **we** **they**
b. **me** **him** **her** **us** **them**

Joe looked at . . . .

Which pronouns could be used as the object of the preposition **at**—those in group *a* or *b*? ____

1903

Church, Theater

2121

The El Dorado parents' club bought uniforms for our school band.

2122

---

girl,

2340

Insert any necessary commas:

Lois has wanted to be a doctor ever since she was a little girl.

2341

Who's, whose

2559

______ **heart beats faster when** ______ **running.**
(You're, Your) (you're, your)

2560

noun

145

Any word that is a noun can be used as the subject of a verb.

If a word can't be used as the subject of a verb, it is not a ________.

146

---

water

365

The car and the trailer went into the ditch.

This sentence also has two subjects.

The second of the two subjects is ________.

366

---

hospital

585

rushed **hospital**

There is no word to tell us the **relationship** between the noun **hospital** and the verb ________.

586

---

although

805

We protect the young plants ________ *frost will not injure them.*

Underline the adverb clause signal that shows the relationship between the two ideas most clearly:

since **while** **so that** **as if**

806

---

first

1025

a. **Unless you have had rain, you can't have a rainbow.**
b. **You can't have a rainbow, unless you have had rain.**

The comma should be omitted from sentence ___.

1026

–n

1245

have broken	**have given**	**have flown**	**have seen**
have driven	**have spoken**	**have grown**	**have thrown**
have eaten	**have taken**	**have known**	
have fallen	**have written**		

All the helper forms of these thirteen verbs end either with the letters ______ or the letter ___.

1246

are

The houses are new.

We know that the verb **are** is plural because its subject **houses** is (*singular, plural*).

1465 1466

---

pens

These pens write well.

Well is an adverb because it describes the action of the verb ______.

1684 1685

---

b

The object form is also used for any pronoun that is the object of a preposition. Here are the nine most common prepositions:

in to of at on by for from with

A pronoun that follows any of these prepositions should be in the (*subject, object*) form.

1903 1904

Parents' Club

The Vollmer Baking company supplies bread to the Weldon Children's hospital and to the Clifton high school.

2122 2123

None

Insert any necessary commas:

With icy shivers in my spine I reached for my flashlight.

2341 2342

Your, you're

______ (Let's, Lets) **find out why Mr. Diaz** ______ (let's, lets) **some students go home early.**

2560 2561

noun

146

The . . . disappeared.

Underline the word that could be used as the subject of the verb **disappeared:**

often **against** **letter**

147

---

trailer

366

We can also make two (or more) statements about the same subject by using two (or more) verbs.

EXAMPLE: **Bert dived into the water and disappeared.**

Both verbs—**dived** and **disappeared**—make statements about the subject ________.

367

---

rushed

586

rushed {*to* / *from* / *toward*} **hospital** **rushed** {*past* / *around* / *through*} **hospital**

Each time we change the word between **rushed** and **hospital,** we change the ________*ship* between the verb and the noun.

587

---

so that

806

Mother always spoke to us children ________ *we were adults.*

Underline the adverb clause signal that shows the relationship between the two ideas most clearly.

because **as if** **although** **unless**

807

---

b

1026

Eliminate the **and** in this sentence by changing the italicized part to an adverb clause. Write the full sentence.

Noreen took vocal lessons, **and her singing improved a great deal.** ________

____

1027

–en, –n

1246

Whenever you are doubtful about which verb form to use after the various forms of **have** or **be,** look for a form that ends with **–en** or **–n.** If there is one, use it.

We had . . . since early morning.

Is there a form of the verb **drive** that ends with **–en** or **–n?** (*Yes, No*)

1247

plural 1466	**The house is new.** We know that the verb **is** is singular because its subject **house** is (*singular, plural*). 1467
write 1685	**good** **well** Which of these words can be used to modify a verb? ______ 1686
object 1904	Other prepositions you will need to recognize are— **about** **among** **beside** **near** **above** **before** **between** **over** **after** **behind** **except** **toward** **against** **below** **like** **without** Be sure to use the object form for objects of verbs and ______________. 1905
Company, Hospital, High School 2123	Lesson **69** **Various Other Uses of Capitals** [Frames 2125–2163]
spine, 2342	**Seeing nothing ahead of me on the road I increased my speed.** 2343
Let's, lets 2561	________ **house looks as if** ________ **not at home.** (They're, Their) (they're, their) 2562

letter 147	**The letter disappeared.** **Letter,** the subject of the verb **disappeared,** is a ________. 148
Bert 367	**A blue jay swooped down and pecked at our cat.** The two verbs in this sentence are **swooped** and ________. 368
relation(ship) 587	A word that **relates** a noun or pronoun which follows it to some other word in the sentence is called a **preposition.** Learn to spell **preposition** correctly. Just write **pre** in front of the word **position** and you have the word ________________. 588
as if 807	In this and the following frames, combine each pair of sentences by changing the italicized sentence to an adverb clause. Write the full sentence. Be sure to put a comma after each adverb clause that begins a sentence. *I was taking his picture.* **He suddenly moved.** ____ 808
After (Because, When) Noreen took vocal lessons, her singing improved a great deal. 1027	A clause that is used to modify a noun or pronoun is an ________________ clause. 1028
Yes 1247	The form of the verb **drive** that ends with **–en** or **–n** is ____________. 1248

singular

1467

a. **This sweater *is* warm.**
b. **These sweaters *are* warm.**

Which sentence contains a plural verb? ____

1468

---

well

1686

WRONG: **These pens write good.**

This sentence is wrong because the adjective **good** cannot be used to modify the verb __________.

1687

---

prepositions

1905

When a single pronoun is the object of a verb or preposition, mistakes are very rare. We are not likely to hear such mistakes as "Paul invited *I*" or "Dad is waiting for *we*."

The dog followed (*she, her*) **home.**

1906

Capitalize the names of particular brands of products.

Wheaties **Chrysler** **Listerine** **Rinso**

I brush my teeth with (*freshie, Freshie*).

2125

---

road,

2343

More than half the Pilgrims had died by the end of the first winter.

2344

Their, they're

2562

__________ **the neighbor who** __________ **his dog**
(Who's, Whose) (let's, lets)

run loose on the street?

2563

noun

148

The loud noise suddenly stopped.

The noun in this sentence is ________.

149

---

pecked

368

Two or more subjects with the same verb are called a **compound subject.**

The word *compound* means "having more than one part."

All the doors and windows were locked.

This sentence has a ________ subject.

369

---

preposition

588

The grass under the tree was dead.

The **grass** was not *above, beyond,* or *around* the **tree.**

The **grass** was ________ the **tree.**

589

As (When, While) I was taking his picture, he suddenly moved.

808

Jane can speak Spanish. **She can't speak it fluently.**

____

____

809

---

adjective

1028

a. **who (whom, whose), which, that**
b. **because, when, if, unless, although**

In which group can the words be used as signals for adjective clauses? ____

1029

---

driven

1248

We had driven since early morning.

We use **driven** rather than **drove** because the verb follows the helping verb ______.

1249

b	An important rule of English is that a subject and a verb must **agree** (be alike) in number. This rule means that with a singular subject we must use a singular verb, and that with a plural subject we must use a __________ verb.
1468	1469
write	**The pitcher was good. He pitched well.** **Good** modifies the noun **pitcher,** but **well** modifies the verb __________.
1687	1688
her	When a verb or preposition has compound objects—either two pronouns or a noun and a pronoun—mistakes often occur. a. **The dog followed <u>her</u> home.** b. **The dog followed <u>Al</u> and** (*she, her*) **home.** In sentence *b*, which pronoun is correct? ______
1906	1907
Freshie	**Don't use ordinary paint—use** (*Durex, durex*).
2125	2126
None	**By the end of the first winter more than half the Pilgrims had died.**
2344	2345
Who's, lets	__________ (They're, Their) **going to raise** __________ (it's, its) **price again.**
2563	2564

noise 149	**The ________________ of this child surprises me.** Underline the word that is a noun and that could therefore be used as the subject of this sentence: **lazy lazily laziness** 150
compound 369	Two or more verbs that make statements about the same subjects are called **compound verbs.** **The blazing fire crackled and snapped.** This sentence has ________________ verbs. 370
under 589	**The grass under the tree was dead.** The preposition **under** shows the relationship between the noun **tree,** which follows it, and the noun ____________, which comes before it. 590
Although Jane can speak Spanish, she can't speak it fluently. 809	*Pure gold is soft.* **It is generally mixed with a harder metal.** ____ ____ 810
a 1029	Do not use the pronoun **which** as a clause signal to refer to (*persons, things, animals*). 1030
had 1249	**Many windows were . . . by the explosion.** Is there a form of the verb **break** that ends with **–en** or **–n?** (*Yes, No*) 1250

plural 1469	When the subject and verb are of the **same** number, as they should be, we say that they **agree** in number. a. **Tom** *was* **absent.** b. **Tom** *were* **absent.** The verb agrees with its subject in sentence ____. 1470
pitched 1688	**The driver was good.** **She drove well.** Which word is an adverb—**good** or **well?** ________ 1689
her 1907	**The dog followed Al and her home.** The object form **her** is correct because **her,** as well as **Al,** is the object of the verb ____________. 1908
Durex 2126	**Your dog will just love** (*krunchies, Krunchies*). 2127
winter, 2345	**If the Yankees win another game will be played.** 2346
They're, its 2564	**I can guess** __________ **manners** __________ **discussing.** (who's, whose) (you're, your) 2565

laziness 150	**My wild ____________________ worried my parents.** Underline the word that is a noun and that could therefore be used as the subject of this sentence: **imagine** **imagination** **imaginary** **imagined** 151
compound 370	Direct objects, indirect objects, and subject complements can also be compound. **Kim quickly changed her** *shirt* **and** *jeans.* The words *shirt* and *jeans* are compound (*direct objects, subject complements*). 371
grass 590	**The children played under the tree.** The **children** didn't play *in, near, behind,* or *above* the **tree.** They played __________ the **tree.** 591
Because (Since, As) pure gold is soft, it is generally mixed with a harder metal. 810	*We were eating dinner.* **Some company arrived.** ____ ____ 811
persons 1030	Which kind of clause can be farther away from the word it modifies—an adverb clause or an adjective clause? An __________________ *clause* can be farther away. 1031
Yes 1250	The form of the verb **break** that ends with **-en** or **-n** is _______________. 1251

a

1470

Tom *were* absent.

This sentence is wrong because the subject and verb do not agree in number.

The subject **Tom** is singular, but the verb **were** is ______.

1471

---

well

1689

WRONG: **She drove good.**

This sentence is wrong because **good** is an adjective, and an adjective cannot modify the verb __________.

1690

---

followed

1908

When two pronouns (or a noun and a pronoun) are used as objects, choose the same form of the pronoun that you would choose if the pronoun were used alone.

Betty showed <u>him</u> her gifts. Betty showed <u>me</u> her gifts.

Betty showed <u>him</u> and (*I, me*) her gifts.

1909

Krunchies

2127

Notice that although brand names are capitalized, the products that they identify are *not* capitalized.

Ford station wagon　**Esterbrook pens**　**Speed King skates**

Write the capital letters you would need to use in writing **red arrow batteries.** __________

2128

---

win,

2346

Looking for a place to park we drove around the block several times.

2347

---

whose, you're

2565

________________ (Let's, Lets) **meet at** ________________ (you're, your) **house.**

2566

imagination

151

A word is printed in parentheses after each sentence that follows. This word is not a noun. Write the *noun form* of this word that would fit in as the subject of the sentence.

EXAMPLE: **His** *strength* **surprised everyone. (strong)**

The ______________ started over a nickel. (argue)

152

direct objects

371

The Holdens lent *Howard* **and** *me* **their boat.**

Two words in this sentence show *to whom* something was done.

The words **Howard** and **me** are compound (*direct objects, indirect objects*).

372

under

591

The children played under the tree.

The preposition **under** shows the relationship between the noun **tree,** which follows it, and the verb ______________, which comes before it.

592

While (When, As) we were eating dinner, some company arrived.

811

The actor wore dark glasses. *People would not recognize him.* ____

____

812

adverb

1031

Combine these two sentences by changing the italicized sentence to an adjective clause. Write the full sentence.

Rosa has several savings bonds. *She is keeping them for her education.* ____

____

1032

broken

1251

Many windows were . . . by the explosion.

We use **broken** rather than **broke** because the verb follows the helping verb __________.

1252

plural

1471

The car *stopped.* **The plane** *disappeared.*

The verbs in these sentences show (*present, past*) time.

1472

---

drove

1690

The main point to remember is that the adjective **good** should never be used to describe *how an action is performed.*

An adjective cannot modify a (*noun, verb*).

1691

---

me

1909

You can ride with them. You can ride with us.

Choose the correct pronouns in the following sentence:

You can ride with (*them, they*) **or** (*us, we*).

1910

R, A

2128

a. **These cookies were made with Tastee Peanut Butter.**
b. **These cookies were made with Tastee peanut butter.**

Which sentence is correctly capitalized? ____

2129

---

park,

2347

You should always wash your hands before you handle food.

2348

Let's, your

2566

__________ **car looks good when** __________ **cleaned up.**
(Their, They're) (it's, its)

2567

argument

152

Write the *noun form* of the word in parentheses that will fit in as the subject of this sentence:

His __________________ came to a sudden end. (happy)

153

---

indirect objects

372

The pears were *small* **but very** *sweet.*

The two words—*small* and __________—describe the subject **pears.**

373

---

played

592

A **preposition** can relate a noun or pronoun that follows it to a **noun, pronoun,** or __________ in some other part of the sentence.

593

The actor wore dark glasses so that people would not recognize him.

812

I put down the right answer. **I foolishly changed it.**

____

____

813

Rosa has several savings bonds which (*or* that) she is keeping for her education.

1032

After each sentence, write *adverb* or *adjective* to show what kind of clause the sentence contains:

a. **Bananas are always harvested when they are green.** ________________

b. **Most people who have seen the movie recommend it**

1033

---

were

1252

PRESENT	SIMPLE PAST	PAST WITH HELPER
eat	**ate**	**have eaten**

The entire cake was ____________ last night.

Which form of the verb is required?

1253

past 1472	**The car** *stopped.* **The plane** *disappeared.* The subjects of these sentences are singular. Now read these sentences again, substituting the plural subjects **cars** and **planes.** Did you need to change the verbs to make them agree with the plural subjects? (*Yes, No*) 1473
verb 1691	**Well** is the word to use if you want to say that something is done *in a good or satisfactory manner.* a. **The water is good.** b. **The motor runs good.** In which sentence is the adjective **good** wrong? ___ 1692
them, us 1910	Be just as careful to choose the correct pronoun when the pronoun is paired with a noun. Choose the same pronoun that you would choose if the pronoun were used alone. **The car splashed mud over Grace and** (*I, me*). 1911
b 2129	a. **I removed the stain with Zippo spot remover.** b. **I removed the stain with Zippo Spot Remover.** Which sentence is correctly capitalized? ___ 2130
None 2348	**When we first met Harvey was a sophomore in high school.** 2349
Their, it's 2567	Lesson **82** **Quotation Marks to Make Words Talk** [Frames 2569–2610] *page 306*

happiness 153	Write the *noun form* of the word in parentheses that will fit in as the subject of this sentence: **My ____________ improved a great deal. (spell)** 154
sweet 373	**The pears were** *small* **but very** *sweet.* *Small* and *sweet* are compound (*direct objects, subject complements*). 374
verb 593	Many prepositions show relationships in **position.** POSITION: *in, on, under, beneath, below, over, above, by, beside, across, behind, between,* etc. **The fog <u>over</u> the airport was very thick.** The preposition **over** shows the *pos*________ of the **fog** with reference to the **airport.** 594
After I put down the right answer, I foolishly changed it. 813	Lesson **27** **Using Adverb Clauses to Improve Sentences** [Frames 815–839]
a. adverb b. adjective 1033	Adverb or adjective clause? a. **People seldom like foods which they are not accustomed to eating.** ________ b. **All food seems to taste better when it is eaten out-of-doors.** ________ 1034
eaten 1253	PRESENT **fall** — SIMPLE PAST **fell** — PAST WITH HELPER **have fallen** **The brush has ________ into the paint.** Which form of the verb is required? 1254

No

1473

SINGULAR	PLURAL
The car *stopped.*	**The cars** *stopped.*
The plane *disappeared.*	**The planes** *disappeared.*

The same simple past verb is used whether the subject is singular or plural. (*True, False*)

1474

---

b

1692

a. **I always sleep good.**
b. **I always sleep well.**

Which sentence is correct? ____

1693

---

me

1911

The car splashed mud over Grace and me.

In the above sentence, the object form **me** is correct because if we used each object separately, what would we say?

The car splashed mud over Grace.
The car splashed mud over (*I, me*).

1912

---

a

2130

a. **the Chrysler Building**
b. **a Chrysler Car**

Which item is incorrect because the type of product, as well as the brand name, is capitalized? ____

2131

---

met,

2349

From the beginning of recorded time people have observed strange objects in the sky.

2350

To quote means to report what a person said *in his or her own words.*

a. **The child replied that his name was Martin.**
b. **The child replied, "My name is Martin."**

Which sentence reports directly the child's own words? ____

2569

spelling

154

Write the *noun form* of the word in parentheses that will fit in as the subject of this sentence:

________________ **increases in stormy weather. (tardy)**

155

---

subject complements

374

Chris and Dad built a small sailboat.

What *connecting word* connects the two parts of the compound subject?

375

(pos)ition

594

Some prepositions show **direction.**

DIRECTION: *from, to, toward, down, up, at*

Isabel walked toward the corner

The preposition **toward** shows that Isabel **walked** in the direction of the ____________.

595

---

a. **and, but, or**
b. **when, because, if, before, unless, although**

Which words can be used as adverb clause signals—those in group *a* or *b*? ____

815

---

a. adjective
b. adverb

1034

a. **Don worked there for two weeks, and he decided to find a better job.**
b. **After Don worked there for two weeks, he decided to find a better job.**

Which sentence brings out more clearly the relationship between the two ideas? ____

1035

---

fallen

1254

PRESENT	SIMPLE PAST	PAST WITH HELPER
fly	**flew**	**have flown**

Food and medicine were __________ to the flooded area.

1255

True

When we use simple past verbs, there is almost no problem of making verbs agree with their subjects.

The only exception is the verb **be.**

Unlike all other verbs, the verb **be** has two simple past forms—**was** and **were.**

1474 **Was** is singular, and **were** is __________. 1475

---

b

I always sleep (*good, well*).

To describe *how* you **sleep,** you should choose the adverb

__________.

1693 1694

---

me

Be especially careful not to say, **"for you and *I*."** This is probably the most widespread of all pronoun blunders.

Since you would never say, **"for *I*,"** do not say, **"for you and *I*,"** which is the same mistake.

1912 **Mother bought two tickets for you and** (*me, I*). 1913

---

b

Capitalize the names of the days of the week, months, holidays, and special days.

Wednesday **February** **Thanksgiving Day**

Write the capital letters you would need to use in writing

2131 **fourth of july.** __________ 2132

---

time,

I found a dollar bill at the very bottom of the wastebasket.

2350 2351

---

b

a. **The child replied that his name was Martin.**
b. **The child replied, "My name is Martin."**

Which sentence reports indirectly in someone else's words

2569 what the child said? ____ 2570

Tardiness

155

careless **carelessly** **carelessness**

Which one of these words is the *noun form*?

____

156

---

and

375

Andy caught but dropped the ball.

What *connecting word* connects the compound verbs?

____

376

---

corner

595

The space between the two cars was small.

The preposition **between** shows (*position, direction*).

596

---

b

815

The plane took off.

To change this simple sentence to an adverb clause, we would need to (*drop, add*) a word.

816

---

b

1035

A sentence that contains an adverb clause or an adjective clause is a (*compound, complex*) sentence.

1036

---

flown

1255

Is there a form of the verb **speak** that ends with **–en** or **–n?** (*Yes, No*)

1256

plural

1475

The verb **be** has two simple past forms—**was** for singular subjects and **were** for plural subjects.

a. **talked** **saw** **laughed** **gave**
b. **was** **were**

Which simple past verbs *cannot* be used with both singular and plural subjects—those in *a* or *b*? ____ 1476

---

well

1694

a. **Shake the bottle well.**
b. **Shake the bottle good.**

Which sentence is correct because an adverb modifies the verb **Shake?** ____

1695

---

me

1913

Mother bought two tickets for you and me.

The object form **me** is correct because **me** is the object of the preposition ______.

1914

F, J

2132

Fill each blank with a small or capital letter, as the word requires:

Schools will open on the ____uesday after Labor ____ay.

2133

None

2351

When Martha returned to law school she worked part-time as a legal aide.

2352

---

a

2570

The child replied, *"My name is Martin."*

Because the italicized words quote directly the child's *own words,* we call them a **direct quotation.** We surround the quotation with quotation marks—or **quotes,** for short.

We use quotes only when we quote a person's ______ words. 2571

carelessness 156	**announces** **announcement** **announced** Which one of these words is the *noun form*? ______________ 157
but 376	**Linda or Gail has your notebook.** What *connecting word* connects the compound subjects? _____ 377
position 596	**We flew to Miami.** The preposition **to** shows (*position, direction*). 597
add 816	An adverb clause can come before or after the main statement of a sentence. (*True, False*) 817
complex 1036	A **suffix** is an ending added to a word to make a new word. Underline the suffix that makes the following statement true: We can turn any verb into an adjective by adding the suffix (*-ful, -ing, -ous*) to it. 1037
Yes 1256	**The customer had ____________ to the manager.** Which form of the verb **speak** is required? 1257

b 1476	A very serious error is the use of the singular verb **was** with a plural subject. WRONG: **The roads was good.** **Was the roads good?** The subject and verb do not agree in number. The subject **roads** is plural; the verb **was** is ______. 1477
a 1695	A person or thing is **good,** but an action is performed ______. 1696
for 1914	In this and the following frames, select the correct pronouns. Always choose the same form of the pronoun that you would use if the pronoun were used by itself. **The only two runs were made by Lopes and** (*he, him*). 1915
T, D 2133	**Can you name two ___olidays in ___ebruary?** 2134
school, 2352	**Although he shouted the name could not be heard.** 2353
own 2571	One of the following sentences requires quotes: a. **The doctor said that I should take a deep breath.** b. **The doctor said now take a deep breath.** Which sentence requires quotes because it reports what the person said *in his own words*? ___ 2572

announcement

157

The same word can often be used as either a *noun* or a *verb*. Which it is depends on how it is used in the sentence.

If the word is used as the subject of the sentence, it is used as a *noun*.

If the word makes a statement about the subject, it is a

_______.

158

---

or

377

The three connecting words used to connect the compound parts of sentences are **and, but,** and **or.**

Words that connect words or groups of words are called **conjunctions.**

Three **conjunctions** are _______, **but,** and **or.**

378

---

direction

597

A few prepositions show relationships in **time.**

TIME: *before, during, after, until, till*

The excitement before the game was tremendous.

The **time** relationship between the **excitement** and the **game** is shown by the preposition _______.

598

True

817

A comma is needed between the adverb clause and the main statement when the adverb clause comes (*first, last*).

818

–ing

1037

Eliminate the **and** in this sentence by changing the italicized part to an *–ing* word group. Write the full sentence.

I tore a page from my notebook **and left a note at the door.**

____

____

1038

---

spoken

1257

PRESENT	SIMPLE PAST	PAST WITH HELPER
speak	**spoke**	**have spoken**

a. **The customer had spoke to the manager.**

b. **The customer had spoken to the manager.**

Which sentence is wrong because the simple past form, instead of the helper form, is used with the helper **had?** ____

1258

singular

Dale's parents (*wasn't, weren't*) **at home.**
(*Wasn't, Weren't*) **Dale's parents at home?**

Both sentences are alike except that one is a statement and the other is a question.

Which verb agrees in number with the plural subject **parents?** ______________

1477 1478

---

well

In this and the following frames, underline the two correct modifiers in each sentence. (Don't assume that one **good** and one **well** are required in each sentence. Some sentences may call for two of the same word.)

You can't study (*good, well*) **when the light isn't** (*good, well*).

1696 1697

---

him

The gift from (*her, she*) **and Bert came on Christmas Eve.**

1915 1916

---

h, F

This year, ___alloween will fall on a ___aturday.

2134 2135

---

shouted,

An introductory word group makes sense by itself—apart from the sentence. (*True, False*)

2353 2354

---

b

Don't use quotes unless you are quoting someone directly *in his own words*. The word **that** is often a signal that we are reporting someone's remark indirectly *in our words*.

a. **Dad said you sit in front, Bob.**
b. **Dad said that I should sit in front.**

Which sentence requires quotes? ____

2572 2573

verb

158

In one of the following two sentences, the italicized word is used as a noun; in the other, as a verb. Write *noun* or *verb* after each sentence.

The *fight* begins at nine o'clock. ________

Children often *fight* over trifles. ________

159

---

and

378

Learn to spell **conjunction.** It has three syllables.

con-junc-tion

The middle syllable of this word is ________.

379

---

before

598

We fished <u>until</u> nightfall.

The preposition **until** shows a relationship in (*time, position*).

599

---

first

818

Earlier in this unit, we learned how to combine two simple sentences into a compound sentence by using the conjunction **and, but,** or **or.**

Hong Kong is an island, *and* Victoria is its main city.

In this compound sentence, the conjunction is ______.

819

Tearing a page from my notebook, I left a note at the door.

1038

An appositive is a noun or pronoun set (*after, before*) another noun or pronoun to explain it.

1039

---

a

1258

PRESENT	SIMPLE PAST	PAST WITH HELPER
give	**gave**	**have given**

a. **The cashier had given me the wrong change.**
b. **The cashier had gave me the wrong change.**

Which sentence is wrong because the simple past form, instead of the helper form, is used with the helper **had?** ____

1259

weren't

1478

The pronoun **you** always requires a plural verb in English—even when it refers to only one person. Therefore, we should always say, "You *were*"—never "You *was*."

You (*was, were*) **driving too fast.**
(*Was, Were*) **you driving too fast?**

Which verb agrees with the subject **you?** ________ 1479

---

well, good

1697

Underline the correct modifier in each pair:

If the cloth is (*good, well*), **a suit will wear** (*good, well*).

1698

---

her

1916

Ann Redcloud will meet the Kirks and (*we, us*) **at town hall.**

1917

H, S

2135

Do not capitalize the names of the four seasons.

spring summer fall winter

They spent the ___ummer in Wisconsin and the ___inter in Florida.

2136

False

2354

Unless it is very short, an introductory word group should generally be followed by a comma. (*True, False*)

2355

---

a

2573

Dad said, "You sit in front, Bob."

What punctuation mark separates the quotation from the words that introduce it (**Dad said**)? ________

2574

noun
verb

159

Is the italicized word a *noun* or a *verb*?

Sandra's *studies* **take most of her time.** ________

Sandra *studies* **Spanish after dinner.** ________

160

---

junc

379

Conjunctions are a kind or *class* of words.

We have now become acquainted with four different classes of words: (1) **nouns,** (2) **pronouns,** (3) **verbs,** (4) **conjunctions.**

Nouns, pronouns, verbs, and other words can be connected by ________________.

380

---

time

599

Still other prepositions like *of, for, about, with,* and *except* show many different kinds of relationship between the words they relate.

EXAMPLES: **a glass of milk** **a book about dogs**
a gift for Ruth **a boy with freckles**

Each of the underlined words is a ________________.

600

---

and

819

When we merely wish to add one idea to another idea, we can connect them with **and.**

If the two ideas are *similar* and *of equal importance,* the result is a good ____________ sentence.

820

---

after

1039

Must an appositive word group—like a clause—have a subject and a verb? (*Yes, No*)

1040

---

b

1259

The form of **grow** that ends with **–en** or **–n** is ________.

1260

were 1479	In this and the following frames, only one of the three subjects in parentheses agrees in number with the verb. Underline this subject. (*You, The sailors, The dog*) **was without water.** 1480
good, well 1698	**A person who reads** (*good, well*) **can't always spell** (*good, well*). 1699
us 1917	**Ellen and** (*him, he*) **spoiled the concert by talking.** (Are you checking each pronoun by trying it by itself in the sentence?) 1918
s, w 2136	**Next ____riday is the first day of ____pring.** 2137
True 2355	It gives variety to your writing to put an introductory word group occasionally ahead of your main statement. (*True, False*) 2356
comma 2574	Use a comma to separate the quotation from the **he said** (or similar expression). **He said, "Stop teasing the dog."** The separating comma comes (*before, after*) the quotes. 2575

noun verb 160	Is the italicized word a *noun* or a *verb*? **This pencil** ***breaks*** **too easily.** ________ **Some bad** ***breaks*** **in the pavement slowed down traffic.** ________ 161
conjunctions 380	a. **He and she joined the same club.** b. **Carol and Ken joined the same club.** In which sentence does the conjunction **and** connect two pronouns that are used as subjects? ___ 381
preposition 600	The word **but** is a preposition when it means **except.** **Everybody went except Nancy.** In this sentence, we can replace the preposition **except** with the preposition ______. 601
compound 820	However, by using an adverb clause, we can often point out a more specific relationship than the word **and** expresses. a. **Phil dropped my radio,** *and* **it wouldn't play.** b. *After Phil dropped my radio,* **it wouldn't play.** Which sentence brings out more clearly the relationship between the two ideas? ___ 821
No 1040	Combine these two sentences by changing the italicized sentence to an appositive word group: **Alva was practicing her piano lesson.** *She is my younger sister.* ____________________ ____________________ 1041
grown 1260	PRESENT — SIMPLE PAST — PAST WITH HELPER **grow** — **grew** — **have** ________ Fill in the helper form of this verb. 1261

The dog

1480

Underline the only subject that agrees in number with the verb:

(*The bank, Schools, Stores*) **was closed on Monday.**

1481

well, well

1699

I can't sleep (*good, well*) **unless the ventilation is** (*good, well*).

1700

he

1918

The flat tire made the Todds and (*us, we*) **late.**

1919

F, s

2137

Do you know why we celebrate ___hanksgiving ___ay in the ___all rather than in another season?

2138

True

2356

Lesson 76 Commas for Setting Off Interrupters

[Frames 2358–2395]

before

2575

He said, "Stop teasing the dog."

The separating comma comes before the quotes.

The period at the end of the sentence comes (*before, after*) the quotes.

2576

verb
noun

161

plant **forget**

Which one of the above words could be used as both a *noun* and a *verb*? (Think of actual sentences before writing your answer.) ________

162

---

a

381

Bruce either forgot or broke his date.

In this sentence, the conjunction **or** connects two ________.

382

---

but

601

The train goes ______________ a tunnel.

Underline the preposition that would make good sense in the above sentence.

among **with** **through** **of**

602

---

b

821

A sentence that contains a clause is called a **complex sentence.**

After Phil dropped my radio, **it wouldn't play.**

Because the above sentence contains a clause, it is a *compound, complex*) sentence.

822

Alva, my younger sister, was practicing her piano lesson.

1041

UNIT 5: **UNDERSTANDING THE SENTENCE UNIT**

Lesson 34 Avoiding Sentence Fragments

[Frames 1043–1077]

---

grown

1261

These tomatoes were . . . in our own backyard.

Which form of the verb **grow** is required? __________

1262

The bank 1481	Underline the only subject that agrees in number with the verb: (*You, I, We*) **was watching the game.** 1482
well, good 1700	**Our seats were** (*good, well*), **and we heard very** (*good, well*). 1701
us 1919	**Mr. Bailey sat behind Verna and** (*me, I*) **at the play.** 1920
T, D, f 2138	Capitalize the names of historical events and documents (but not **the** when it precedes these names). **the Korean War** **the Battle of Gettysburg** **the Bill of Rights** **the Declaration of Independence** Write the capital letters you would need to use in writing **the war of independence.** ________ 2139
	We often use expressions that interrupt the smooth flow of the sentence. In speaking them, we drop our voices and pause before and after to set them off from the main idea. **John,** *however,* **is much older.** **The breakfast,** *for example,* **costs fifty cents.** The interrupting expressions are set off with ________. 2358
before 2576	Now let's turn the sentence around and put the quotation first instead of last. **"Stop teasing the dog," he said.** Look at the point where the comma and quotes come together. Does the comma still come before the quotes? (*Yes, No*) 2577

plant

Is the italicized word a *noun* or a *verb*?

The *plant* **needs water.** ________

Many farmers *plant* **corn.** ________

162

163

verbs

The words **and, but,** and **or** are ____________________.

382

383

through

The plane ______________ **New York was late.**

Underline the preposition that would make good sense in the above sentence.

against **from** **during** **except**

602

603

complex

a. **Ted insisted on diving,** *and* **the water was too shallow.**
b. **Ted insisted on diving** *although the water was too shallow.*

Which sentence is a complex sentence? ____

822

823

A **fragment** means "a broken piece"—like a fragment of glass or wood.

A **sentence fragment** is a piece of a sentence that is written as though it were a complete ______________.

1043

grown

PRESENT	SIMPLE PAST	PAST WITH HELPER
grow	**grew**	**have grown**

We (*grew, growed*) **these tomatoes in our own back yard.**

1262

1263

I

1482

Underline the only subject that agrees in number with the verb:

Was (*your sister, you, they*) **at Saturday's game?**

1483

good, well

1701

When business is (*good, well*), **employment is** (*good, well*).

1702

me

1920

The Fields and (*us, we*) **have been neighbors for years.**

1921

W, I

2139

Copy only the words that need to be capitalized, adding the capitals:

Delaware was the first state to ratify the constitution.

2140

commas

2358

The commas that set off interrupting expressions help your reader to keep his mind on the main idea.

Underline the interrupter and set it off with commas:

It happened I suppose on an icy pavement.

2359

Yes

2577

He said, "Stop teasing the dog."
"Stop teasing the dog," he said.

When a comma and quotes or a period and quotes come together, always put the comma or period first.

Punctuate this sentence completely:

The farmer replied These eggs were laid today

2578

noun
verb

Lesson 6 Pronouns Take the Place of Nouns

[Frames 165–192]

163

conjunctions

Three common conjunctions used to connect compound subjects, verbs, and other parts of the sentence are **and,** ________, ________.

383

384

from

Our dog jumped __________ the fence and escaped.

Underline the preposition that would make good sense in the above sentence.

in **around** **near** **over**

603

604

b

a. **Ted insisted on diving,** *and* **the water was too shallow.**
b. **Ted insisted on diving** *although the water was too shallow.*

Which sentence shows more clearly how the two ideas are related? ____

823

824

sentence

To be a sentence, a group of words must pass two tests:

1. Does it have a subject and a predicate?
2. Does it make sense by itself?

A little man in a big hat.

The above word group is a (*fragment, sentence*).

1043

1044

grew

The form of **know** that ends with **–en** or **–n** is __________.

1263

1264

your sister 1483	Underline the only subject that agrees in number with the verb: **Was** (*the tickets, the refreshments, the game*) **free?** 1484
good, good 1702	**These scissors used to be** (*good, well*), **but now they don't cut** (*good, well*). 1703
we 1921	**We didn't see** (*them, they*) **or the Masons at church today.** 1922
Constitution 2140	Copy only the words that need to be capitalized, adding the capitals: **One of the fiercest battles of World war II was the Battle of the bulge.** ____________________ 2141
, I suppose, 2359	Here are other common interrupters that must be fenced off by commas from the sentences in which they occur: **of course by the way on the whole on the other hand** **it seems if possible nevertheless as a matter of fact** Underline the interrupter and set it off with commas: **English on the other hand is easier for me.** 2360
replied, "These . . . today." 2578	Punctuate this sentence completely: **These eggs were laid today replied the farmer.** 2579

Another kind of word that can serve as the subject of a verb is the **pronoun.** The name *pronoun* comes from a Latin word which means "in place of a noun."

As their name suggests, pronouns are words used in place of ________.

165

---

but, or

384

We can buy or rent a tent.

This sentence has compound ________.

385

---

over

604

(This problem is different. Read the directions carefully.)

We walked ________ the park.

Underline the *one* preposition that would *not* make good sense in the above sentence.

across around with toward

605

---

b

824

a. **Ted insisted on diving,** *and* **the water was too shallow.**
b. **Ted insisted on diving** *although the water was too shallow.*

The relationship between the two ideas is made clearer by using an adverb clause in a (*complex, compound*) sentence.

825

---

fragment

1044

A little man in a big hat . . .

This word group is a fragment because it names something (man) but makes no statement about it.

In other words, this word group is not a sentence because it lacks a (*subject, predicate*).

1045

---

known

1264

The causes of tuberculosis have been . . . for a long time.

Which form of the verb **know** is required? ________

1265

the game

1484

An even more common error is the use of **don't** for **doesn't. Don't** is a short cut for **do not; doesn't** is a short cut for **does not.**

My dad *doesn't* **smoke.**

The word **doesn't** takes the place of the two words ________ ________.

1485

good, well

1703

This motor runs (*good, well*) **if the gasoline is** (*good, well*).

1704

them

1922

The police had trailed his partner and (*he, him*) **across the state.**

1923

War, Bulge

2141

Copy only the words that need to be capitalized, adding the capitals:

The United Nations charter went into effect on october 24, 1945. ____________________

2142

, on the other hand,

2360

When an interrupter begins or ends a sentence, we need, of course, only one comma to set it apart from the main idea.

Punctuate this sentence:

As a matter of fact he was telling the truth.

2361

"These . . . today,"

2579

The first word of a quotation is always capitalized because it is the beginning of someone's sentence.

The farmer replied, "These eggs were laid today."

The first letter in the above quotation is capital ____.

2580

nouns

165

Notice how a pronoun can take the place of a noun:

a. **The *dog* ran away.**
b. ***It* ran away.**

The pronoun *It* in sentence *b* takes the place of the noun _______ in sentence *a*.

166

---

verbs

385

Mia and the new boy soon became friends.

This sentence has a compound ______________.

386

---

with

605

Joan hid the money ____________ a book.

Underline the *one* preposition that would *not* make good sense in the above sentence.

in under behind until

606

---

complex

825

It is easy to change a **compound** sentence to a **complex** sentence.

although

Paul can play the piano, ~~and~~ he has never taken lessons.

We put the clause signal *although* in place of the conjunction *and*. In this way the (*first, second*) part of the compound sentence becomes an adverb clause.

826

---

predicate

1045

A little man in a big hat . . .

Which of the following items could make a sentence of the above fragment by providing a predicate? ____

a. **with a gray band**
b. **and a long raincoat**
c. **boarded the bus**

1046

---

known

1265

PRESENT	SIMPLE PAST	PAST WITH HELPER
know	**knew**	**have known**

a. **I should have knew better than to depend on Tommy.**
b. **I should have known better than to depend on Tommy.**

Which sentence is right? ____

1266

does not

1485

Eric's parents *don't* speak English.

The word **don't** takes the place of the two words ______ ______.

1486

well, good

1704

Lesson 56 Modifiers After "Sense" Verbs

[Frames 1706–1742]

him

1923

Mother had kept the secret from Bert and (*me, I*).

1924

Charter, October

2142

With two exceptions, which will be explained shortly, the general subjects taught in schools should not be capitalized.

arithmetic algebra history biology

Ron is excellent in (*math, Math*).

2143

fact,

2361

a. **I was worried** *by the way* **he acted.**
b. **This model** *by the way* **is more expensive.**

In one sentence, the italicized phrase is a necessary part of the sentence; in the other, it is an interrupter that might be omitted.

In which sentence is it an interrupter—*a* or *b*? ____

2362

T

2580

a. **The heroic Harriet Tubman always said, "Keep going."**
b. **The heroic Harriet Tubman always said, "keep going."**

Which sentence is correct? ____

2581

dog

166

a. **Bob drove the car.**
b. **He drove the car.**

In place of the noun **Bob** in sentence *a*, we have the pronoun ______ in sentence *b*.

167

---

subject

386

Fred stayed in his room and studied.

This sentence has compound __________.

387

---

until

606

The explosion occurred ____________ the fire.

Underline the *one* preposition that would *not* make good sense in the above sentence.

before of after during

607

---

second

826

COMPOUND: **Paul can play the piano,** *and* **he has never taken lessons.**
COMPLEX: **Paul can play the piano** *although he has never taken lessons.*

The contrast between the two ideas is brought out more clearly by the (*compound, complex*) sentence.

827

---

c

1046

A little man in a big hat boarded the bus.

This is now a complete sentence because it has both a subject and a ______________.

1047

---

b

1266

If an irregular verb has a form that ends with **-en** or **-n,** use it after any form of the helping verb **be** or ________.

1267

do not

1486

Before using **don't,** see if you can fit **do not** in its place.

He *don't* **like oysters.** *Don't* **he like oysters?**

Can we substitute **do not** for **don't** in these sentences? (*Yes, No*)

1487

Here are five well-known senses that human beings have:

1. We *hear* with our ears. 2. We *smell* with our noses.
3. We *look* with our eyes. 4. We *taste* with our tongues.
5. We *feel* with our hands.

I looked at my watch.

The verb **looked** means an action of the (*ears, eyes, nose*).

1706

---

me

1924

Vincent and (*me, I*) **played the parts of the two brothers.**

1925

---

math

2143

a. **Ann likes History better than Algebra.**
b. **Ann likes history better than algebra.**

Which sentence is correctly capitalized? ____

2144

---

b

2362

a. **I was worried by the way he acted.**
b. **This model by the way is more expensive.**

In which sentence should the phrase **by the way** be set off with commas? ____

2363

---

a

2581

a. **The waiter replied, "the pie is all gone."**
b. **The waiter replied, "The pie is all gone."**

Which sentence is correct? ____

2582

He

a. **The** *coat* **fits better.**
b. *This* **fits better.**

Is the italicized word a pronoun in sentence *a* or *b*? ____

167 168

---

verbs

Minneapolis and St. Paul are on opposite sides of the Mississippi River.

This sentence has a compound ____________.

387 388

---

of

Write in the blank a preposition that would make good sense in each sentence:

a. **Judy looked** _____ **herself in the mirror.**

b. **The address** _____ **the envelope was not clear.**

607 608

---

complex

Now let's change the **first** part of a compound sentence to an adverb clause:

Because ____ **The road was under repair,** ~~and~~ **we had to turn back.**

We drop the conjunction *and*. Then we add the clause signal ____________ at the beginning of the sentence.

827 828

---

predicate

Now we shall add a clause to our sentence:

A little man *who was wearing a big hat* **boarded the bus.**

The clause *who was wearing a big hat* modifies the noun **man.**

It is therefore an (*adjective, adverb*) clause.

1047 1048

---

have

The cashier gave me the wrong change.

If you added the helper **had** to the verb, you would need to change the verb **gave** to ____________.

1267 1268

No	a. **He** *don't* **like oysters.** b. **They** *don't* **like oysters.** In which sentence is **don't** wrong because the words **do not** would be wrong? ____
1487	1488
eyes	**look smell taste feel hear** When these "sense" verbs mean the actions we perform with our eyes, nose, hands, etc., we should use *adverbs* to describe these actions. **Luisa looked** (*sad, sadly*) **at the dent in her new car.**
1706	1707
I	**Between you and** (*I, me*), **it doesn't make any difference.** (**Between** is a preposition.)
1925	1926
b	We do, however, capitalize the names of language subjects. **English Latin French Spanish** Underline the names of subjects you would capitalize in the following sentence: **I'm now taking english, algebra, french, and history.**
2144	2145
b	a. **The guard** *it seems* **was asleep.** b. *It seems* **to be warmer today.** In which sentence should *it seems* be set off with commas because it is an interrupter? ____
2363	2364
b	a. **"You can't hunt on this land", warned the farmer.** b. **"You can't hunt on this land," warned the farmer.** Which sentence is correct? ____
2582	2583

b

a. *Ours* **won the game.**
b. **The** *team* **won the game.**

Is the italicized word a pronoun in sentence *a* or *b*? ____

168 | 169

---

subject

My favorite subjects are math and science.

This sentence has compound (*subject complements, subjects*).

388 | 389

---

a. at
b. on

Write in the blank a preposition that would make good sense in each sentence:

a. **Vicky is still talking** ________ **her travels.**

b. **Everyone in our family** ________ **Ken has had the mumps.**

608 | 609

Because

________ **Sonja was giving a lecture,** *and* **a plane passed overhead.**

How would we change the **first** part of this compound sentence to an adverb clause?

Drop the conjunction *and*. Then put the clause signal *while* or *as* before the word ________.

828 | 829

---

adjective

Do not mistake a modifier for a predicate.

A little man *who was wearing a big hat . . .*

This is not a sentence. It is just a subject with an adjective clause that modifies it.

To make a sentence of this fragment, we would need to add a ________.

1048 | 1049

---

given

PRESENT	SIMPLE PAST	PAST WITH HELPER
throw	**threw**	**have thrown**

My test was (*threw, thrown, throwed*) **out by mistake.**

1268 | 1269

a 1488	Never use **don't** unless you can put the two words _____ _____ in its place. 1489
sadly 1707	**Mr. Roe felt the material** (*careful, carefully*). **Felt** is an action performed with one's hands. To describe the action of the verb **felt,** we should choose the adverb ________________. 1708
me 1926	**The Devil's Ride made Leora and** (*him, he*) **sick.** 1927
English, French 2145	When the name of a language is combined with the word **history** or **literature,** capitalize only the name of the language. **English literature** **American history** Underline the words you would capitalize: **Ellen enjoys american literature and english history.** 2146
a 2364	When the word **yes, no,** or **well** begins a sentence, it should be followed by a comma. **Yes, we do own a dog.** **No, I don't agree.** **Well, this is all the news I have to tell.** Supply *three* necessary commas: **Yes I shall if possible give Iris your message.** 2365
b 2583	One set of quotes (**"..."**) will take care of any number of sentences as long as the same person continues to speak. Punctuate the following quotation: **Rhoda said I have known Lee for several years. She has a lot of ability. She's a hard worker. You can't elect a better class president.** 2584

a

169

The boys washed the car.

Underline the *pronoun* that could take the place of the noun **(The) boys** in the above sentence.

neighbors **women** **they**

170

---

subject complements

389

The high wind blew down many trees and dead branches.

This sentence has compound (*direct objects, subject complements*).

390

---

a. about
b. but *or* except

609

Underline the preposition in each sentence:

a. **A small sign pointed to the lunchroom.**
b. **The paper printed the names of the winner.**

610

Sonja

829

__________ **I looked over my paper,** *and* **I noticed several mistakes.**

After you drop the conjunction *and,* what clause signal would you put at the beginning of the sentence? __________

830

---

predicate

1049

a. **A little man** *who was wearing a big hat.*
b. **A little man** *who was wearing a big hat* **boarded the bus.**

A subject followed by a modifying word group is not a sentence.

The complete sentence is ____.

1050

---

thrown

1269

The catcher should have . . . the ball to second base.

Which form of the verb **throw** is required? __________

1270

do not 1489	In this and the following frames, only one of the three subjects in parentheses agrees in number with the verb. Underline this subject. (*The cover, The bolts, The hat*) **don't fit.** 1490
carefully 1708	**Richard tasted his first cake very** (*hopeful, hopefully*). **Tasted** is an action performed with one's tongue. To describe the action of the verb **tasted,** we should choose the adverb ________________. 1709
him 1927	**Here's a snapshot of** (*he, him*) **and his dog.** 1928
American, English 2146	a. **Our coach also teaches American history.** b. **Our coach also teaches American History.** Which sentence is correctly capitalized? ____ 2147
Yes, shall, possible, 2365	a. **No I have never been to Florida.** b. **No small boat could survive in such a gale.** In which sentence should a comma follow the word **No?**____ 2366
said, "I . . . president." 2584	In this and the following frames, supply all the necessary commas and quotes. A few sentences do not require quotes because they do not give the actual words of the speaker. **You meet us in the gym said Inez.** 2585

they

170

Underline the *noun* that the pronoun **she** could take the place of:

girls **Peggy** **sisters**

171

---

direct objects

390

My topcoat is light but warm.

This sentence has compound (*direct objects, subject complements*).

391

---

a. to
b. of

610

I dropped my coin into the slot.

What is the preposition that shows the relationship between **dropped** and **slot?** ________

611

As (When, While)

830

A complex sentence is not always better than a compound sentence with **and.** It is better only when there is a more specific relationship than the word **and** can express.

a. **Pat's hair is red,** *and* **his eyes are blue.**
b. **Don is very bright,** *and* **he gets poor grades.**

Which compound sentence would you leave as it is? ____

831

---

b

1050

The old wooden bridge.

This word group is a (*sentence, fragment*).

1051

---

thrown

1270

The form of the verb **write** that ends with **–en** or **–n** is ________________.

1271

The bolts 1490	Underline the only subject that agrees in number with the verb: (*The tires, It, The car*) **don't look new.** 1491
hopefully 1709	**look smell taste feel hear (sound)** Besides meaning actions of parts of our bodies, these words have another and more common meaning. a. **Connie smelled the roses.** b. **The roses smelled fragrant.** **Smelled** means an action of the nose in sentence ____. 1710
him 1928	In this and the following frames, underline the two correct pronouns in each sentence: (*She, Her*) **and** (*I, me*) **first met at Alice's party.** 1929
a 2147	**Next semester we study ^ literature.** If you inserted the word **American** at the point indicated, would you need to capitalize the noun **literature?** (*Yes, No*) 2148
a 2366	When the word **why** begins a sentence that does not ask a question, it should be followed by a comma. a. **Why did you change your mind?** b. **Why this story is ridiculous!** In which sentence does **Why** require a comma? ____ 2367
"You . . . gym," 2585	**Inez said You meet us in the gym.** 2586

Peggy

171

The noun **elephant** can mean only one *definite* kind of animal. The pronoun **it,** on the contrary, could mean almost anything—an elephant, a cat, a city, or a cake.

A pronoun is generally (*more, less*) definite than a noun.

172

---

subject complements

391

His aunt and uncle play both golf and tennis.

Besides having compound subjects, this sentence also has compound (*direct objects, subject complements*).

392

---

into

611

Coffee without sugar has a bitter taste.

What is the preposition that shows the relationship between **coffee** and **sugar?** ______________

612

---

a

831

Pat's hair is red, *and* **his eyes are blue.**

This is a good compound sentence. We merely wish to state two facts about Pat's appearance, and we connect them with *and.* There is no other relationship between the two facts.

Could you improve this sentence by making it complex? (*Yes, No*)

832

---

fragment

1051

The old wooden bridge . . .

Which one of the following word groups could change this fragment to a sentence—*a, b,* or *c*? ____

a. **which was built 50 years ago**
b. **collapsed**
c. **across the shallow stream**

1052

---

written

1271

Supply the right form of the verb **write:**

The new teacher's name was ______________ **on the board.**

1272

The tires

1491

Underline the only subject that agrees in number with the verb:

(*Archie, We, My dad*) **don't like spinach.**

1492

---

a

1710

Besides meaning an action of the nose, the verb **smelled** has another use.

The roses smelled (= were) fragrant.

In this sentence, **smelled** serves as a linking verb—like **were**—to show that the adjective **fragrant** modifies the subject ____________. 1711

She, I

1929

There isn't room in Eileen's car for both (*them, they*) **and** (*us, we*).

1930

No

2148

We also capitalize any school subject that is followed by a *course number*. The course number pins it down as a *particular* course in a general subject.

algebra—Algebra (1) **literature—Literature II**

Underline the words you would capitalize:

After completing typewriting (2), I began shorthand. 2149

---

b

2367

Another type of sentence interrupter is the appositive. An **appositive** is a noun or pronoun—often with modifiers—set after another noun or pronoun to explain it.

Mrs. Chen, *my English teacher,* **coaches the tennis team.**

The appositive explains who ____________________ is.

2368

---

said, "You . . . gym."

2586

Inez said that we should meet him in the gym.

2587

less

The noun **teachers** is (*more, less*) definite than the pronoun **they.**

172 173

direct objects

392

Lesson 14 Verbs of More Than One Word

[Frames 394–429]

The lamp on the table is broken.
The lamp beside the table is broken.

without

In these two sentences, the relationship between **lamp** and **table** is different because the ______________ are different.

612 613

COMPOUND: **Don is very bright,** *and* **he gets poor grades.**
COMPLEX: **Don is very bright** *although he gets poor grades.*

No

The contrast between the two facts is expressed more clearly in the (*compound, complex*) sentence.

832 833

The old wooden bridge collapsed.

b

Now the meaning is complete because the verb __________ makes a statement about the subject **bridge.**

1052 1053

written

In rapid conversation, the verb **have** and the preposition **of** sound very much alike. Be careful not to write **of** when you mean **have.**

a. **You should have started earlier.**
b. **You should of started earlier.**

Which sentence is correct? ___

1272 1273

We 1492	Underline the only subject that agrees in number with the verb: (*The ladies, My mother, Mr. Henry*) **don't play bridge.** 1493
roses 1711	**The roses were fragrant.** **The roses smelled fragrant.** The verbs **were** and **smelled** both serve the same purpose. They *link* the adjective **fragrant** with the subject **roses,** which it describes. **Were** and **smelled** are, therefore, ________*ing* verbs. 1712
them, us 1930	**Mr. Thomas always gave** (*she, her*) **and** (*I, me*) **the same grades.** 1931
Typewriting (2) 2149	**We are having a test in math ‸ today.** If you inserted the number **(2)** at the point indicated, would you need to capitalize the noun **math?** (*Yes, No*) 2150
Mrs. Chen 2368	**Mrs. Chen,** *my English teacher,* **coaches the tennis team.** Read the above sentence, omitting the italicized appositive. Is it still a complete sentence without the appositive? (*Yes, No*) 2369
None 2587	**The man turned around and said Please don't rattle your program.** 2588

more

173

Which **won the first prize?**

We do not know whether *which* refers to a story, a dog, a car, or what.

The word *which* is a (*noun, pronoun*).

174

A verb often needs the help of one or more other verbs to express our exact meaning.

He might study.

He should study.

These sentences have (*the same, different*) meanings.

394

---

prepositions

613

A preposition shows the ______________*ship* between the noun or pronoun that follows it and some other word in the sentence.

614

---

complex

833

In this and the following frames, improve each sentence by changing the italicized part to an adverb clause. In other words, change each compound sentence to a complex sentence. Write the full sentence.

I start to eat popcorn, **and it is hard to stop.**

____

834

---

collapsed

1053

a. **The old wooden bridge collapsed.**

b. **Because the old wooden bridge collapsed.**

Although both word groups have a subject and a verb, which one does *not* make sense by itself? ____

1054

---

a

1273

When **have** is a helping verb, it is followed by the main verb. The preposition **of,** on the other hand, is followed by a noun or pronoun.

I could (*of, have*) **done this better myself.**

Have should be used because it is followed by a (*verb, noun*).

1274

The ladies

1493

Underline the only subject that agrees in number with the verb:

Don't (*Fred, he, the boys*) **want the job?**

1494

---

link(ing)

1712

The roses smelled (*fragrant, fragrantly*).

Because the word that follows the linking verb **smelled** describes the subject **roses,** we should choose the adjective ____________.

1713

---

her, me

1931

(*They, Them*) **and** (*we, us*) **are on the same party line.**

1932

Yes

2150

Paula does well in Mechanical Drawing (3).

If you dropped the number **(3)** from this sentence, would you still write **Mechanical Drawing** with capital letters? (*Yes, No*)

2151

Yes

2369

The appositive is an "extra" which may be omitted without damaging the completeness of the sentence.

a. **Our target,** *a small tin can,* **was nailed to a post.**
b. *A small tin can* **was nailed to a post for our target.**

In which sentence are the italicized words an appositive? ____

2370

---

said, "Please . . . program."

2588

It's like squeezing blood out of a turnip   **sighed Rita.**

2589

pronoun 174	a. **Three** *eggs* **broke.** b. *Some* **broke.** Is the italicized word a pronoun in sentence *a* or *b*? ____ 175
different 394	**He might study.** **He should study.** The words that give these sentences different meanings are **might** and ____________. 395
relation(ship) 614	Lesson **21** **The Prepositional Phrase as a Modifier** [Frames 616–646]
When (Whenever, After, If) I start to eat popcorn, it is hard to stop. 834	**These coins are valuable,** *and very few of them exist.* ________________________________ ________________________________ 835
b 1054	a. **The old wooden bridge collapsed.** b. **Because the old wooden bridge collapsed . . .** By adding the clause signal **because** to sentence *a*, we changed it from a sentence to an adverb ____________, which needs a main statement to give it meaning. 1055
verb 1274	**Virginia must** (*of, have*) **waited for over an hour.** Which word is correct in this sentence? __________ 1275

the boys 1494	Underline the only subject that agrees in number with the verb: **Don't** (*the neighbors, your father, she*) **object to the noise?** 1495
fragrant 1713	a. **Mr. Roe felt the material.** b. **Mr. Roe felt happy.** In which sentence does **felt** mean an action of the hands—*a* or *b*? ____ 1714
They, we 1932	**Are you going to vote for** (*he, him*) **or** (*she, her*)**?** 1933
No 2151	**There is more to remember in American History II.** If you dropped the number **II,** would you still write **American** with a capital letter? (*Yes, No*) 2152
a 2370	An appositive always comes *after* the noun or pronoun it explains. a. **Harriet Gomez, the editor of our paper, is graduating.** b. **The editor of our paper, Harriet Gomez, is graduating.** In which sentence is **Harriet Gomez** an appositive? ____ 2371
"It's . . . turnip," 2589	**I told the driver that one of his headlights was out.** 2590

b

175

a. *People* **wanted their money back.**
b. *Customers* **wanted their money back.**
c. *Many* **wanted their money back.**

In which sentence is the subject a pronoun, not a noun? ____

176

---

should

395

a. **He might study.**

b. **He should study.**

In sentence *a*, the verb consists of two words—**might study.**

In sentence *b*, the verb consists of two words— __________ __________.

396

The noun or pronoun that follows a preposition is called its **object.**

Cindy works for her aunt.

The object of the preposition **for** is the noun __________.

616

These coins are valuable because (since, as) very few of them exist.

835

The winners were being announced, **and everyone held his breath.**

____

____

836

---

clause

1055

Because the old wooden bridge collapsed, **we took the longer road.**

The adverb clause answers the question (*How? Why?*) about the action of the verb in the main statement.

1056

---

have

1275

Fill in the right word:

Nobody could __________ **tried harder.**

1276

the neighbors

1495

Lesson 48 The Useful "Rule of *S*"

[Frames 1497–1520]

a

1714

Mr. Roe felt the material (*careful, carefully*).

In this sentence, **felt** means an action of the hands.

To describe this action, we should choose the adverb

_________________.

1715

him, her

1933

Lesson 63 The Problem of Omitted Words

[Frames 1935–1968]

Yes

2152

In this and the following frames, cross out each capital letter that is not correct:

We study the Bill Of Rights in American History.

2153

b

2371

Because an appositive interrupts the sentence, it is set off with commas (or with a comma if it ends the sentence).

Punctuate this sentence:

Colgate Clock the largest clock in the world is in New York.

2372

None

2590

Miss Gaines said You look out the window. You play with your pen. You talk to your neighbors. You do everything except pay attention.

2591

c

176

a. *Everybody* **liked this program.**
b. *Roger* **liked this program.**

In which sentence is the subject a pronoun, not a noun?

____

177

---

should study

396

Verbs that help the main verb to express our meaning more exactly are called **helping verbs** or **helpers.**

He must study.

The main verb is **study;** the helping verb is ________.

397

---

aunt

616

The sound of heavy footsteps awoke me.

The object of the preposition **of** is the noun ________.

617

As (While, When) the winners were being announced, everyone held his breath.

836

We fed our cat salmon, **and it would eat no other food.**

____

____

837

Why?

1056

Because the old wooden bridge collapsed, **we took the longer road.**

The adverb clause modifies the verb ________ in the main statement.

1057

---

have

1276

One of the pupils must of lost some of the tickets.

There are three **of**'s in this sentence.

Write the word which follows the **of** which should have been **have.** ________

1277

The dog barked.

If we made the subject **dog** plural, would we need to change the simple past verb **barked?** (*Yes, No*)

1497

---

carefully

1715

a. **Mr. Roe felt the material.**
b. **Mr. Roe felt happy.**

In which sentence is **felt** a linking verb which links an adjective with the subject **Mr. Roe?** ____

1716

A comparison expressed by the word **than** or **as** is usually an abbreviated sentence. By supplying the omitted words, you will see instantly which pronoun to choose.

Gerald stayed later than I (stayed).

The omitted verb in this sentence is ____________.

1935

~~O~~f, ~~H~~istory

2153

Cross out each capital letter that is not correct:

We shall have tests in English and Algebra when we return from our Spring vacation.

2154

Clock, world,

2372

Punctuate this sentence:

A heavy snowstorm held up our train the Lexington Express.

2373

---

said, "You . . . attention."

2591

This wasn't my lucky day groaned Mike.

2592

a 177	a. **Wayne and Gary were absent.** b. **Both were absent.** How many names in sentence *a* does the word **Both** in sentence *b* take the place of? ______ 178
must 397	Learn to recognize these important helping verbs. Each has its own special meaning. HELPING VERBS: **shall, will** **may, can** **could, would, should** **must, might** Two helping verbs that rhyme with **could** are ______ and ______. 398
footsteps 617	**The band marched across the muddy field.** The object of the preposition **across** is the noun ______. 618
After (Since, Because, If, When) we fed our cat salmon, it would eat no other food. 837	**Bob is always broke,** *and he gets a good salary.* ______ ______ 838
took 1057	a. *Because the old wooden bridge collapsed,* **we took the longer road.** b. *Because the old wooden bridge collapsed.* **We took the longer road.** Which is correct because the adverb clause is in the same sentence with the verb it modifies? ____ 1058
lost 1277	Lesson 41 **Straightening Out *Lie* and *Lay*** [Frames 1279–1317] *page 355*

No

1497

SINGULAR: **The dog barked.**

PLURAL: **The dogs barked.**

We use the same simple past verb whether its subject is singular or ______________.

1498

---

b

1716

Mr. Roe felt (= was) happy.

In this sentence, **felt** is a linking verb which links the adjective **happy** with the subject ______________, which it describes.

1717

---

stayed

1935

Gerald stayed later than I (stayed).

The subject form **I** is correct because it is the (*subject, object*) of the omitted verb **stayed.**

1936

~~A~~lgebra, ~~S~~pring

2154

Cross out each capital letter that is not correct:

Myra's Painting teacher got her a job with the Company that manufactures Treetop Greeting Cards.

2155

---

train,

2373

Punctuate this sentence:

With the help of Eva Rivera the girl across the street I built a model jet plane.

2374

"This . . . day,"

2592

Ali announced firmly that he was going to retire.

2593

Two 178	**Both were absent.** The word **Both** is a ______________. 179
would, should 398	HELPING VERBS: **shall, will** / **could, would, should** / **may, can** / **must, might** Two helping verbs that begin with **m** and end with **t** are ______________ and ______________. 399
field 618	A group of words that begins with a preposition and ends with its object is called a **prepositional phrase.** **The sound of heavy footsteps awoke me.** In this sentence, the **prepositional phrase** begins with the preposition **of** and ends with its object ______________. 619
Bob is always broke although he gets a good salary. 838	**We'll mark our route on the map,** *and we won't lose our way.* ______________________________ ______________________________ 839
a 1058	**The kettle whistles. When the water boils.** The second word group is not a sentence. It is an adverb clause that modifies the verb ______________ in the main statement to which it should be attached. 1059
	The verbs **lie** and **lay** are often confused. First, let's see how these slippery little verbs differ in meaning. **To lie** means "to rest in a flat position" or "to be in place." **Don't** __________ **in the hot sun.** 1279

plural

1498

Except for the verb **be,** all verbs have one simple past form that is used with both singular and plural subjects.

SINGULAR: **The dog was hungry.**
PLURAL: **The dogs were hungry.**

The verb **be,** however, has two simple past forms: the singular form **was** and the plural form ______. 1499

Mr. Roe

1717

Mr. Roe felt (*happy, happily*).

Because the word that follows the linking verb **felt** describes the subject **Mr. Roe,** we should choose the word ______.

1718

---

subject

1936

We live closer to the school than they (____).

The omitted verb in this sentence is ______.

1937

---

painting, company, greeting cards

2155

George plans to take Chemistry and Geometry (2) at Summer School.

2156

Eva Rivera, street,

2374

Here is another type of interrupter that requires commas. When we address (talk to) a person directly, we often interrupt a sentence to insert his name or other words that identify him. This is called **direct address.**

Donna **wants you to write her,** *Nancy,* **about your plans.**

The name used in direct address is (*Donna, Nancy*). 2375

None

2593

A sign on the lawn says Your feet are killing me.

2594

pronoun

179

To show ownership, nouns and pronouns have a **possessive** form. Possessive pronouns take the place of possessive nouns.

a. **Sharon's hair is red.**
b. **Her hair is red.**

What pronoun in sentence *b* takes the place of **Sharon's** in sentence *a*? ______

180

---

must, might

399

HELPING VERBS: **shall, will** **may, can**
could, would, should **must, might**

Two helping verbs that end with **-ll** are ________ and ________.

400

---

footsteps

619

My cousin lives on a very large ranch.

In this sentence, the **prepositional phrase** begins with the preposition **on** and ends with its object ________.

620

We'll mark our route on the map so that we won't lose our way.

839

Lesson 28 Understanding the Adjective Clause

[Frames 841-875]

---

whistles

1059

a. **The kettle whistles. When the water boils.**
b. **The kettle whistles when the water boils.**

Because an adverb clause should be in the same sentence as the verb it modifies, (*a*, *b*) is correct.

1060

---

lie

1279

A rug **lies** on the floor, a letter **lies** on the desk, and a person ________ in bed.

1280

were

1499

Now we shall change to present time.

SINGULAR: **The dog** *barks.*
PLURAL: **The dogs** *bark.*

The verbs in both sentences show present time.

Is the same form of the verb used with both a singular and a plural subject? (*Yes, No*)

1500

---

happy

1718

When the "sense" verbs **look, smell, taste, feel,** and **hear** mean actions of the body, we use (*adjectives, adverbs*) to describe the action.

1719

---

live (*or* do)

1937

We live closer to the school than <u>they</u> (live).

The subject form **they** is correct because **they** is the (*subject, object*) of the omitted verb **live.**

1938

---

c̸hemistry, s̸ummer s̸chool

2156

In this and the following frames, underline the words that lack required capitals:

My birthday is on the first sunday in april.

2157

Nancy

2375

Because words of direct address interrupt the sentence, they are set off with commas.

Punctuate this sentence:

I am happy ladies and gentlemen to be here tonight.

2376

---

says, "Your . . . me."

2594

Now let's see what happens when the quotation is a question rather than a statement of fact.

"Have you heard the news?" he asked.

The question mark is at the end of the (*quotation, sentence*).

2595

Her

180

a. **Cleo finished her homework.**
b. **Cleo finished hers.**

The pronoun **hers** in sentence *b* takes the place of two words in sentence *a*. What are these two words? ________ ________ 181

---

shall, will

400

HELPING VERBS: **shall, will** **may, can** **could, would, should** **must, might**

One helping verb besides **may** that has only three letters is ______. 401

---

ranch

620

a. **Mary was raised by an aunt.**
b. **Mary was raised by a very strict aunt.**

How many words does the **prepositional phrase** in sentence *a* contain? ___ In sentence *b*? ___ 621

He consulted *important* people.

The adjective *important* modifies the noun __________. 841

---

b

1060

We have bought new equipment. Which saves us much time.

The second word group is not a sentence. It is an adjective clause that modifies the noun __________ in the main statement. 1061

---

lies

1280

To lay means "to put or to place something."

Never use this word unless you name the "something" that is put or placed somewhere (or use a pronoun in its place).

You can lay (put) the box on the shelf.

What is the "something" that you can **lay (put)** on the shelf? It is the ______. 1281

No 1500	**The dog barks.** The subject **dog** is singular, and the verb **barks** is singular. Which word ends in *s*—the *subject* or the *verb*? ________ 1501
adverbs 1719	If we can substitute for the "sense" verb some form of **be (am, is, are—was, were, been),** it is used as a linking verb and should be followed by an (*adjective, adverb*) which describes the subject. 1720
subject 1938	Here, to fill in the sentence, we must add two words, not just a verb: **The dress fits you better than (it fits) her.** The two omitted words in this sentence are ______ and ________. 1939
Sunday, April 2157	Underline the words that need to be capitalized: **After the Merrills bought their new pontiac, Dick's grades in latin and history went down.** 2158
happy, gentlemen, 2376	Punctuate this sentence: **I have decided my friend to take your advice.** 2377
quotation 2595	**"Have you heard the news?" he asked.** Because the quotation itself is a question, the question mark is placed (*inside, outside*) the quotes. 2596

her homework

181

Hers is newer than yours.

How many pronouns are there in this sentence? ______

182

---

can

401

a. **write, sell, swim, bring**
b. **shall, would, may, might**

Which group of words consists of helping verbs? ___

402

---

a. 3
b. 5

621

The smoke from this great fire darkened the sky.

The **prepositional phrase** begins with the preposition ________ and ends with its object ________.

622

---

people

841

A **prepositional phrase** can be used exactly like an adjective.

We consulted people *of importance.*

The prepositional phrase *of importance* is an adjective phrase because it modifies the ________ **people.**

842

---

equipment

1061

a. **We have bought new equipment which saves us much time.**
b. **We have bought new equipment. Which saves us much time.**

An adjective clause should not be cut off from the word it modifies. Therefore, (*a, b*) is correct.

1062

---

box

1281

Once again, **to lie** means "to rest in a flat position" or "to be in place."

In which of the following sentences does this definition fit? ___

a. **You will get sunburnt if you . . . on the beach.**
b. **Don't . . . the hot pan on the table.**

1282

verb

1501

The dogs bark.

Now the subject **dogs** is plural, and the verb **bark** is plural. Which word ends in *s*—the *subject* or the *verb*? ________

1502

adjective

1720

a. **Jennifer's make-up looked very** (*curious, curiously*).
b. **Everyone looked at Jennifer very** (*curious, curiously*).

In which sentence does **looked** mean an action of the eyes—*a* or *b*? ____

1721

it, fits

1939

The dress fits you better than (it fits) her.

The object form **her** is correct because it is the object of the omitted verb ________.

1940

Pontiac, Latin

2158

Underline the words that need to be capitalized:

The speaker expressed the idea that the constitution was inspired by god.

2159

decided, friend,

2377

Punctuate this sentence:

How wisely you spend your money you clever girl!

2378

inside

2596

"Have you heard the news?" he asked.

Is the separating comma used between the quotation and **he asked?** (*Yes, No*)

2597

Two

182

Is the italicized word in each sentence a *noun* or a *pronoun?*

a. *Corn* **grows fast in hot weather.** ______________

b. *It* **grows fast in hot weather.** ______________

183

---

b

402

The three helping verbs below have several forms.

HELPING VERBS: **be (is, am, are—was, were, been)**
have (has, had)
do (does, did)

Has and **had** are forms of the verb ________.

Does and **did** are forms of the verb ________.

403

---

from, fire

622

a. **healthy people**
b. **people in good health**

In *a*, the adjective **healthy** modifies the noun **people.**

In *b*, the prepositional phrase **in good health** also modifies the noun ____________.

623

---

noun

842

A **clause,** too, can do the work of an adjective by modifying a noun or pronoun.

We consulted people *who are important.*

Because the clause *who are important* modifies the noun **people,** it is an (*adjective, adverb*) clause.

843

---

a

1062

Sue read until midnight. And finished the book.

The (*first, second*) word group is a sentence fragment.

1063

---

a

1282

You will get sunburnt if you . . . on the beach.

The meaning we want is "to rest in a flat position."

Therefore, the correct word is _______.

1283

subject 1502	**The boy swims.** The subject **boy** is singular, and the verb **swims** is singular. Which word ends in *s*—the *subject* or the *verb*? ________ 1503
b 1721	**Everyone looked at Jennifer very** (*curious, curiously*). In this sentence, **looked** means an action of the eyes. To describe this action of the eyes, we should choose the word ________________. 1722
fits 1940	Write in the omitted words: **The collision hurt the car more than (______ __________) us.** 1941
Constitution, God 2159	**The Vogue shop on Washington boulevard is showing the newest fall fashions.** 2160
money, 2378	Because names are often used as appositives and direct address, some pupils thoughtlessly put commas around every name they write. Don't use commas unless the words interrupt the sentence and could be omitted. **The next time you come Dave you must bring Earl along.** 2379
No 2597	**"Have you heard the news?" he asked.** The comma that usually separates the quotation from the rest of the sentence is no longer needed. The question mark alone is enough to separate the quotation from **he asked.** Punctuate the following sentence: **Where did you put the car keys asked Sally.** 2598

noun
pronoun

183

Is the italicized word a *noun* or a *pronoun*?

a. ***Who*** **reported the fire?**____________

b. ***Jane*** **reported the fire.**____________

184

---

have
do

403

a. **Tom is my brother.**

b. **Tom is washing the car.**

Is the verb **is** used by itself as the *main verb* in sentence *a* or *b*? ____

404

---

people

623

a. **healthy people**

b. **people in good health**

Because the prepositional phrase **in good health** serves the same purpose as the adjective ____________, we call it an **adjective phrase.**

624

---

adjective

843

a. **We consulted** *important* **people.**

b. **We consulted people** *who are important.*

The adjective clause *who are important* does the same job in sentence *b* that the adjective ____________ does in sentence *a*.

844

---

second

1063

Sue read until midnight. And finished the book.

The second word group is a sentence fragment because the verb **finished** lacks a ____________.

1064

---

lie

1283

PRESENT	SIMPLE PAST	PAST WITH HELPER
lie	**lay**	**have lain**

Last night I ____________ down on the sofa and fell asleep.

Supply the right form of the verb **lie.**

1284

verb

1503

The boys swim.

Now the subject **boys** is plural, and the verb **swim** is plural.

Which word ends in *s*—the *subject* or the *verb*? __________

1504

---

curiously

1722

a. **Jennifer's make-up looked very** (*curious, curiously*).
b. **Everyone looked at Jennifer very** (*curious, curiously*).

In which sentence can we substitute **was** for **looked?** ____

1723

---

it hurt

1941

Underline the correct pronoun:

The collision hurt the car more than (*we, us*).

1942

Shop,
Boulevard

2160

Pulaski and Kosciusko were young officers who served general Washington in the American revolution.

(Remember that historical events are capitalized.)

2161

---

come, Dave,

2379

In this sentence, only one of the two names is used as an appositive and, therefore, requires commas.

Insert the necessary commas:

The hero of this story Dick Crothers saves Allan Merrick from drowning.

2380

"Where . . . keys?"

2598

a. **"Does coffee ever keep you awake," asked Mr. Horn?**
b. **"Does coffee ever keep you awake?" asked Mr. Horn.**

Which sentence is correct? ____

2599

pronoun noun 184	Is the italicized word a *noun* or a *pronoun*? a. ***These* won prizes.** ______ b. **The *stories* won prizes.** ______ 185
a 404	a. **I have the measles.** b. **I have caught the measles.** Is the verb **have** used as a *helping verb* in sentence *a* or *b*? ___ 405
healthy 624	**people in good health** We call **in good health** an **adjective phrase** because it does exactly the same work as an ______. 625
important 844	Think of an adjective clause as a "stretched-out" adjective of several words that modifies a noun or pronoun, like any ordinary ______. 845
subject 1064	a. **Sue read until midnight. And finished the book.** b. **Sue read until midnight and finished the book.** A verb should be in the same sentence as its subject. Therefore, (*a*, *b*) is correct. 1065
lay 1284	This little rhyme will help you to remember that the simple past form of **lie** is **lay:** Yes-ter-**day** In bed I **lay.** Write the correct past form of the verb **lie:** **I don't know how long I ______ there.** 1285

subject

1504

Add an *s* where it will make the sentence plural:

The tree____ grow____.

1505

---

a

1723

Jennifer's make-up looked (= was) (*curious, curiously*).

Because **looked** is a linking verb here, it must be followed by a word that modifies the subject.

Therefore, we should choose the word ________________.

1724

---

us

1942

Sometimes the meaning of a sentence depends on whether we use the subject or object form of a pronoun.

a. **I like her sister more than she (likes her sister).**
b. **I like her sister more than (I like) her.**

In which sentence does the pronoun come before the omitted verb as its subject? ____

1943

General,
Revolution

2161

The American legion presented a flag to our high school on Veterans day.

2162

---

story,
Dick Crothers,

2380

Punctuate the appositive in this sentence:

The winners of the game Kent High had never defeated Marston High before.

2381

---

b

2599

We follow the same procedure with a quotation that requires an exclamation point **(!)**.

"What a beautiful sunset!" exclaimed Virginia.

Punctuate the following sentence:

Look out for the car shouted Ken

2600

pronoun
noun

185

Is the italicized word a *noun* or a *pronoun*?

a. **The** ***car*** **broke down.** ______________

b. ***Ours*** **broke down.** ______________

186

---

b

405

a. **Judy does her lessons.**
b. **Yes, Judy does study her lessons.**

Is the verb **does** used by itself as the *main verb* in sentence *a* or *b*?

406

---

adjective

625

a. **The Hopi live in adobe houses.**
b. **The Hopi live in houses of adobe.**

In *a,* **adobe** is an adjective.

In *b,* the phrase **of adobe** is an *adjective* ______________.

626

---

adjective

845

a. **A** ***friendly*** **squirrel comes to our door.**
b. **A squirrel** ***that is friendly*** **comes to our door.**

The adjective clause *that is friendly* does the same job in sentence *b* that the ______________ *friendly* does in sentence *a.*

846

---

b

1065

a. **Vern had many opportunities but threw them all away.**
b. **Vern had many opportunities. But threw them all away.**

Which is correct—*a* or *b*? ____

1066

---

lay

1285

(An object can *lie* on a chair, table, or floor just as a person can *lie* on a bed.)

My missing wallet (*lay, laid*) in the snow all winter.

1286

(tree)s

1505

Add an *s* where it will make the sentence singular:

The tree____ grow____.

1506

curious

1724

The doctor felt my ankle very gently.

The adverb **gently** is correct because it modifies the verb ________.

1725

a

1943

a. **Cliff likes dogs more than <u>she</u> (. . .).**
b. **Cliff likes dogs more than (. . .) <u>her</u>.**

Each of the above sentences has a different meaning. To see this difference, think of the missing words in each sentence. Which sentence means that Cliff likes dogs more than the girl likes them? ____

1944

Legion, Day

2162

A boy in my english class found a presto camera on the Woodlawn avenue bus.

2163

game,
Kent High,

2381

Don't put commas around the titles of books, stories, poems, etc., unless they are used as appositives.

a. **I am reading *Laughing Boy* for my book report.**
b. **I am reading an interesting book *Laughing Boy* for my book report.**

In which sentence does the title require commas? ____

2382

"Look . . . car!" shouted Ken.

2600

a. **"We've won again!" screamed Betty.**
b. **"We've won again," screamed Betty!**

Which sentence is correct? ____

2601

noun
pronoun

186

Is the italicized word a *noun* or a *pronoun*?

a. **Do you want** *mustard*? ______________

b. **Do you want** *any*? ______________

187

---

a

406

The bus will be leaving soon.

The main verb **leaving** has two helpers—________ and ________.

407

---

phrase

626

Think of an **adjective phrase** as being a stretched-out **adjective** consisting of two or more words.

a. **The team with the greater strength will win.**
b. **The stronger team will win.**

Is the **adjective phrase** in sentence *a* or *b*? ___

627

---

adjective

846

a. **A** *friendly* **squirrel comes to our door.**
b. **A squirrel** *that is friendly* **comes to our door.**

In sentence *a*, the adjective *friendly* comes *before* the noun it modifies.

In sentence *b*, the adjective clause *that is friendly* comes (*before, after*) the noun it modifies.

847

---

a

1066

In this and the following frames, write an **S** for each word group that is a **sentence,** and an **F** for each word group that is a **fragment.** Write your answers in the same order as the two word groups.

I feel sorry for Judy. Because her birthday comes on Christmas. ___ ___

1067

---

lay

1286

PRESENT	SIMPLE PAST	PAST WITH HELPER
lie (be in place)	**lay**	**have lain**

The boat lies on the beach all summer.

If we changed this sentence from present to past time, we would need to change **lies** to _______.

1287

(grow)s

SINGULAR: **The boy swims.** SINGULAR: **The tree grows.**
PLURAL: **The boys swim.** PLURAL: **The trees grow.**

When we add an *s* to the subject, we do not add an *s* to the verb.

When we add an *s* to the verb, we do not add an *s* to the ________.

1506 1507

felt

This wood feels too rough to use.

The adjective **rough** is correct because it modifies the noun ________.

1725 1726

a

Cliff likes dogs more than she (likes them).

The subject form **she** is the subject of the omitted verb ________.

1944 1945

English, Presto, Avenue

2163

Lesson 70 Learning to Capitalize Titles

[Frames 2165–2201]

b

In this and the following frames, supply the necessary commas. Some of the sentences do not require commas.

Wilma Rudolph for example won a gold medal in the Olympics.

2382 2383

a

When the question or exclamation comes at the end of the sentence, the usual comma is needed as a separator.

Terry asked, "Did you finish the test?"

Punctuate this exclamation the same way:

Judy exclaimed What a beautiful sunset

2601 2602

noun
pronoun

187

Pronouns help us to avoid the tiresome repetition of nouns.

Connie **denied that the writing was** *Connie's.*

Avoid this repetition by substituting a pronoun:

Connie denied that the writing was ________.

188

---

will, be

407

a. **Frank is working.**
b. **Frank has been working.**
c. **Frank should have been working.**

In which sentence does the main verb **working** have three helpers? ____

408

---

a

627

a. **spoke angrily**
b. **spoke with anger**

In *a*, the adverb **angrily** modifies the verb **spoke.**

In *b*, the prepositional phrase **with anger** also modifies the verb __________.

628

---

after

847

A squirrel *that is friendly* **comes to our door.**

Now let's remove the adjective clause from this sentence and look at it more closely:

that is friendly

Although this clause has both a subject and a verb, does it form a complete sentence by itself? (*Yes, No*)

848

S F

1067

Put down an **S** (for **sentence**) or an **F** (for **fragment**) for each of the two word groups:

I feel sorry for Judy. Her birthday comes on Christmas.

____ ____

1068

---

lay

1287

PRESENT	SIMPLE PAST	PAST WITH HELPER
lie (in bed)	**lay**	**have lain**

Lee had ________ down after dinner.

1288

Answer	Frame
subject 1507	**The tree grows.** **The trees grow.** When the subject is singular, there is no *s* on the subject, but there is an *s* on the verb. When the subject is plural, there is an *s* on the subject but none on the ________. 1508
wood 1726	In this and the following frames, underline the adverb **(–ly)** if the subject is smelling with his nose, looking with his eyes, feeling with his hands, etc., and if the word describes this action. **The cashier looked at the check** (*suspicious, suspiciously*). 1727
likes 1945	a. **Cliff likes dogs more than she.** b. **Cliff likes dogs more than her.** Which sentence means that Cliff likes dogs more than he likes the girl? ____ 1946
	Capitalize the first word and all important words in titles of books, stories, poems, etc. ***The Sea Wolf*** ***"A Worn Path"*** ***"Through the Tunnel"*** ***"Paul Revere's Ride"*** Write the capital letters you would need to use in writing ***the red pony.*** ____________ 2165
Rudolph, example, 2383	Insert any necessary commas: **Those two writers Clifton and Giovanni are famous poets.** 2384
exclaimed, "What . . . sunset!" 2602	In this and the following frames, supply the necessary punctuation. Each sentence requires either a question mark or an exclamation point. **When do we eat asked Charlie.** 2603

hers

188

Stanley **is training** *Stanley's* **dog to obey** *Stanley's* **commands.**

Avoid this repetition by substituting pronouns:

Stanley is training ______ dog to obey ______ commands.

189

---

c

408

The two or more words that make up the verb may come together, or they may be interrupted by other words that are not verbs.

a. **The bus will be leaving** *soon.*

b. **The bus will** *soon* **be leaving.**

The verb is interrupted by another word in sentence (*a, b*).

409

---

spoke

628

a. **spoke angrily**
b. **spoke with anger**

Because the prepositional phrase **with anger** in sentence *b* does exactly the same work as the adverb **angrily** in sentence *a*, we call it an ______ *phrase.*

629

No

848

ADJECTIVE CLAUSE SIGNALS

The following pronouns are often used to start adjective clauses: **who (whom, whose), which, that.**

Lisa owns a collie *which has won many prizes.*

The adjective clause in this sentence begins with the pronoun ______.

849

S S

1068

Unless you are willing to care for a dog properly. You should not get one.

___ ___

1069

---

lain

1288

Another little rhyme will help you to remember that the helper form of **lie** is **have lain:**

In **pain**
I **have lain.**

The cow had . . . down on the railroad track.

Write the correct helper form: ______

1289

verb 1508	**The store closes.** **The stores close.** Which verb is singular—**closes** or **close?** __________ 1509
suspiciously 1727	Underline the adjective (without **-ly**) if the verb is used as a linking verb and the word that follows it describes the subject. **Your dress looks** (*beautiful, beautifully*) **on you.** 1728
b 1946	**Cliff likes dogs more than (he likes) her.** The object form **her** is the object of the omitted verb __________. 1947
T R P 2165	a. ***The Covered Wagon*** b. ***the Covered Wagon*** Which title is correctly capitalized? ____ 2166
writers, Giovanni, 2384	Insert any necessary commas: **Yes that was the last time that I saw Tom Chapman.** 2385
"When . . . eat?" 2603	Supply the necessary punctuation, including either a question mark or an exclamation point: **Just look at your paper exclaimed Mrs. Lee.** 2604

his, his

189

The boys **washed** *the boys* **in the lake.**

Avoid repeating *the boys* by substituting a pronoun:

The boys washed ______________ **in the lake.**

190

b

409

Dad has always collected stamps.

The main verb is separated from its helper by the word ______________.

410

adverb

629

a. **Tom ate hurriedly.**
b. **Tom ate in a hurry.**

In sentence *a*, **hurriedly** is an adverb.

In sentence *b*, **in a hurry** is an *adverb* ______________.

630

which

849

Lisa owns a collie *which has won many prizes.*

The adjective clause *which has won many prizes* modifies the noun ______________.

850

F S

1069

Gunpowder was invented by the Chinese. Who used it only for fireworks.

____ ____

1070

lain

1289

I lay down and couldn't get up.

If we added the helper **had** to the verb, what word would we need to put in place of **lay?** ______________

1290

closes 1509	**The store closes.** **The stores close.** Adding an *s* to the noun makes it plural. Adding an *s* to the verb makes it ________. 1510
beautiful 1728	**This perfume smells** (*different, differently*) **from the last.** (*Hint:* Perfume has no nose for smelling.) 1729
likes 1947	We use the word **as,** as well as **than,** in making comparisons. **I have as many friends as she (has).** The subject form **she** is correct because it is the subject of the omitted verb ______. 1948
a 2166	Unless they are the first word in a title, do not capitalize: ARTICLES: **a, an, the** CONJUNCTIONS: **and, but, or** SHORT PREPOSITIONS: **of, in, to, for, with,** etc. Underline the words you would capitalize in the following title: ***the call of the wild.*** 2167
Yes, 2385	**It won't be easy to win old boy with Luis Tiant pitching for the Yankees.** 2386
"Just . . . paper!" 2604	Supply the necessary punctuation, including either a question mark or an exclamation point: **Pam Mitchell inquired Is parking allowed here** 2605

themselves

190

A noun is the name of a person, place, thing, or an idea. A word used in place of a noun is a ______________.

191

always

410

I could hardly read the address.

The main verb is separated from its helper by the word ______________.

411

phrase

630

We drove <u>over a very shaky bridge</u>.

The prepositional phrase **over a very shaky bridge** modifies the verb **drove**—just like an ordinary *adverb.* We therefore call it an ______________ ______________.

631

collie

850

which has won many prizes

The verb of this clause is *has won;* the subject is the pronoun ____________.

851

S F

1070

Ellen put the key in the lock. And tried to turn it.

____ ____

1071

lain

1290

To lay means "to put or to place something."

You can't just put—you have to put *something.* Unless the sentence names this "something," this is not the word you want.

Don't lay the hot pan on the table.

The "something" in this sentence is ________.

1291

singular 1510	People frequently make mistakes in the agreement of subject and verb because they think that a verb that ends in *s* is plural. **My friend lives in Florida.** A present-tense verb that ends in *s* is always (*singular, plural*). 1511
different 1729	**We now smelled smoke very** (*distinct, distinctly*). 1730
has 1948	Underline the correct pronoun: **We made as many hits as** (*they, them*). 1949
the call of the wild 2167	Copy the following title, adding the needed capitals: ***a raisin in the sun*** ______________________________ 2168
win, boy, 2386	**Well this is all the news I have Steve.** (More than one comma is needed.) 2387
inquired, "Is . . . here?" 2605	**Alex bawled angrily I told you to shut off the water** (Use an !) 2606

pronoun

191

A pronoun is usually (*more, less*) definite than a noun.

192

---

hardly

411

Alison will surely visit us this summer.

The verb **will visit** is interrupted by the word ________.

412

---

adverb phrase

631

Think of an adverb phrase as being a stretched-out adverb consisting of two or more words.

a. **I glued the broken pieces together carefully.**
b. **I glued the broken pieces together with great care.**

Is the **adverb phrase** in sentence *a* or *b*? ___

632

---

which

851

Lisa owns a collie *which has won many prizes.*

An adjective clause signal is always a pronoun. This pronoun stands for the word which the clause modifies. In the above sentence, the pronoun *which* stands for the noun ________, as the arrow shows.

852

S F

1071

After Ellen put the key in the lock. She tried to turn it.

___ ___

1072

---

pan

1291

PRESENT	SIMPLE PAST	PAST WITH HELPER
lay (put)	**laid**	**have laid**

This verb is the simpler of our two verbs.

The two past forms of **lay** are (*alike, different*).

1292

singular 1511	This is the **"Rule of S"** that we have been building up: When the subject ends in *s*, the verb does not; when the verb ends in *s*, the ______________ does not. 1512
distinctly 1730	**Chad's scheme sounded rather** (*dishonest, dishonestly*) **to me.** 1731
they 1949	**We made as many hits as <u>they</u> (made).** The subject form **they** is correct because it is the subject of the omitted verb __________. 1950
A Raisin in the Sun 2168	Copy and capitalize this title: ***the prince and the pauper*** ______________________________________ 2169
Well, have, 2387	**The article stated that Dr. Ralph Bunche was awarded the Presidential Medal of Freedom.** 2388
angrily, "I . . . water!" 2606	**Can't you read that sign shouted the police officer.** 2607

less

192

Lesson 7 Unit Review

[Frames 194–215]

surely

412

The words **not** and **never** make a statement negative. They are never a part of the verb.

Alison will not visit us this summer.
Alison will never visit us this summer.

In both sentences, the verb consists of only two words—

________ ________.

413

b

632

An **adjective phrase** is used like a single adjective.

An **adverb phrase** is used like a single ________.

633

collie

852

which has won many prizes

really means:

collie *has won many prizes*

In this clause, the pronoun ________ stands for the noun **collie.**

853

F S

1072

Ellen tried to turn the key. Which she had put in the lock.

___ ___

1073

alike

1292

Mother . . . a cold cloth on my forehead.

This sentence names the "something" that Mother put on my forehead. It was a cloth.

Therefore, our verb should be a form of (*lay, lie*).

1293

subject

1512

Our rule does *not* state that there must always be an *s* on either the subject or the verb.

Women work. **I dive.**
Children play. **We swim.**

In these sentences, do either the subjects or the verbs end in *s*? (*Yes, No*) 1513

---

dishonest

1731

I tasted the hot soup (*cautious, cautiously*).

1732

---

made

1950

a. **We must invite the Kirks as well as <u>they</u>.**
b. **We must invite the Kirks as well as <u>them</u>.**

Which sentence means that we must invite both the Kirks and the other family? ____

1951

The Prince and the Pauper

2169

Capitalize, too, the titles of movies, works of art, musical compositions, etc.

Wings of the Eagle **"Tea for Two"**
"After the Rain" **"March of the Toy Soldiers"**

Write the capital letters you would need to use in writing the movie title ***the shadow of a doubt.*** ____________ 2170

None

2388

Don't forget you lucky gal that I voted for you.

2389

"Can't . . . sign?" (*or*) !"

2607

What a ridiculous idea exclaimed George

2608

A sentence normally consists of two parts.

The *predicate* makes a statement about the ________.

194

will visit

Supply a suitable helping verb:

Someone ______ taken your seat.

413

414

adverb

An adverb phrase—just like an adverb—can tell **when, where, how,** or **how much** about the ________.

633

634

which

The fish *that we caught* **were too small to keep.**

The adjective clause *that we caught* modifies the noun ________.

853

854

S F

Rivers caught the ball. And made the third out.

___ ___

1073

1074

lay

PRESENT	SIMPLE PAST	PAST WITH HELPER
lay (put)	**laid**	**have laid**

Write in the correct verbs:

a. **Mother ________ a cold cloth on my forehead.**

b. **Mother had ________ a cold cloth on my forehead.**

1293

1294

No

1513

In this and the following frames, underline the verb that agrees in number with the subject. Avoid having an *s* on both the subject and the verb.

school (*open, opens*)

1514

cautiously

1732

The customer felt the cloth very (*rough, roughly*).

1733

b

1951

We must invite the Kirks as well as (invite) them.

The pronoun **them** is the (*object, subject*) of the omitted verb **invite.**

1952

T S D

2170

a. **"On The Road To Mandalay"**
b. **"On the Road to Mandalay"**
c. **"On the road to Mandalay"**

Which song title is correctly capitalized? ____

2171

forget, gal,

2389

Ray Charles then played my favorite song "The St. Louis Blues."

2390

"What . . . idea!" exclaimed George.

2608

I called to Mother **Is this sketch pad for me**

2609

subject 194	a. **disappeared into the clouds** b. **the man on third base** c. **escaped from its cage** Which group of words could be the subject of a sentence? ___ 195
has *or* had 414	Supply a suitable helping verb: **Every driver ____________ have a license.** 415
verb 634	**We reached Niagara Falls in the late afternoon.** The adverb phrase tells (*how, when*) about the verb **reached.** 635
fish 854	**The fish** *that we caught* **were too small to keep.** The clause signal *that* is a pronoun. The pronoun *that* stands for the noun ________, the word that the clause modifies. 855
S F 1074	**If there were no such thing as gravity. A person would weigh nothing at all.** ___ ___ 1075
a. laid b. laid 1294	Here are the two verbs to compare: PRESENT / SIMPLE PAST / PAST WITH HELPER **lie** (in bed) / **lay** / **have lain** **lay** (put) / **laid** / **have laid** The simple past form of **lie** is ________. The simple past form of **lay** is ________. 1295

opens 1514	Underline the verb that agrees in number with the subject: **schools** (*open, opens*) 1515
roughly 1733	**Mayor Kearney felt** (*unhappy, unhappily*) **about his defeat.** (This does not mean an action of the hands.) 1734
object 1952	a. **We must invite the Kirks as well as they.** b. **We must invite the Kirks as well as them.** Which sentence means that we, as well as the other family, must invite the Kirks? ____ 1953
b 2171	Now we turn to another kind of title—the titles of **people,** like **Doctor Klein, Captain Craig,** or **Aunt Ruth.** **a doctor** **Doctor Klein** Which words mean a *particular* doctor? ____________ 2172
song, 2390	**Ray Charles then played "The St. Louis Blues."** 2391
Mother, "Is . . . me?" 2609	**Mr. Kerney cried out** **My feet are killing me** (Use an !) 2610

b

195

a. **most of the new cars**
b. **the decision of the referee**
c. **started on time**

Which group of words could be the predicate of a sentence? ____

196

---

must
or should

415

Supply a suitable helping verb:

If I were George, I __________ find a job.

416

---

when

635

Jack opened the screen door with a wire.

The adverb phrase tells (*how, when*) about the verb **opened.**

636

---

fish

855

that we caught

really means:

fish *we caught* (*we caught* **fish**)

In this clause, the pronoun ________ stands for the noun **fish.**

856

F S

1075

Mr. Bosley would get his own breakfast. Or eat at a drugstore near his office.

___ ___

1076

---

lay
laid

1295

PRESENT	SIMPLE PAST	PAST WITH HELPER
lie (in bed)	**lay**	**have lain**
lay (put)	**laid**	**have laid**

The verb whose two past forms are the same—just like any regular verb—is ________.

1296

open 1515	**stores** (*sell, sells*) 1516
unhappy 1734	**Her playing must have sounded** (*frightful, frightfully*). 1735
a 1953	**We must invite the Kirks as well as <u>they</u> (must invite) them.** The pronoun **they** is the (*object, subject*) of the omitted verb **must invite.** 1954
Doctor Klein 2172	**I called a doctor.** **I called Doctor Klein.** We capitalize the noun **doctor** only when it is used (*with, without*) a person's name. 2173
None 2391	**No our neighbors the Sandovals don't have their collie any more.** 2392
out, "My . . . me!" 2610	Lesson **83** **Unit Review** [Frames 2612–2633] *page 392*

c

196

a. **the hungry dog waited at the door**
b. **the only boy on the committee**
c. **walked briskly across the stage**

Which group of words is a sentence because it has both a subject and a predicate? ____

(The capital letter and the period are omitted to avoid revealing the answer.)

197

---

would

416

Supply a suitable helping verb:

Some animals ______ see in the dark.

417

---

how

636

Ross buys most of his clothes at one store.

The adverb phrase tells *(when, where)* about the verb **buys.**

637

---

that

856

When we remove an adjective clause from a sentence, we should have a complete sentence remaining.

a. **The fish** *that we caught* **were too small to keep.**
b. **The fish** **were too small to keep.**

Is sentence *b*, without the clause, a complete sentence? (*Yes, No*)

857

S F

1076

In this frame there are three word groups to be judged.

Although the novel is long. The reader never loses interest. Because the plot is loaded with suspense.

____ ____ ____

1077

---

lay

1296

PRESENT	SIMPLE PAST	PAST WITH HELPER
lie (in bed)	**lay**	**have lain**

Write in the missing words:

Ken ________ on the beach longer than I had ________ there.

1297

sell 1516	**show** (*start, starts*) 1517
frightful 1735	**This snapshot looks more** (*natural, naturally*) **than the other.** 1736
subject 1954	In this and the following frames, underline the correct pronoun. Make sure that you select the correct pronoun by thinking of the omitted word or words in each comparison. **You live closer to the school than** (*they, them*). 1955
with 2173	Capitalize titles that show a person's profession, rank, or position when they are used as part of a person's name. a. **The order was given by major Stokes.** b. **The order was given by Major Stokes.** Which sentence is correctly capitalized? ____ 2174
No, neighbors, Sandovals, 2392	**The courage of one soldier Private William Thompson saved the platoon.** 2393
	Apostrophes are used with nouns to show ownership. Place the apostrophe so that the letters that come before it indicate the owner. a. **one boy's test** b. **one boys' test** Because the test belongs to one **boy,** the apostrophe is correctly placed in (*a, b*). 2612

a

197

The most important word in the predicate is called the ________.

198

can *or* do

417

Fill each blank with a suitable helping verb.

You ________ ________ started earlier to get a good seat.

418

where

637

An adverb phrase does not need to be next to the verb it modifies.

Ross buys most of his clothes at one store.

How many words stand between the adverb phrase and the verb which it modifies? ____

638

Yes

857

Let's look at the adjective clause signals once again:

who (whom, whose) which that

These words are used to start adjective clauses, which modify ________ and pronouns.

858

F S F

1077

Lesson 35 More Types of Sentence Fragments

[Frames 1079–1106]

lay, lain

1297

PRESENT	SIMPLE PAST	PAST WITH HELPER
lay (put)	**laid**	**have laid**

Write in the missing words:

Paul ________ his books where he always had ________ them.

1298

starts

1517

doctors (*agree, agrees*)

1518

natural

1736

When the "sense" verb means action, use the adverb *well* to describe this action.

When the "sense" verb links a word that follows it to the subject, use the adjective *good* to describe the subject.

You can't smell (*good, well*) **when you have a cold.**

1737

they

1955

Mosquitoes always bit Dad more than (*I, me*).

1956

b

2174

a. **Pam saluted captain Marsh.**
b. **Pam saluted the captain.**

In which sentence should **captain** be capitalized? ____

2175

soldier,
Thompson,

2393

It was the courage of Private William Thompson that saved the platoon.

2394

a

2612

a. **several student's tests** b. **several students' tests**

Because the tests belong to several **students,** the apostrophe is correctly placed in (*a, b*).

2613

verb 198	When we change a sentence from present to past time, or from past to present time, the only word that usually changes its form is the ________. 199
should (could, might) have 418	In the following frames, write the *initials* (first letters) only of the words that make up the *complete* verb. EXAMPLE: **I should have followed your advice.** Initials of verb: *s h f* The initials of the verb **may be waiting** are ________. 419
4 638	**With no hesitation, the owner of the store refunded my money.** How many words stand between the adverb phrase and the verb which it modifies? ___ 639
nouns 858	**The couple** *whose baby was crying* **left the theater.** The adjective clause starts with the word ________ and ends with the word ________. 859
	Here, again, are the two tests for a complete sentence: 1. Does it have a subject and a predicate? 2. Does it make sense by itself? Adverb and adjective clauses fail to pass the (*first, second*) of these tests. 1079
laid, laid 1298	**to lie** **to lay** Which of these verbs means "to rest in a flat position" or "to be in place"? ________ 1299

Answer	Frame
agree 1518	**glue** (*stick, sticks*) 1519
well 1737	**A hot drink tastes** (*good, well*) **after ice-skating.** 1738
me 1956	**Are you as old as** (*he, him*)? 1957
a 2175	**Our dentist is doctor Chavez.** In this sentence, capitalize (*dentist, doctor*). 2176
None 2394	**If you want to read a good book about horses Joan read *My Friend Flicka.*** 2395
b 2613	a. **The men's department is having a sale.** b. **The mens' department is having a sale.** Look at the letters that come before the apostrophe. Since the department belongs to **men**—not **mens,** the apostrophe is correctly placed in sentence (*a, b*). 2614

verb

199

PRESENT: **My dad takes many pictures.**

To change this sentence to past time, we would need to change the verb **takes** to ________.

200

---

m b w

419

Sonny did not wipe his feet on the mat.

Initials of verb: ________

(Be careful not to include a word that is not part of the verb.)

420

5

639

An adverb phrase—just like an adverb—can often be moved to another part of the sentence.

We reached Niagara Falls <u>in the late afternoon</u>.

<u>In the late afternoon</u>, we reached Niagara Falls.

The fact that the prepositional phrase can be moved shows that it is an (*adjective, adverb*) phrase. 640

---

whose, crying

859

The couple *whose baby was crying* **left the theater.**
The couple **left the theater.**

When we omit the adjective clause from this sentence, do we have a complete sentence remaining? (*Yes, No*)

860

---

second

1079

Now we will look at other types of sentence fragments.

The young man apologized. Realizing his mistake.

The sentence fragment is the (*first, second*) word group.

1080

---

to lie

1299

Remember these rhymes. They will help to straighten you out when using the two past forms of **lie.**

Yes-ter-**day** In **pain**
In bed I **lay.** I **have lain.**

The two past forms of **lie** are (*alike, different*). 1300

sticks

1519

dogs *(have, has)*

1520

---

good

1738

Feel the paint (*good, well*) **to make sure that it's dry.**

1739

---

he

1957

I bake my bread much longer than (*she, her*).

1958

Doctor

2176

Sam introduced lieutenant Romero to the major.

In this sentence, capitalize *(lieutenant, major).*

2177

---

horses, Joan,

2395

Lesson 77 Commas in Addresses and Dates

[Frames 2397–2421]

---

a

2614

Be sure that the letters coming before the apostrophe spell the owner or owners correctly.

Underline the correct word:

These *(ladys', ladies')* **handkerchiefs are very expensive.**

2615

took

PAST: **The old map showed the location of the treasure.**

To change this sentence to present time, we would need to change the verb from __________ to __________.

200

201

---

d w

The meeting will surely end by ten o'clock.

Initials of verb: __________

420

421

---

adverb

Jack opened the screen door with a wire.
With a wire, Jack opened the screen door.

The prepositional phrase **with a wire** is an (*adverb, adjective*) *phrase.*

640

641

Yes

The couple *whose baby was crying* **left the theater.**

Because the clause *whose baby was crying* modifies the noun **couple,** it is an (*adjective, adverb*) clause.

860

861

---

second

The young man apologized. *Realizing his mistake.*

Realizing his mistake is an **-ing** word group. It is not a complete sentence because it has neither a subject nor a __________.

1080

1081

---

different

In this and the following frames, underline the correct verb in each pair:

Keith must (*lie, lay*) **in bed for several days.**

1300

1301

have

1520

Lesson 49 Keeping Track of the Subject

[Frames 1522–1543]

well

Home certainly looked (*good, well*) **to me after living in a tent.**

1739

1740

she

The referee penalized them more often than (*we, us*).

1958

1959

Lieutenant

Our superintendent appealed to mayor Kirby.

In this sentence, capitalize (*superintendent, mayor*).

2177

2178

The following sentence gives only one part of Bob's address—the street address:

Bob has lived at *464 Oak Street* **for ten years.**

Is this one-part address set off with commas? (*Yes, No*)

2397

ladies'

Place the apostrophe accurately in each italicized word:

My *mothers* **calendar shows all her** *friends* **birthdays.**

2615

2616

showed, shows

201

It is better to find the verb before looking for the subject.

Underline just the verb with two lines:

A tall, husky guard in uniform stood at the entrance to the camp.

202

---

w e

421

The use of safety glass has saved many lives.

Initials of verb: ______

422

---

adverb

641

a. **A herd of cows blocked the road.**
b. **Edith delivers papers after school.**

Can the prepositional phrase be moved to another position in sentence *a* or *b*? ____

642

---

adjective

861

The pupil __________ *name the teacher called* **was absent.**

Underline the pronoun that would serve as an adjective clause signal in this sentence.

who which whose that

862

---

predicate (*or* verb)

1081

The young man apologized. *Realizing his mistake.*

The **-ing** word group *Realizing his mistake* modifies the noun ______ in the main statement.

1082

---

lie

1301

Where did Peggy (*lie, lay*) **her coat?**

1302

Now we shall study a type of sentence that often leads people to choose the wrong verb.

One (*is, are*) **broken.**

Which verb agrees with the singular subject **One?** ______

1522

---

good

1740

I looked at his face (*good, well*) **so that I would recognize him the next time we met.**

1741

---

us

1959

My brother gets home much earlier than (*me, I*).

1960

Mayor

2178

The judge is a friend of superintendent Welch.

In this sentence, capitalize (*judge, superintendent*).

2179

No

2397

Now to make Bob's address more complete, we add a second part—the city.

Bob has lived at 464 Oak Street, *Columbus,* **for ten years.**

Is the second part of the address set off with commas? (*Yes, No*)

2398

---

mother's, friends'

2616

Place the apostrophe accurately in each italicized word:

Two other *fellows* **scores were higher than my** *dads*.

2617

stood

202

A tall, husky guard in uniform stood at the entrance to the camp.

Now that you have found the verb **stood,** ask yourself, "Who **stood?**" The answer to this question tells you the subject, which is ______.

203

---

h s

422

The other car must have been speeding.

Initials of complete verb: ______

423

---

b

642

Edith delivers papers after school.

The prepositional phrase **after school** is an ______ *phrase.*

643

---

whose

862

The pupil whose name the teacher called was absent.

Write the sentence that remains when we omit the adjective clause. ______

863

---

man

1082

a. **The young man apologized,** *realizing his mistake.*
b. **The young man apologized.** *Realizing his mistake.*

An **–ing** word group should be in the same sentence as the word it modifies.

Therefore, (*a*, *b*) is correct.

1083

---

lay

1302

The doctor told me to (*lie, lay*) **down.**

1303

is 1522	a. **One is broken.** b. **One (of the eggs) is broken.** In sentence *a*, we don't know whether **One** means an egg, a window, a chair, or a cup. We therefore add a prepositional phrase **(of the eggs)** to make our meaning clear. The subject in both *a* and *b* is the pronoun ______. 1523
well 1741	**A cold shower feels** (*good, well*) **on a hot day.** 1742
I 1960	**The sudden storm caught us as well as** (*them, they*). 1961
Superintendent 2179	Also capitalize a word that shows family relationship, like **uncle, cousin,** or **grandmother,** when used with a person's name. a. **This gift was from my uncle Juan.** b. **This gift was from my Uncle Juan.** Which sentence is correctly capitalized? ____ 2180
Yes 2398	To make the address still more complete, we now add a third part—the state. **Bob has lived at 464 Oak Street, Columbus,** *Ohio,* **for ten years.** Is the third part of the address set off with commas? (*Yes, No*) 2399
fellows', dad's 2617	When apostrophes are used with nouns to measure time (*a week's work*) or money (*ten cents' worth*), apply the same rule that you follow to show ownership. Place the apostrophe accurately in each italicized word: **In less than an** *hours* **time, my customer selected over two hundred** *dollars* **worth of books.** 2618

guard

203

First, underline the verb with two lines. Then underline the subject with one line:

The owner of this car drove it only on weekends.

204

---

m h b s

423

This could never have happened to anyone else.

Initials of complete verb: ___________

424

---

adverb

643

A blind man with a cane was waiting at the curb.

This sentence contains both an adjective phrase and an adverb phrase.

The **adverb phrase** is the (*first*, *second*) phrase.

644

The pupil was absent.

863

There are many interesting hobbies which are not expensive.

The adjective clause starts with the word ___________ and ends with the word ___________.

864

---

a

1083

Sliding into third base. **Sally twisted her ankle.**

The sentence fragment is the (*first*, *second*) word group.

1084

---

lie

1303

Don't (*lie*, *lay*) **near the open window.**

1304

One 1523	A verb agrees with its subject, not with another noun that may come between the subject and the verb. **One (of the eggs) is broken.** **Eggs** is not the subject of the verb. It is the object of the preposition ____. 1524
good 1742	Lesson **57** **Making Comparisons Correctly** [Frames 1744–1779]
them 1961	**Eleanor doesn't spend as much as** (*me, I*) **on movies.** 1962
b 2180	a. **My aunt owns an airplane.** b. **My aunt Jean owns an airplane.** In which sentence should **aunt** be capitalized? ____ 2181
Yes 2399	**Bob has lived at 464 Oak Street, Columbus, Ohio, for ten years.** After the first part of the address, is there a comma both *before* and *after* each additional part? (*Yes, No*) 2400
hour's, dollars' 2618	Apostrophes have very exact uses. Do not insert an apostrophe before the final *s* on a verb or on an ordinary plural noun that does not show ownership. Place an apostrophe in the *one* word that requires it: **One of our neighbors sometimes prunes and sprays my fathers apple trees.** 2619

owner drove

204

A word used to name a person, place, thing, or an idea is a ________.

205

---

c h h

424

A crowd of people were asking Maya Angelou for her autograph.

Initials of complete verb: ________

425

---

second

644

The smell of fresh bread came from the kitchen.

This sentence contains both an adjective phrase and an adverb phrase.

The **adjective phrase** is the (*first, second*) phrase.

645

---

which, expensive

864

People who live in glass houses should not throw stones.

The adjective clause starts with the word ________ and ends with the word ________.

865

---

first

1084

Sliding into third base, **Sally twisted her ankle.**

Sliding into third base is an **–ing** word group. It modifies the noun (*Sally, ankle*) in the second word group.

1085

---

lie

1304

(*Lie, Lay*) **your packages on the back seat.**

1305

of 1524	**One (of the eggs) is broken.** The subject of this sentence is not the plural noun **eggs** but the singular pronoun ______. 1525
	John is tall. Here we are talking about only one boy. If we were to compare the tallness of John with the tallness of another boy, how would we need to change the word **tall?** **John is ____________ than Fred.** 1744
I 1962	**We have lived in Nashville as long as** (*they, them*). 1963
b 2181	**My aunt lives with grandma Olson.** In this sentence, capitalize (*aunt, grandma*). 2182
Yes 2400	After writing the first part of an address, put a comma both *before* and *after* each additional part. Of course, if an added part ends the sentence, a period—not a comma—is used. Punctuate the following sentence: **The package was sent to 94 Park Avenue Portland Oregon.** 2401
father's 2619	SINGULAR: **Mr. Jones** **Mrs. Sims** **Miss Barnes** PLURAL: **the Joneses** **the Simses** **the Barneses** In forming the possessive of names ending in *s*, be sure that the letters before the apostrophe spell the name of the owner or owners correctly. (*Jame's, James's*) **aunt fixed the** (*Joneses', Jone's*) **car.** 2620

noun

205

A good test for a noun is to see if it can be used as the subject of a sentence.

If a word cannot be used as a subject, it (*is, is not*) a noun.

206

w a

425

Someone must have carelessly dropped this pen.

Initials of complete verb: ___________

426

first

645

During the summer, I read a book about the Cheyenne.

The **adverb** phrase is the (*first, second*) phrase.

646

who, houses

865

In a previous lesson, we saw that an **adverb clause** can often be moved from one position to another in a sentence.

A squirrel *that is friendly* **comes to our door.**

Can the adjective clause *that is friendly* be moved to another position in this sentence? (*Yes, No*)

866

Sally

1085

a. *Sliding into third base.* **Sally twisted her ankle.**
b. *Sliding into third base,* **Sally twisted her ankle.**

An **–ing** word group should be in the same sentence as the word it modifies.

Therefore, (*a, b*) is correct.

1086

Lay

1305

lay **laid**

Which one of these past forms means that someone or something "rested in a flat position" or "was in place"?

____

1306

One

1525

One of the tires . . . flat.

We are not making a statement about all four tires but about only one of them.

Is the subject of this sentence the singular pronoun **One** or the plural noun **tires?** ________

1526

---

taller

1744

John is taller than Fred.

To show that John has more tallness than Fred, we add the letters ________ to the word **tall.**

1745

---

they

1963

Although they both did the same work, Mrs. Todd paid Linda more than (*she, her*).

(Think of the omitted words before making your choice.)

1964

Grandma

2182

My aunt Gloria inherited the farm from her grandmother.

In this sentence, capitalize (*aunt, grandmother*).

2183

Avenue,
Portland,

2401

If an address is put right after a name with no preposition like **at, in, on,** or **of** to tie it in with the name, even a one-part address is set off with commas.

a. **Mr. Wanatee** *of* **461 Avery Road is the owner.**
b. **Mr. Wanatee 461 Avery Road is the owner.**

The street address requires commas in sentence ____.

2402

James's,
Joneses'

2620

Unlike nouns, possessive pronouns show ownership without the addition of apostrophes.

POSSESSIVE PRONOUNS: **his, hers, yours**
its (belonging to **it**), **ours, theirs**

Add the *one* necessary apostrophe:

Neither yours nor hers will open Carols locker.

2621

is not

206

His ________________ surprised me.

Underline the word that is a noun and could therefore be used as the subject of the above sentence:

generous **generosity** **generously**

207

m h d

426

never **shall** **will** **soon**

The two helping verbs in the above group are __________ and __________.

427

first

646

Lesson 22 Unit Review

[Frames 648–669]

No

866

An adjective clause, generally, is fixed in position.

a. **Gwen arrived** *as I was leaving.*
b. **We took the road** *which was shorter.*

In which sentence can the clause be moved to another position? ___

867

b

1086

Don't mistake an *-ing* word group for a predicate.

My friend, *wanting to please me . . .*

Wanting to please me is not a predicate. It merely describes the subject ______________, as any ordinary adjective might do.

1087

lay

1306

He (*lay, laid*) **awake and counted sheep most of the night.**

1307

One

1526

One of the tires (*was, were*) **flat.**

The subject **One** is singular.

Therefore, we choose the singular verb ________.

1527

–er

1745

John is tall.
John is taller than Fred.

When we speak about the tallness of one boy, we use the word **tall.**

When we compare the tallness of two boys, we use the word ________.

1746

---

her

1964

The other team made twice as many touchdowns as (*us, we*).

1965

Aunt

2183

My grandfather Shaw put my cousin through college.

In this sentence, capitalize (*grandfather, cousin*).

2184

---

b

2402

a. **The Speedy Cleaners, 666 Belmont Avenue, give 4-hour service.**
b. **The Speedy Cleaners, at 666 Belmont Avenue, give 4-hour service.**

From which sentence should the commas be omitted? ____

2403

Carol's

2621

In writing contractions, always put the apostrophe in place of the missing letter or letters.

a. **doesn't, couldn't, hasn't, wasn't**
b. **does'nt, could'nt, has'nt, was'nt**

Which group of words is correct—*a* or *b*? ____

2622

generosity

207

Underline the one word which is a noun:

eager **eagerly** **eagerness**

208

---

shall, will

427

should **surely** **make** **would**

The two helping verbs in the above group are __________ and __________.

428

Adjectives can modify two classes of words: __________ and __________.

648

---

a

867

a. **Gwen arrived** *as I was leaving.*
b. **We took the road** *which was shorter.*

In sentence *a,* the clause modifies the verb **arrived.**

In sentence *b,* the clause modifies the __________ **road.**

868

---

friend

1087

My friend, *wanting to please me . . .*

Which one of the following word groups could make a sentence of the above fragment by providing a predicate? _____

a. **on my birthday**
b. **and my sister**
c. **bought me a book.**

1088

---

lay

1307

I can't remember where I (*lay, laid*) **the car keys.**

1308

was 1527	**One of the tires** (*was, were*) **flat.** In sentences like this, don't let a noun that follows the subject run off with the verb. The plural noun **tires** is not the subject of the sentence. It is the object of the preposition ______. 1528
taller 1746	When we compare the tallness of three (or more) boys, how would we need to change the word **tall?** **John is tall.** (one) **John is taller than Fred.** (two) **John is the** ______________ **boy in the class.** (three or more) 1747
we 1965	**Although I was just as guilty, the teacher scolded Fred more often than** (*me, I*). 1966
Grandfather 2184	When **Mother, Father, Dad,** etc., are used as names, you may capitalize them or not, as you please. **Hello, Mother (mother). How is Father (father)?** In the following sentence, which word is used as a name—**Dad** or **mother?** ____________ **Dad, I'd like you to meet Jim's mother.** 2185
b 2403	**Janice Suzuki** *of* **2211 Pinecrest Road is in charge of ticket sales.** If you omitted the preposition *of* from this sentence, should commas be added? (*Yes, No*) 2404
a 2622	Do not confuse contractions with possessive pronouns that sound exactly like them. CONTRACTIONS: **you're they're it's who's** POSSESSIVE PRONOUNS: **your their its whose** (*You're, Your*) **always thinking about** (*you're, your*) **mistakes.** 2623

eagerness

208

Some words can be used as either nouns or verbs.

a. **The Chens** *travel* **every summer.**
b. *Travel* **provides interesting experiences.**

In which sentence is the italicized word used as a noun?

___

209

---

should, would

428

always may not can

The two helping verbs in the above group are ____________ and ____________.

429

---

nouns, pronouns

648

The most common position of adjectives is right before the nouns they modify.

Underline *three* adjectives:

Several students received perfect scores on this test.

649

---

noun

868

a. **Gwen arrived** *as I was leaving.*
b. **We took the road** *which was shorter.*

Which sentence contains an adjective clause? ___

869

---

c

1088

A subject followed by only an *–ing word group* is not a sentence. An *–ing word group* has no power to make a statement about a subject.

a. **My friend,** *wanting to please me.*
b. **My friend,** wanting to please me, **bought me a book.**

The complete sentence is ___.

1089

---

laid

1308

A hundred miles of bad roads still (*lay, laid*) **ahead of us.**

1309

of

1528

The tricky phrases that make people choose the wrong verb often begin with the following prepositions:

of (of the car) (of the books) (of the voters)
on (on the floor) (on his clothes) (on the field)

The spots (on the floor) were ink.

Is the subject of this sentence **spots** or **floor?** ________

1529

---

tallest

1747

John is the tallest boy in the class.

To show that John has the most tallness of all the boys in the class, we add the letters ________ to the word **tall.**

1748

---

me

1966

I am taking just as many subjects as (*her, she*).

1967

Dad

2185

When **mother, father, dad,** etc., are used merely to show family relationship, do not capitalize them.

My mother knew his dad at college.

In the following sentence, which word is used to show family relationship—**mother** or **dad?** ________

Dad, I'd like you to meet Jim's mother.

2186

Yes

2404

Joe Rivera, Union City, is the newly elected chairman.

If you inserted the preposition **of** after the name **Joe Rivera,** would you keep the commas? (*Yes, No*)

2405

You're, your

2623

a. *Their* **trying to sell** *they're* **farm.**
b. *They're* **trying to sell** *their* **farm.**

In which sentence are the italicized words correct? ____

2624

b

209

a. **The new** *shop* **opened yesterday.**
b. **Many people** *shop* **in the new store.**

In which sentence is the italicized word used as a noun—*a* or *b*? ____

210

may, can

429

Lesson 15 Unit Review

[Frames 431–455]

Several, perfect, this

649

When an adjective is used as a subject complement, it comes (*before, after*) the noun or pronoun it modifies.

650

b

869

One sentence contains an adverb clause, and one sentence contains an adjective clause:

a. **People** *who are selfish* **make poor friends.**
b. **Hilda had many friends** *because she was generous.*

Which sentence contains an adjective clause? ____

870

b

1089

We talked about photography. My favorite hobby.

Which word group does not have both a subject and a predicate—the *first* or *second*? __________

1090

lay

1309

The strikers (*lay, laid*) **down their tools and went home.**

1310

spots

1529

Other tricky phrases begin with these prepositions:

in (in the box) (in the cities) (in the room)
for (for his success) (for his absences)
with (with the case) (with the records)

The reason (for his absences) was illness.

The subject of this sentence is ________. 1530

–est

1748

Most adjectives and adverbs have three degrees (or steps) of power.

The *first degree* merely states the quality—**new, quiet, fast.**

strong stronger strongest

Underline the adjective in the first degree. 1749

---

she

1967

Jimmy is jealous because he thinks that his parents like the new baby better than (*him, he*). 1968

---

mother

2186

Mother, father, dad, etc., show family relationship and should not be capitalized whenever they are used after **a, the,** or any possessive word **(my, his, their, Kim's).**

a. **Are you ready, Mother?**
b. **Their mother was not at home.**

Does **mother** show relationship in sentence *a* or *b*? ___ 2187

No

2405

The name of a state following the name of a city is usually set off with commas.

Supply the necessary commas:

The Tournament of Roses is held in Pasadena California every New Year's Day. 2406

---

b

2624

The word **who's** is a contraction that means *who is.* The word **whose** is a possessive pronoun that means *belonging to whom.*

a. *Who's* **the batter** *whose* **home run won the game?**
b. *Whose* **the batter** *who's* **home run won the game?**

In which sentence are the italicized words correct? ___ 2625

a

A word that can take the place of a noun is called a ______________.

210

211

---

a. **The outfielder has dropped the ball.**
b. **The price of eggs has dropped again.**

In one sentence, the action verb makes a complete statement about its subject. It needs no word to show *what* received the action. This sentence is (a, b). ____

431

---

after

a. **This store is** *generous* **to its employees.**
b. **This store gives** *generous* **treatment to its employees.**

In which sentence does the italicized adjective come after the noun it modifies? ____

650

651

---

a

a. **The telephone rang while I was taking a bath.**
b. **The car which Jerry bought needs new tires.**

Which sentence contains an adjective clause? ____

870

871

---

second

We talked about photography. My favorite hobby.

Which word group does not make sense by itself—the *first* or *second*? ______________

1090

1091

---

laid

has lain **has laid**

Which of these helper forms is a form of the verb **lie,** which means "to rest in a flat position" or "to be in place"?

____

1310

1311

reason

1530

Remember the **"Rule of S"**:

When we add an *s* to the subject, we do not add an *s* to the verb.

When we add an *s* to the verb, we do not add an *s* to the ________________.

1531

---

strong

1749

The *second degree* shows that one thing has *more* of this quality than another thing—**newer, quieter, faster.**

cold colder coldest

Underline the adjective in the second degree.

1750

---

him

1968

Lesson 64 Pronouns That Show Ownership

[Frames 1970–1992]

---

b

2187

a. **Why don't you ask your father?**
b. **Why don't you ask Father?**

Is **father** used to show family relationship, and not as a name, in sentence *a* or *b*? ____

2188

Pasadena, California,

2406

We drove from Atlanta to Detroit in only one day.

If we inserted **Georgia** after **Atlanta,** and **Michigan** after **Detroit,** how many commas would we need to add? ____

2407

---

a

2625

Be especially careful to use the contraction **it's** only when you can substitute the two words **it is.** To show ownership, use the possessive pronoun **its** without an apostrophe.

a. *It's* **owner is sure that** *its* **genuine.**
b. *Its* **owner is sure that** *it's* **genuine.**

In which sentence are the italicized words correct? ____

2626

pronoun

211

a. **The *lock* broke.**
b. ***It* broke.**
c. ***One* broke.**
d. **The *window* broke.**

In which two sentences is the italicized word used as a pronoun? ____ and ____

212

---

b

431

An action verb often needs to be completed with another word. This word shows *who* or *what* receives its action or shows the result of this action.

Such a word is called a ________ ________.

432

---

a

651

Some words can be used as either adjectives or nouns.

a. **The *road* was very winding.**
b. **The *road* map showed a detour.**

In which sentence is the italicized word used as an adjective? ____

652

---

b

871

a. **because, when, if, unless, although, after**
b. **who (whom, whose), which, that**

Which words can be used as adjective clause signals—those in group *a* or *b*? ____

872

Second

1091

We talked about photography. My favorite *hobby*.

The noun *hobby* in the second word group means the same thing as the noun ____________ in the first word group.

1092

---

has lain

1311

Gail caught cold because she had (*lain, laid*) in a draft.

1312

subject

1531

The cost of the repairs (*seem, seems*) **too high.**

Since **cost,** the subject of the sentence, does not end in *s*, which verb would you choose? __________

1532

---

colder

1750

The *third degree* shows that one thing has this quality to the *highest* degree—**newest, quietest, fastest.**

Write the third degree of the adjective **cheap.** __________

1751

Apostrophes are needed to make nouns show ownership or possession.

My <u>sister's</u> coat is dark.

The noun that shows the ownership of the coat is __________.

1970

---

a

2188

a. **A mother has many responsibilities.**
b. **I invited mother to our meeting.**

In which sentence would it be wrong to capitalize **mother** because it is used to show family relationship? ____

2189

4

2407

We punctuate **dates** in the same way as addresses. If only one part of a date is given, no commas are used.

It was decided that *October 4* **would be the date of the Lloyd and Austin match.**

Is a one-part date set off with commas? (*Yes, No*)

2408

---

b

2626

Use quotation marks only when you report what a person said directly in his own words.

a. **Bob said I'll be home by ten.**
b. **Bob said that he would be home by ten.**

Which sentence requires quotation marks? ____

2627

b, c

The *wind* **damaged** *some* **of the** *trees.*

Which one of the italicized words is a pronoun? ________

212 213

---

direct object

a. **They started after a short** *delay.*

b. **They started the** *game* **on time.**

In which sentence is the italicized word a direct object? ___

432 433

---

b

Although adverbs can modify three classes of words, they usually modify ________.

652 653

---

b

who (whom, whose) which that

Because these adjective clause signals stand for a noun in the main statement of the sentence, they are (*adverbs, pronouns*).

872 873

---

photography

We talked about photography. *My favorite hobby.*

Because the noun *hobby* comes after the noun **photography** and explains it, it is (*a clause, an appositive*).

1092 1093

---

lain

Where could I have (*lain, laid*) **my keys?**

1312 1313

seems 1532	**The windows in the kitchen** (*need, needs*) **washing.** Since **windows,** the subject of this sentence, ends in *s*, which verb would you choose? ________ 1533
cheapest 1751	FIRST DEGREE: **high**, **happy** — SECOND DEGREE: **higher**, **happier** — THIRD DEGREE: **highest**, **happiest** With short words of one and sometimes two syllables, the second degree is formed by adding **–er;** the third degree is formed by adding ________. 1752
sister's 1970	a. **My <u>sister's</u> coat is dark.** b. **<u>Yours</u> is light.** In sentence *a*, the word that shows ownership is the noun **sister's.** In sentence *b*, the word that shows ownership is the pronoun ________. 1971
a 2189	**I should have phoned Mother or Dad.** Since **Mother** and **Dad** are used as names in the above sentence, you may capitalize them or not, as you wish. If you inserted the pronoun **my** before **Mother** and **Dad,** would you still capitalize these words? (*Yes, No*) 2190
No 2408	If the date consists of more than one part, put a comma both *before* and *after* each additional part. **October 4,** *1966,* **was the date of the Lloyd and Austin match.** Punctuate the following sentence: **On April 10 1947 Jackie Robinson joined the Dodgers.** 2409
a 2627	a. **Dad said to Henry "Don't read while you eat."** b. **Dad said to Henry, "Don't read while you eat."** Which sentence is correct? ____ 2628

some

213

They **bought a new** *house* **on our** *street.*

Which one of the italicized words is a pronoun? ________

214

---

b

433

A word that shows by its position alone *to whom* or *for whom,* or *to what* or *for what,* something is done is called a(n) ________________ *object.*

434

---

verbs

653

We form many adverbs by adding the suffix (*-ly, -ous*) to adjectives.

654

---

pronouns

873

If a clause can be moved from one position to another, it is likely to be an (*adverb, adjective*) clause.

874

---

appositive

1093

a. **We talked about photography.** *My favorite hobby.*
b. **We talked about photography,** *my favorite hobby.*

Which is correct because the appositive is in the same sentence with the noun it explains? ____

1094

---

laid

1313

Gordy must have (*lain, laid*) **the paint on too thick.**

1314

need

1533

In this and the following frames, underline the verb that agrees with its subject. Don't be fooled by an object of a preposition that might come between the subject and the verb.

The weight of the big trucks (*injure, injures*) **the pavement.**

1534

–est

1752

Let's see what happens when we make comparisons with longer words:

María is more intelligent than Pat.

To avoid such a clumsy word as **intelligenter,** we do not add **–er.** Instead, we form the second degree of longer words by using the adverb ______________. 1753

Yours

1971

My sister's coat is dark.
Yours is light.

The word that shows ownership without the use of an apostrophe is the (*noun, pronoun*).

1972

No

2190

I enjoy talking to ^ Mom.

If you inserted **Val's** at the point indicated, would you capitalize the word **Mom?** (*Yes, No*)

2191

April 10, 1947,

2409

A period used after an abbreviation in an address or a date does not take the place of a required comma. Use commas just as you would with the complete words.

Punctuate the following sentence:

We moved to 1700 Lakeshore Ave. Oakland CA on Sept 5 1965.

2410

---

b

2628

a. **"Where did you get your facts?," asked Mr. Reagan.**
b. **"Where did you get your facts?" asked Mr. Reagan.**

Which sentence is correct? ____

2629

They

214

The *soldier* **camouflaged** *himself* **with** *branches.*

Which one of the italicized words is a pronoun? ________

215

---

indirect

434

Mrs. Rey bought a dress *for* **Marta.**

If you changed the phrase *for Marta* to an indirect object, you would insert the indirect object right after the word ________.

435

–ly

654

When? Where? How? How much? How often?

Words that answer these questions about the actions of verbs are called ________.

655

---

adverb

874

Only *one* of the following statements is correct:

a. An adjective clause is one that does the work of a single adjective.
b. An adjective clause is one that begins with an adjective.

Which definition of an adjective clause is correct? ____

875

---

b

1094

In this and the following frames, write an **S** for each word group that is a **sentence,** and an **F** for each word group that is a **fragment.** Write your answers in the same order as the two word groups.

Grabbing the ball. Jabbar ran down the court.

____ ____

1095

---

laid

1314

You shouldn't have (*lain, laid*) **down in your best suit.**

1315

injures

1534

One of the car's headlights (*is, are*) **out.**

1535

---

more

1753

María is the most intelligent girl in the class.

To avoid such a clumsy word as **intelligentest,** we form the third degree of longer words not by adding **–est,** but by using the adverb ________.

1754

---

pronoun

1972

Although nouns need apostrophes to show ownership, pronouns show ownership *without apostrophes.* The ownership idea is built right into the pronouns themselves.

My sister's coat is darker than yours.

Do both of the underlined words in this sentence show ownership? (*Yes, No*)

1973

No

2191

a. **Tommy was raised by his Grandma.**
b. **Tommy was raised by his Grandma Schultz.**

Which sentence is correctly capitalized—*a* or *b*? ____

2192

Ave., Oakland,
CA, Sept. 5,

2410

In this and the following frames, supply the necessary commas. Several sentences do not require commas.

The Dionne quintuplets were born on May 28 1934 in Callender Ontario.

2411

---

b

2629

a. **Mr. Dobbs said that we had only five minutes left.**
b. **Mr. Dobbs said, "That we had only five minutes left."**

Which sentence is correct? ____

2630

himself

215

UNIT 2: **PATTERNS OF THE SIMPLE SENTENCE**

Lesson 8 The Subject–Verb and Direct Object Patterns

[Frames 217–248]

bought

435

Only one of the following statements is true:

a. An *action verb* must always be completed by a direct object.
b. A *linking verb* must always be completed by a subject complement.

The true statement is (*a*, *b*). ____

436

adverbs

655

Underline *two* adverbs:

My polite friend graciously stepped aside for the lady.

656

a

875

Lesson 29 How to Make Adjective Clauses

[Frames 877–911]

F S

1095

I saw the Illinois game. The biggest game of the season.

____ ____

1096

lain

1315

Lay and **have lain** are past forms of the verb (*lie*, *lay*).

1316

is

The reasons for his dismissal (*has, have*) **not been stated.**

1535 1536

most

a. **Our backyard is more beautiful than our front yard.**
b. **Our backyard is beautifuller than our front yard.**

In which sentence is the comparison made correctly—*a* or *b*? ____

1754 1755

Yes

My sister's coat is darker than yours.

Which underlined word shows ownership without the use of an apostrophe—the *noun* or the *pronoun*? __________

1973 1974

b

In this and the following frames, cross out each capital letter that is not correct:

Many famous actors had small parts in the movie *Around The World In Eighty Days.*

2192 2193

May 28, 1934,
Callender,

Insert any necessary commas:

We drove from El Paso Texas to Phoenix Arizona in a single day.

2411 2412

a

a. **"How did the movie end?" asked Rita.**
b. **"How did the movie end," asked Rita?**

Which sentence is correct? ____

2630 2631

Many action verbs are able to make *complete statements* about their subjects without the help of other words.

EXAMPLES: **Birds fly.** **The motor stalled.**
Ice melts. **The game began.**

The verbs in these sentences make (*complete, incomplete*) statements about their subjects. 217

---

b

436

The most common linking verbs are the various forms of the verb (*have, be, do*). ________

437

---

graciously, aside

656

Underline *two* adverbs:

Some fans usually come early to get good seats.

657

Adjective clauses are useful for combining sentences.

We had a large *map. It* **showed all the small towns.**

First, find a word in the second sentence (*It*) that means the same as a word in the first sentence (________).

877

S F

1096

I saw the Illinois game. It was the biggest game of the season.

1097

---

lie

1316

Laid and **have laid** are past forms of the verb (*lie, lay*).

1317

have

1536

The footprints in the snow (*was, were*) the only clue.

1537

---

a

1755

a. **This is the wonderfullest trick I have ever seen.**
b. **This is the most wonderful trick I have ever seen.**

In which sentence is the comparison made correctly? ____

1756

---

pronoun

1974

<u>His</u> is next to <u>hers</u>.

The two pronouns in this sentence that show ownership are **His** and ________.

1975

~~T~~he, ~~I~~n

2193

Cross out each capital letter that is not correct:

Our High School band is rehearsing Scott Joplin's "Maple Leaf Rag" for our Spring concert.

2194

El Paso, Texas,
Phoenix,
Arizona,

2412

Insert any necessary commas:

Your complaint should be sent to the Longwear Tire Company in Akron.

2413

---

a

2631

a. **"That's what friends are for", smiled Paul.**
b. **"That's what friends are for," smiled Paul.**

Which sentence is correct? ____

2632

complete

217

PATTERN 1: *Subject—Action Verb*
A sentence built around a subject and an action verb is our first and simplest sentence pattern.

The exciting game with Knox began on time at two o'clock.

This entire sentence of 11 words is built around a two-part framework—the subject __________ and the action verb __________.

218

---

be

437

a. **is, am, are**
b. **does, can, make**
c. **has, may, will**
d. **was, were, been**

The various forms of the verb **be** are found in lines ____ and ____.

438

---

usually, early

657

Besides modifying verbs, adverbs can also modify other modifiers: ______________ and other ______________.

658

---

map

877

We had a large *map.* ~~*It*~~ *which* **showed all the small towns.**

Next, put the adjective clause signal *which* in place of the word *It*, thus changing the second sentence into an __________________ *clause.*

878

S S

1097

Homer was in the basement. Trying to iron his shirt.

____ ____

1098

---

lay

1317

Lesson 42 Learning the Difference Between *Sit* and *Set*

[Frames 1319–1347]

page 435

were

1537

One of the wheels (*squeak, squeaks*).

1538

---

b

1756

FIRST DEGREE	SECOND DEGREE	THIRD DEGREE
expensive	**more expensive**	**most expensive**
skillfully	**more skillfully**	**most skillfully**

The second degree of **successful** would be ______ **successful.**

1757

---

hers

1975

His is next to hers.

Pronouns show ownership without apostrophes. To write **hers** with an apostrophe **(her's)** is just as incorrect as to write **his** with an apostrophe **(hi's).**

Should either **his** or **hers** be written with an apostrophe? (*Yes, No*)

1976

~~H~~igh ~~S~~chool, ~~S~~pring

2194

Cross out each capital letter that is not correct:

For my Birthday, my Aunt gave me a copy of *Lightning On Ice*.

2195

None

2413

F. W. Woolworth opened his first five-and-ten store in Utica NY on Feb. 22 1879.

2414

---

b

2632

a. **"What a perfect day for a picnic," exclaimed Alison!**
b. **"What a perfect day for a picnic!" exclaimed Alison.**

Which sentence is correct? ____

2633

game (subject)
began (verb)

218

Some action verbs, however, are *not* able to make complete statements about their subjects.

a. **The rain stopped.**

b. **The dog needs . . .**

Does the verb in sentence *a* or *b* fail to make a complete statement about its subject? ___ 219

---

a, d

438

We can often substitute another verb for a form of the linking verb **be.** This word would also be used as a linking verb.

The trip *was* **tiresome.**

Underline *two* of the following verbs that could be used as linking verbs in the above sentence.

became **drove** **seemed** **planned** 439

---

adjectives,
adverbs

658

Special adverbs such as **very, quite, rather, extremely,** and **too** can modify either adjectives or adverbs. (*True, False*)

659

---

adjective

878

a. **It showed all the small towns.**

b. *which showed all the small towns*

We have now changed *a,* which is a sentence, to *b,* which is a ________.

879

S F

1098

Homer was in the basement. He was trying to iron his shirt.

___ ___

1099

To sit means "to take a sitting position" or "to be in place."

Dick sits next to Julia.
The clock sits on his desk.

The children like to ______ in the front row.

1319

squeaks 1538	**The effects of sunburn** (*is, are*) **often quite serious.** 1539
more 1757	FIRST DEGREE / SECOND DEGREE / THIRD DEGREE **expensive** / **more expensive** / **most expensive** The third degree of **courteous** would be ________ **courteous.** 1758
No 1976	**Hers writes better than Karens.** Both the underlined words in this sentence show ownership. Which of these words requires an apostrophe? ________ 1977
~~B~~irthday, ~~A~~unt, ~~O~~n 2195	Cross out each capital letter that is not correct: **My Uncle Steve was promoted from Captain to Major.** 2196
Utica, NY, Feb. 22, 2414	**The Pickwick Restaurant at 851 Concord Avenue was sold to Joy Evans in March 1959.** (Only one comma is needed.) 2415
b 2633	

b

219

After an incomplete action verb, we keep wondering "What?" or "Whom?" until another word is added.

The dog needs . . . (What?)

The dog needs a bath.

The word that completes the meaning of the verb **needs** is ________.

CONTINUED WITH FRAME 221 ON PAGE 1 220

---

became, seemed

439

The coat *is* too tight.

Underline *two* of the following verbs that could be used as linking verbs in the above sentence.

sells feels looks makes

CONTINUED WITH FRAME 441 ON PAGE 1 440

True

659

a. **The train made *very* frequent stops.**
b. **The train stopped *very* frequently.**

In which sentence does the italicized adverb modify another adverb? ____

CONTINUED WITH FRAME 661 ON PAGE 1 660

---

clause

879

We had a large map *which showed all the small towns.*

The clause *which showed all the small towns* is an adjective clause because it modifies the noun ________.

CONTINUED WITH FRAME 881 ON PAGE 1 880

S S

1099

The camp is on Lake Superior. The largest of the Great Lakes.

____ ____

CONTINUED WITH FRAME 1101 ON PAGE 1 1100

---

sit

1319

A person **sits** on a chair, a kettle **sits** on the stove, and a radio ________ on the table.

CONTINUED WITH FRAME 1321 ON PAGE 2 1320

WRITING APPLICATIONS

Contents

The Writing Process

In the first part of this textbook, you followed a step-by-step program, or process, to study grammar and usage. You were first given a bit of information in a frame; then you tried to apply it. If you did not get the correct answer the first time, you were given another opportunity to get the correct answer in another frame. You completed entire sections of this book using this process. When you write, you can also use a process that will give you additional opportunities to improve your writing. This process is called the **writing process.**[1] In this section of your textbook, you will be introduced to the six basic stages of the writing process. Once you have mastered these basic stages, you should be able to apply them in any writing task.

WHY STUDY THE WRITING PROCESS?

Knowing how to use this process will enable you to compose more quickly and accurately. Since an important part of the writing process is evaluating and revising, you always have several opportunities to analyze and improve your writing before you prepare the final version.

Following this introduction (pages 443-448), you will find writing applications that correspond to each of the units in the first part of this book. The applications are designed to give you practice in applying the principles of grammar and usage that you studied in the first part of this textbook. They will also enable you to practice the writing process and to improve your writing skills. In addition, you may find that they help you organize your thoughts and give you practice in analyzing information.

HOW TO USE THIS SECTION OF THE BOOK

After you read this section, refer to it to help you complete the writing applications. Use the basic models presented here whenever you need help composing. In this section, you will learn about and practice the six stages of the writing process. These six stages are (1) prewriting, (2) writing the first draft, (3) evaluating, (4) revising, (5) proofreading, and (6) writing the final version.

Prewriting

The prewriting stage enables you to formulate ideas before you write. During this thinking and planning stage, you determine most of the information you need to write your first draft. During this stage, you determine your purpose and audience; choose and limit your topic; establish your tone; and gather, classify, and arrange information.

[1] Adapted from pp. 3–35 in *English Composition and Grammar,* Benchmark Edition, Fourth Course, by John E. Warriner. Copyright © 1988 by Harcourt Brace Jovanovich, Inc. Reprinted by permission of Harcourt Brace Jovanovich, Inc.

SELECTING A PURPOSE

Before you begin writing, you should have in mind a clear purpose. Your purpose will guide your writing and help determine the content and language you use. There are four basic purposes for writing: to tell a story, to inform or explain, to describe, or to persuade. Writing to tell a story is called **narrative** writing. Writing to inform or explain is called **expository** writing. Writing to describe is called **descriptive** writing. Finally, writing that attempts to persuade or convince is called **persuasive** writing.

DETERMINING YOUR AUDIENCE

You will always write for an audience, but audiences may vary widely in age, background, and opinion. Like purpose, your audience will help guide your writing since you do not write the same way for all people. Determine carefully who your reading audience will be. Then decide whether they will need background information and whether your subject will interest them. Also, decide how simple or difficult the language you use should be.

CHOOSING AND LIMITING A SUBJECT

Before you write, choose a subject that is interesting to you and your audience and draws on your experiences. Then limit your subject so that you can write about it adequately in the time and space you have. To limit your subject, consider your purpose and the form of writing you have chosen. A broad, general subject that has been limited is called a **topic.**

ESTABLISHING TONE

Determining your feelings toward your topic will help you establish your tone. Decide what attitude you want to convey and how it will influence your writing. You create tone in your writing through the details you choose to include.

GATHERING INFORMATION

Gather information to include in your writing that is appropriate to your purpose. For example, if your purpose is to describe someone famous, you may want to gather facts about that person's life, appearance, and mannerisms. You can use several methods in gathering information. A few that are described here include brainstorming, clustering, asking the *5 W-How?* questions, and asking point-of-view questions.

Brainstorming. In brainstorming, you gather information by writing down ideas that come freely to mind. First, write your topic at the top of a sheet of paper. Then, think about your topic, listing any ideas that you associate with your topic. Do not worry if some of the ideas seem silly or incomplete. You will be able to eliminate or expand these ideas later.

EXAMPLE *Topic:* Family picnic last summer

Ideas: Uncle Tim played banjo.
Uncle Tim, Aunt Mary, and cousin Lee made Irish stew—delicious!
Ants crawled on blankets and on some of our sandwiches.
held at Patterson Park
played volleyball
rained towards evening
hot day in August—everyone sweating
so hot that we drank all our fruit punch right away
families reunited: Uncle Tim, Aunt Mary, and Lee came all the way from County Cork, Ireland.

Clustering. Clustering is like brainstorming in that you write down ideas as they come to mind. In clustering, however, you arrange the ideas in groups, or clusters. To begin clustering ideas, write your topic in the center of your paper and circle it. Then begin thinking about ideas that relate to the topic. Write down and circle these ideas also. Draw lines to connect ideas to the topic.

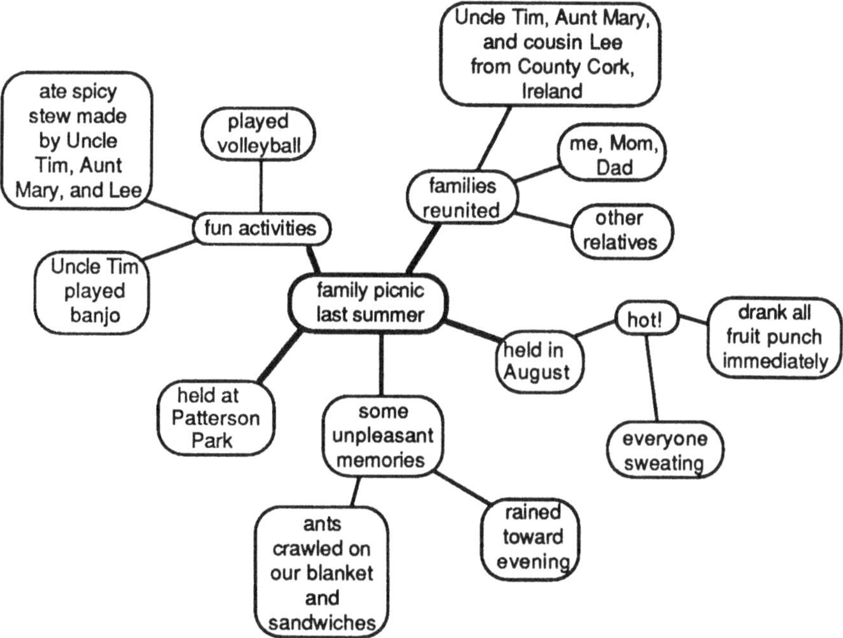

Asking the 5 *W-How?* Questions. Another technique for gathering information is asking the *5 W-How?* questions. The *5 W-How?* questions are *Who? What? When? Where? Why?* and *How?* Ask yourself these questions to find out specific details about your topic. You may not be able to use every question with every topic, but you will always be able to use at least several of the questions.

EXAMPLE *Topic: Family picnic last summer*

Who came? (Mom, Dad, I, and other relatives)
What special things did we do? (ate spicy Irish stew, played volleyball, listened to Uncle Tim play banjo)
When was the picnic? (last August)
Where was the picnic held? (Patterson Park)
Why was this picnic held? (to reunite families; Uncle Tim, Aunt Mary, and cousin Lee came all the way from County Cork, Ireland)
How did the picnic turn out? (fun, except ants crawled on our blanket and on some of our sandwiches; rained towards evening)
How was the weather generally? (so hot that everyone was sweating until it rained)

Asking Point-of-View Questions. Still another technique that can be used to gather information is to look at a topic from three different points of view. To determine the point of view, ask three questions: (1) What is it? (2) How does it change or vary? (3) What are its relationships?

EXAMPLE *Topic:* Family picnic last summer

1. What is a family picnic? (In our family, it is a reunion of family members from around the world.)
2. How did our family picnic start? (Since it was so hot, we drank all our fruit punch right away.)
   How did the picnic progress? (played volleyball, listened to Uncle Tim play banjo, ate homemade Irish stew)
   How did the picnic end? (Towards evening, we sat around talking before leaving.)
3. What events were most pleasant? (eating spicy stew, playing volleyball, listening to Uncle Tim play banjo)
   What events were unpleasant? (rained later in afternoon, ants crawled on blanket and on some sandwiches)

CLASSIFYING INFORMATION

Once you have gathered your information, you need to classify, or sort, it into groups. Classifying helps you organize your information for writing. One of the simplest ways to classify information is to look for similarities and differences. Another way is to determine which ideas are more important than others. The more important ideas may become the main ideas of your paragraphs. The less important ideas will become supporting details.

EXAMPLE

Topic: Family picnic last summer

Time and Place	Weather	Pleasant Memories	Unpleasant Memories
August	Hot	Ate spicy stew	Rained later in day
Patterson Park	Everyone sweating	Played volleyball	Ants on sandwiches
	Rained later	Uncle Tim played banjo	Too hot
		Family reunited	

ARRANGING INFORMATION

The last step in the prewriting process is to arrange the ideas you have classified into a logical order or sequence. Usually your purpose will determine your order. For example, if you are writing a narrative paragraph, you will write your paragraph in chronological order. If you are writing a persuasive paragraph, you might write your argument first and follow it with supporting sentences that provide evidence. Sometimes, however, your purpose will not dictate an exact order. In these cases, you should present your information in any way that will be clear and interesting.

EXAMPLE *Topic:* Family picnic last summer
Purpose: Narrative, to tell a story
Order: Chronological

1. Family members reunited at park
2. Drank all fruit punch right away because so hot
3. Listened to Uncle Tim play banjo
4. Played volleyball
5. Rained, so took cover; sat around talking
6. Ate spicy Irish stew

Writing a First Draft

The next stage of the writing process is to write a first draft based on the information you prepared in the prewriting stage. In this stage, you put your ideas into sentences and paragraphs. Remember that this draft will not be your final one. Therefore, you should evaluate and revise your writing as many times as you need. Keep your prewriting notes in front of you as you write, and write freely.

Evaluating

Evaluating is the third stage of the writing process. In this stage, you review your first draft for content, organization, and style. You determine your weaknesses and decide what works and what does not. Use the following guidelines to help you evaluate your writing.

1. Do the ideas help to achieve a main purpose: to explain, to describe, to persuade, or to tell a story?
2. Is the topic limited enough?
3. Are the topic and details suitable and interesting for the audience?
4. Are enough details provided so that the topic can be easily understood? Are too many unnecessary details provided?
5. Does the order of the information make the main ideas clear?
6. Is the choice of words appropriate for the audience? Does the writing sound serious without sounding angry? Is the tone used light enough, or is it too light?
7. Are the words used specific and precise rather than vague?

Revising

Once you have evaluated your writing and have determined its weaknesses, you are ready to revise it. Revising your writing means making changes to it to improve it. Four basic techniques are used when revising: adding, cutting, replacing, and reordering. Note how this paragraph has been revised using these techniques.

EXAMPLE

picnic
Our family ~~reunion~~ was extra special this year beqause we were
an uncle, an aunt, and a cousin
reunited with ~~relatives~~ from Ireland. Unfortunately, that day was so
we had already drunk
hot that ~~the the first thing we did was drink~~ our entire supply of fruit
punch and had nothing to drink with the stew. Early in the afternoon,
~~drink for the day. Then~~ we sat around and talked and listened to
a fierce game of
Uncle Tim play the banjo. Later in the afternoon, we played volleyball.
When it began to rain towards evening,
~~Although it rained later in the day,~~ we gathered under a covered picnic
again h
area and talked for ours. Uncle Tim, Aunt Mary, and my cousin Lee,
a hot, spicy
from County Cork, ~~Ireland, even~~ made ~~homemade~~ Irish stew ~~there,~~
at the picnic — and it
~~which~~ was delicious. What a wonderful day that was!

Proofreading

In the proofreading stage of the writing process, you reread your revised draft one last time to find and correct errors. Proofreading means finding and correcting mistakes in grammar, usage, and mechanics (spelling, capitalization, and punctuation). Special standardized marks called revising and proofreading symbols are used in making the corrections. You will find a complete list of these marks on the inside of the back cover of this textbook.

Writing the Final Version

Writing the final version is the last step of the writing process. This step includes preparing a clean copy of your revised and proofread paper. Although your teacher will provide you with specific directions, you can use these general guidelines when completing any of the writing applications.

1. Write on lined 8 1/2 x 11-inch composition paper.
2. Write on only one side of each sheet.
3. Write in blue or black ink.
4. Leave top, bottom, and side margins of one inch.
5. Indent the first line of each paragraph.

UNIT 1 The Verb and Its Subject

WRITING APPLICATION A: Using Specific Nouns

Have you ever tried to leave a message on a telephone answering machine? If you have, you know that you are given only a few seconds to state your message. After that, the machine stops recording what you are saying. Therefore, you need to use words that are precise and specific to state your message in the time allotted. When you write, you also need to use specific words. If you use too many words with general, nonspecific meanings, your reader may decide to stop reading what you have to say. One easy way to keep your reader interested is to use specific nouns.

EXAMPLES
1. In Key West, I saw a *swordfish* leap high into the air.
2. The *falcon* soared high above the forest.
3. Our *chalet* in Switzerland was beautiful.

Writing Assignment: On a separate sheet of paper, write a paragraph about a favorite vacation you have taken. Describe some of the places you visited and the things you saw. Write complete sentences, and include a topic sentence. Use specific nouns in your writing.

Evaluation Checklist: Reread your first draft. Use these guidelines to help you judge the content and organization of your writing.

____ Each of my sentences is complete.
____ Each of my supporting sentences refers to the topic sentence.
____ I have used specific nouns in my paragraph.

Revising, Proofreading, and Writing the Final Version: Revise the first draft of your paragraph based on your evaluation. Then proofread your revised draft. Write your paragraph in final form.

WRITING APPLICATION B: Using Correct Verb Tenses

The idea of time travel may be intriguing to you. However, how intriguing would it be if you could spend only one or two seconds in each time period before moving on to the next period? No doubt, you would soon become confused and disoriented by the sudden time changes. In a similar way, writing can become confusing and disorienting to a reader when verb tenses change in the middle of a paragraph. Any change in tenses is like a sudden change in time for the reader. For this reason, always try to keep your verb tenses consistent within a paragraph.

EXAMPLE Tom, Ann, and I *met* in front of the theater at 6:45 p.m. We *talked* about old times for a few minutes before we *went* inside. After the movie, we *drove* to Freddy's Cafe, where we *shared* a pizza.

Writing Assignment: Think of an interesting social gathering you have attended, such as a dance, a club meeting, a holiday dinner, or even a get-together with a special friend. On a separate sheet of paper, write two or three paragraphs to describe what happened at that gathering. Use logical time order and correct verb tenses in your description. Make sure you have a topic sentence and supporting sentences in each paragraph you write.

Evaluation Checklist: Reread your first draft. Use these guidelines to help you judge the content and organization of your writing.

____ My description follows a logical time order.
____ I have used correct verb tenses in my writing.
____ Each of my supporting sentences refers to the topic sentence.

Revising, Proofreading, and Writing the Final Version: Revise your draft according to your evaluation. Then proofread your revised draft carefully. Write your description in final form.

WRITING APPLICATION C: Using Pronouns in Place of Nouns

To introduce one person to another, you need to make the introduction only once. Writing a paragraph is in some ways like making an introduction. To do it properly, you may only need to introduce your topic noun once. Then you can use pronouns to keep from repeating the same noun too many times in your writing.

EXAMPLE *Melissa* raced downward past all the other skiers on the steep hill. Suddenly *she* lunged forward, as if *she* were about to fall. Then, just as suddenly, *she* did a complete somersault and landed right-side-up on *her* skis. *Melissa* finished this spectacular race in second place.

Writing Assignment: Think of a sports event that you have watched in which something interesting occurred. Write a paragraph that describes what you saw. Use pronouns in place of any repetitive nouns. Use logical order in describing what happened. Also, remember to include a topic sentence in your paragraph.

Evaluation Checklist: Reread your first draft. Use these guidelines to help you judge the content and organization of your writing.

____ My paragraph has a topic sentence and supporting sentences.
____ I have used a pronoun in place of any repetitive noun.
____ I have used logical order in describing what happened.

Revising, Proofreading, and Writing the Final Version: Using your evaluation, revise your first draft. Check carefully that you have not repeated your subject noun too many times in your writing. Then proofread your revised draft. Write your draft in final form.

UNIT 2 Patterns of the Simple Sentence

WRITING APPLICATION A: Using Vivid Action Verbs

Imagine watching a movie in which the characters just stand or walk back and forth across the screen for an hour. You would soon become quite bored and stop watching the movie. The same sort of thing can happen to your writing if you use verbs that show little action. Your reader soon becomes bored with your writing and stops reading. To make your writing more dynamic, replace dull verbs with more vivid ones.

EXAMPLES
1. He *scurried* into the crowded conference room.
2. The parrot *shrieked* at each visitor to the store.
3. Marion *agonized* over her decision.

Writing Assignment: Write a paragraph describing a scene from one of your favorite movies. Use vivid action verbs in your description.

Evaluation Checklist: Reread your first draft. Use these guidelines to help you judge the content and organization of your writing.

____ I have used vivid action verbs in my paragraph.
____ My paragraph has a topic sentence and supporting sentences.

Revising, Proofreading, and Writing the Final Version: Use the results of your evaluation to help you revise your draft. Then proofread your revised draft. Write your paragraph in final form.

WRITING APPLICATION B: Varying Sentence Patterns

When you listen to a song playing on the radio, you hear the song's rhythm as well as its tune and lyrics. If you listen closely, you will notice that the rhythm varies at least a little throughout the song. This is done to keep the song interesting. Good writing is like a good song. Its rhythm must be varied to keep the writing interesting to the reader. To vary the rhythm of your writing, use a variety of sentence patterns. One easy way to vary your sentence patterns is to place the subject of your sentences in different positions.

EXAMPLE *Paul and I* were happy that Joan had come to visit. After she settled into her room, *we* all went fishing. All in all, *we* had a wonderful time together.

Writing Assignment: On a separate sheet of paper, write about a friend's or relative's visit to your home that was particularly special. Use a variety of sentence patterns to help make your writing interesting. Remember to use a topic sentence and supporting sentences in each of your paragraphs.

Evaluation Checklist: Reread your first draft. Use these guidelines to help you judge the content and organization of your writing.

____ I have used a variety of sentence patterns.
____ Each of my paragraphs has a topic sentence and supporting sentences.
____ My writing follows a logical order.

Revising, Proofreading, and Writing the Final Version: Revise your draft based on your evaluation. Then proofread your revised draft. Write your paragraphs in final form.

WRITING APPLICATION C: Using Helping Verbs

Have you ever said to yourself, "I wonder what might have happened if . . ."? The words *might have* are helping verbs that help you express this type of statement. Some other examples of helping verbs are *am, are, be, been, can, could, do, did, has, had, is, may, must, shall, should, was, were, will,* and *would.* You can use helping verbs in your writing to enrich your descriptions and express continuing action.

EXAMPLES I *could have* made the swim team this year if I *had* practiced during the summer. Instead, I spent my summer lounging on the beach. I *have* always wanted to be on our school's swim team. Now I *must* wait another whole year before I can try again. I *will* make sure that next summer I practice every day.

Writing Assignment: On a separate sheet of paper, write about something you could have done or been if circumstances had been different. Use helping verbs to help you express your ideas. Remember to include a topic sentence in each paragraph you write.

Evaluation Checklist: Reread your first draft. Use these guidelines to help you judge the content and organization of your writing.

____ I have used helping verbs to help me express actions or make statements.
____ My writing follows a logical order.
____ Each of my paragraphs has a topic sentence and supporting sentences.
____ I have explained the circumstances that kept me from doing or becoming something.

Revising, Proofreading, and Writing the Final Version: Revise your draft based on your evaluation. Make sure you have used helping verbs correctly in your sentences. Then proofread your revised draft. Write your revised draft in final form.

UNIT 3 The Work of Modifiers

WRITING APPLICATION A: Using Descriptive Adjectives

Good writers use words to paint a picture of what they are describing. The colors in their palette are adjectives. The more dynamic the adjectives, the more interesting and detailed is the picture that they create for the reader. You, too, can paint detailed pictures for your reader by using vivid, dynamic adjectives in your writing.

EXAMPLES
1. The *hungry* panther lurked among the *jagged* rocks.
2. The *brilliant* colors of her *tiny flower* garden made the *plain white* house look cheerful and inviting.
3. The *dilapidated brick* building has been abandoned since 1959.
4. Prepare to turn left onto a *gravel* road when you see the *rusty yellow* mailbox.

Writing Assignment: Pretend that you want to invite a new classmate to visit your home after school. Since your classmate is unfamiliar with your neighborhood, you need to give accurate directions. On a separate sheet of paper, write a paragraph that gives detailed directions from your school to your house. Use adjectives to describe landmarks that will help your classmate find his or her way.

Evaluation Checklist: Reread your first draft. Use these guidelines to help you judge the content and organization of your writing.

____ I have used vivid adjectives to describe landmarks.
____ My paragraph follows a logical order.
____ My paragraph has a topic sentence and supporting sentences.

Revising, Proofreading, and Writing the Final Version: Revise the first draft of your paragraph based on your evaluation. Then proofread your revised draft. Write your paragraph in final form.

WRITING APPLICATION B: Using Precise Adverbs

To teach someone how to do something new, you need to give good directions. To give good directions, you need to tell exactly *when* and *how* to complete certain steps. Adverbs are the part of speech that help you tell how and when to do something. Using precise adverbs in your writing will clarify steps in your directions.

EXAMPLE *Carefully* empty the powdered mix into the bowl. Then *slowly* pour in one cup of hot water. Stir until the mix looks *completely* dissolved in the water. *Gradually* mix in one-half cup of raisins and sliced bananas.

Writing Assignment: Think of something you know how to make or do well. Then write directions for a classmate. Use a step-by-step order so that your classmate can follow your directions easily. Use precise adverbs to clarify your directions.

Evaluation Checklist: Reread your first draft. Use these guidelines to help you judge the content and organization of your writing.

____ I have used precise adverbs to clarify my directions.
____ My directions are in correct order.
____ My directions are accurate and complete.

Revising, Proofreading, and Writing the Final Version: Based on your evaluation, revise the first draft of your directions. Then proofread your revised draft. Write your directions in final form.

WRITING APPLICATION C: Using Prepositions

There are many ways to cross a river. You can go over, under, or around the river, or you can swim across or ride across in a boat. All these methods enable you to get to the other side. In writing, prepositions are the part of speech that enable writers to get to the other side of sentences. They connect nouns or pronouns and verbs with other words in sentences. There is a great variety of prepositions that can be used to make these connections.

EXAMPLES
1. The soldiers marched gallantly *over* the hill.
2. The balloon floated peacefully *above* the tiny village.
3. Michael dives *with* caution *below* the reef.
4. The holiday season is just *around* the corner.
5. The containers *on* the shelves and the flat boxes *in* the attic are used *for* storing winter clothes.

Writing Assignment: Think of a physical barrier you once had to cross. On a separate sheet of paper, describe how you finally crossed that barrier. Use prepositions to help make connections.

Evaluation Checklist: Reread your first draft. Use these guidelines to help you judge the content and organization of your writing.

____ I have used prepositions in my description to make connections.
____ My description follows a logical order.
____ I have included a topic sentence in each of the paragraphs I have written.

Revising, Proofreading, and Writing the Final Version: Revise your first draft based on your evaluation. Then proofread your revised draft. Write your paragraphs in final form.

UNIT 4 Building Better Sentences

WRITING APPLICATION A: Writing Compound Sentences

One of the first things you might do when you shop is to compare items by price and quality. Doing this helps you determine how similar or different various brands are before you make your final selection. You can also compare and contrast items in this way when you write. First, write your topic sentence. Then compare and contrast two things point by point. Use compound sentences to help you combine sentences.

EXAMPLE I like to play volleyball, but I also like to read. I like volleyball because it is a group activity, but I like reading because it is a solitary activity. Volleyball involves doing something with your body, and reading involves doing something with your mind.

Writing Assignment: On a separate sheet of paper, compare and contrast two of your favorite hobbies. Use compound sentences in your writing.

Evaluation Checklist: Reread your first draft. Use these guidelines to help you judge the content and organization of your writing.

____ I have used a point-by-point method of comparison or contrast.
____ I have included a topic sentence in each paragraph I have written.
____ I have correctly punctuated my compound sentences.

Revising, Proofreading, and Writing the Final Version: Revise your first draft based on your evaluation. Then proofread your revised draft. Write your assignment in final form.

WRITING APPLICATION B: Writing Complex Sentences

When factory workers are assembling a car, they are putting together the complex machinery that will enable the car to run smoothly. If the workers have done a good job, the driver of the car will not even think of the machinery as he or she drives. In a similar way, when you write complex sentences in combination with other types of sentences, you are assembling the parts that will make your writing read smoothly. If you do a good job of combining different types of sentences, your reader will not even notice the skillful way you have worked complex sentences into your writing.

EXAMPLE *Although I had always wanted to see the ocean, I did not have the opportunity until this year.* My family and I went on vacation to Kennebunkport, Maine, in July. *Since we arrived at our cabin in Kennebunkport after dark, I could hear the the ocean's waves pounding but could not see them.* At dawn, I woke up my family with shrieks of glee. I could see the ocean from our cabin door.

Writing Assignment: On a separate sheet of paper, write a narrative that explains your reaction to a place or a thing you saw for the first time. You may use your own topic or one of these ideas: sand dunes, mountains, the city, a farm, the Great Lakes, or palm trees. Use complex sentences as well as other types of sentences in your explanation.

Evaluation Checklist: Reread your first draft. Use these guidelines to help you judge the content and organization of your writing.

____ I have used complex sentences as well as simple and compound sentences.
____ I have included a topic sentence in each of the paragraphs I have written.
____ I have written my narrative in chronological order.

Revising, Proofreading, and Writing the Final Version: Revise your draft based on your evaluation. Make some of your compound sentences into complex sentences, if doing so will improve them. Proofread your revised draft. Write your revised draft in final form.

WRITING APPLICATION C: Using Appositives to Explain

When you take notes, you are jotting down important details that help explain something. In a similar way, when you write appositives, you are writing important details that help explain something in your sentences. Appositives identify or tell something about the noun or pronoun they follow. They can also be used to help you combine information in sentences that have similar constructions.

TWO SENTENCES	Louisa May Alcott was a famous author. She wrote *Little Women* more than 100 years ago.
ONE SENTENCE WITH APPOSITIVE	Louisa May Alcott, a famous author, wrote *Little Women* more than 100 years ago.

Writing Assignment: On a separate sheet of paper, write about a famous person who has inspired you in some way. Use appositives to help you combine sentences and explain ideas. Use a variety of sentence types in your writing.

Evaluation Checklist: Reread your first draft. Use these guidelines to help you judge the content and organization of your writing.

____ I have used a variety of sentence types.
____ I have used correct punctuation with appositives.
____ I have included a topic sentence in each of the paragraphs I have written.

Revising, Proofreading, and Writing the Final Version: Revise your draft based on your evaluation. Then proofread your revised draft. Write your draft in final form.

WRITING APPLICATION A: Avoiding Sentence Fragments

How would you like to buy a sweater and later find one sleeve missing? A sentence fragment is like a sweater with only one sleeve. It is missing something important that would make it complete. In a sentence fragment, either the subject or predicate of the sentence is missing. When this happens, a reader cannot form a complete thought from a sentence and cannot make sense of the writing. Always make sure you have a subject and a predicate in each of your sentences.

SENTENCE FRAGMENTS The four Haney children. Leaped over the fence simultaneously.

COMPLETE SENTENCE The four Haney children leaped over the fence simultaneously.

Writing Assignment: On a separate sheet of paper, write about something that happened in your neighborhood last summer. Use two of the three fragments below to compose complete sentences. Then use those sentences in your composition.

one day last summer near the road but did not understand

Evaluation Checklist: Reread your first draft. Use these guidelines to help you judge the content and organization of your writing.

____ Each of my sentences has a subject and a predicate.
____ I have used correct punctuation in each of my sentences.
____ I have used logical order in describing what happened.

Revising, Proofreading, and Writing the Final Version: Revise your draft based on your evaluation. Check carefully that each sentence is complete. Then proofread your revised draft. Write your draft in final form.

WRITING APPLICATION B: Stopping Run-on Sentences

Riding on a roller coaster can be exciting, unless you cannot get off! Reading run-on sentences is like riding on a roller coaster that will not stop. Images go speeding by because there are no pauses or stops to let you enjoy them. You experience the speed but not the meaning of anything around you. As you write, correct run-on sentences by punctuating them in one of four ways: (a) Add a period between sentences. (b) Add a semicolon between sentences. (c) Add a comma and a conjunction between two sentences. (d) Make one part of a sentence dependent on the other, and add a comma.

RUN-ON SENTENCE   Stephanie is getting ready for school Pat is eating.

COMPLETE SENTENCES
1. Stephanie is getting ready for school. Pat is eating.
2. Stephanie is getting ready for school; Pat is eating.
3. Stephanie is getting ready for school, and Pat is eating.
4. While Stephanie is getting ready for school, Pat is eating.

Writing Assignment: On a separate sheet of paper, describe a typical day in your favorite class. Describe what you and your classmates do during class that you particularly enjoy. Use complete sentences.

Evaluation Checklist: Reread your first draft. Use these guidelines to help you judge the content and organization of your writing.

____ Each of my sentences is complete and correctly punctuated.
____ My description follows a logical order.

Revising, Proofreading, and Writing the Final Version: Revise your draft based on your evaluation. Then proofread your revised draft. Write your draft in final form.

WRITING APPLICATION C: Using Transitions in Sentences

To ease the transition, or change, from one year to another, many people attend New Year's Eve celebrations. These celebrations help make the change from the old year to the new year seem less abrupt. In writing, certain words can be used to make the change from one sentence to another seem less abrupt. These words are called transitions. Some examples of transitions are *then, therefore, consequently,* and *as a result*. Transitions help sentences flow logically from one topic to another. Since they frequently connect complete sentences, you should make sure you use periods and semicolons before them rather than commas.

EXAMPLES
1. Peggy and her four friends arrived. *Then* the fun began.
   Peggy and her four friends arrived; *then* the fun began.
2. Kelly misplaced her ticket; *therefore*, she missed the flight.
   Kelly misplaced her ticket. *Therefore*, she missed the flight.

Writing Assignment: On a separate sheet of paper, write about an appointment or event you were late for or missed. Use transitions in your writing to help your sentences flow logically from one topic to another.

Evaluation Checklist: Reread your first draft. Use these guidelines to help you judge the content and organization of your writing.

____ I have used transitional words and phrases to make my sentences flow logically and smoothly.
____ I have used correct punctuation with transitions.

Revising, Proofreading, and Writing the Final Version: Revise your draft based on your evaluation. Then proofread your revised draft. Write your draft in final form.

UNIT 6 Using Verbs Correctly

WRITING APPLICATION A: Choosing Irregular Verb Forms

Many people in business form lasting impressions of other people's abilities from the letters they read. If a businessperson reads a letter that uses words incorrectly, he or she tends to think the writer has poor skills in other areas as well. This is particularly true if the writer has misused simple nouns and verbs. Verbs such as *bring, come, do, give, go, run, see,* and *take* are some of the most commonly used words in the English language. Therefore, you need to know their correct verb forms. Since you will use them frequently in all your writing, you should memorize those verb forms you do not already know.

Present	Simple Past	Past with Helper
bring	brought	have brought
come	came	have come
do	did	have done
give	gave	have given
go	went	have gone
run	ran	have run
see	saw	have seen
take	took	have taken

Writing Assignment: On a separate sheet of paper, write a paragraph about a school or business meeting you have attended. Describe what you had to bring, where you had to go, what you had to do, who else came, and things you saw. Use correct verb forms in your writing.

Evaluation Checklist: Reread your first draft. Use these guidelines to help you judge the content and organization of your writing.

___ I have used correct verb forms in my writing.
___ My paragraph follows a logical order.
___ I have included a topic sentence in my paragraph.

Revising, Proofreading, and Writing the Final Version: Revise your draft based on your evaluation. Then proofread your revised draft. Write your paragraph in final form.

WRITING APPLICATION B: Using Irregular Verbs

Have you ever wondered how two people with completely different personalities end up the best of friends? They are friends because they know and accept each other's differences. Memorizing irregular verb forms is, in a way, like this type of friendship. Once you have memorized irregular verb forms, you will know their differences and feel comfortable writing them. You will be able to use them without effort and can concentrate on other aspects of your writing. Several pairs of irregular verb forms sometimes cause confusion. These verbs are *bring* and *take, leave* and *let, lie* and *lay, raise* and *rise,* and *sit* and *set.* Three of the verb forms for each pair are shown below.

Present	Simple Past	Past with Helper
bring (toward)	brought	have brought
take (away from)	took	have taken
leave (place and go)	left	have left
let (put)	let	have let
lie (recline)	lay	have lain
lay (put)	laid	have laid
raise (lift)	raised	have raised
rise (go up)	rose	have risen
sit (sitting position)	sat	have sat
set (put)	set	have set

Writing Assignment: On a separate sheet of paper, write about one of the following topics in the past tense. As you write, use the verbs in the topic you have chosen at least twice. Remember to include a topic sentence for each paragraph you write.

Setting an Example by Sitting Up Straight

Rising Early to Raise My Grades

Leaving Behind a Good Friend and Letting In New Friends

Laying Down Rules for Lying in the Sun

Bringing and Taking Home an Umbrella

Evaluation Checklist: Reread your first draft. Use these guidelines to help you judge the content and organization of your writing.

____ I have a topic sentence and supporting sentences in each of my paragraphs.
____ I have used the past tense in my writing.
____ I have used the correct verbs in my writing.
____ My paragraphs follow a logical order.
____ I have written about one of the listed topics.

Revising, Proofreading, and Writing the Final Version: Revise your draft based on your evaluation. Write your chosen topic as the title of your paper if you have not already done so. Then proofread your revised draft. Write your draft in final form.

UNIT 7 Agreement of Subject and Verb

WRITING APPLICATION A: Using Subject–Verb Agreement

Even the most brilliant argument can be lost if it is not presented well. Presenting an argument in writing is called persuasive writing. Presenting it well means stating reasons for the argument and supporting those reasons with evidence. It also means using correct subject-verb agreement. Because persuasive writing often uses a variety of subject-verb combinations, extra care should be taken in making sure that verbs agree with their subjects.

EXAMPLE Recent *circumstances reveal* that this *library should be kept* open until 9 p.m. daily. Since *many* of this district's students *work* part-time after school, *they are* unable to get to the library before *it closes* at 7:30 p.m. Our *survey* of area high schools *shows* that 52 *percent* of this year's graduating class *works* part-time after school. In addition, large evening *enrollments* at the new extension center on Jackson Street *mean* more *adults need* to use the library at night. Our most recent *survey* from the extension center *shows* a current enrollment of 206 students.

Writing Assignment: On a separate sheet of paper, write an argument to persuade your classmates that the school year should either be extended or shortened. Give at least three reasons for your argument and support those reasons with evidence. Use correct subject-verb agreement.

Evaluation Checklist: Reread your first draft. Use these guidelines to help you judge the content and organization of your writing.

____ I have supported my argument with at least three reasons.
____ I have supported my reasons with evidence.
____ I have used correct subject-verb agreement.

Revising, Proofreading, and Writing the Final Version: Revise your draft based on your evaluation. In addition, make sure your reasons are arranged in order of importance. Your argument should be serious but not have an angry tone. Proofread your draft after you have revised it. Then write your argument in final form.

WRITING APPLICATION B: Keeping Track of Your Subject

Have you ever momentarily forgotten where you put something? In writing, when a subject in a sentence is separated from its verb by other words, you may momentarily forget the location of the subject. When this happens, you may use a verb that agrees not with the subject but with another noun in the sentence. As you write, carefully check that each verb you write agrees with the subject, no matter how far away it may be.

EXAMPLES 1. High-tech *industries* in this state *have* increased dramatically.
2. Where *are* the *players* for that team?
3. *Neither* of his assistants *is* present today.

Writing Assignment: On a separate sheet of paper, describe how a group in your community or school has helped others. Ideas might include sponsoring a canned-food drive, setting up an election, or welcoming an honored guest. Use correct subject-verb agreement in your description.

Evaluation Checklist: Reread your first draft. Use these guidelines to help you judge the content and organization of your writing.

____ Each of my paragraphs has a topic sentence.
____ I have used correct subject-verb agreement.

Revising, Proofreading, and Writing the Final Version: Revise your rough draft based on your evaluation. Check carefully that the subject in each of your sentences agrees in number with the verbs you have used. Proofread your draft after you have revised it. Then write your draft in final form.

WRITING APPLICATION C: Using Verbs with Combined Subjects

Even though main dishes listed on a restaurant menu are not separated by the word *or,* you are expected to select only one. In a similar way, when you use two or more singular subjects in your sentences and connect them with the word *or,* you are expected to use a singular verb. The word *or* separates singular subjects so that each must be considered individually. Singular subjects connected by the word *and,* however, require a plural verb. The word *and* connects two or more things to make them plural.

EXAMPLES 1. The stage manager, the director, *or* the producer *makes* the final decisions. (Only one of these three makes the decisions.)
2. The stage manager, the director, *and* the producer *make* the final decisions. (The three make the decisions jointly.)

Writing Assignment: On a separate sheet of paper, describe the favorite hobbies of two or three of your friends or relatives. As you write, use *or* or *and* to connect subjects.

Evaluation Checklist: Reread your first draft. Use these guidelines to help you judge the content and organization of your writing.

____ I have used a plural verb with subjects connected by *and.*
____ I have used a singular verb with singular subjects connected by *or.*

Revising, Proofreading, and Writing the Final Version: Revise your draft based on your evaluation. Then proofread your revised draft. Write your draft in final form.

UNIT 8 Choosing the Right Modifier

WRITING APPLICATION A: Choosing Between *Good* and *Well*

You may have heard the adage, "If the shoe fits, wear it." As you write, you sometimes have to decide whether certain words "fit" your sentences. Deciding whether to use *good* or *well* is an example of deciding which word will fit best in your sentences. Since *good* is an adjective, it modifies only nouns and pronouns. *Well* is used primarily as an adverb and answers the question *How? Well,* however, can also be used as an adjective when it refers to health. To determine which word you should use in a sentence, first determine the part of speech. If you are still unsure, test the sentence using *well.* If *well* fits, you should be using that word. If it does not fit, you should be using *good.*

EXAMPLES
1. Andrew did a *good* job of singing at the concert. (adjective)
2. The food they serve is *good.* (adjective)
3. Clara is not feeling *well* today. (adjective)
4. Juan ran *well* in last month's marathon. (adverb)

Writing Assignment: On a separate sheet of paper, write a narrative describing some task that you did particularly well. Use the words *good* and *well* at least twice in your writing.

Evaluation Checklist: Reread your first draft. Use these guidelines to help you judge the content and organization of your writing.

____ I have written my narrative in chronological order.
____ I have used *good* and *well* correctly.

Revising, Proofreading, and Writing the Final Version: Revise your draft based on your evaluation. You may want to check one last time that *well* cannot be substituted for *good* in any of your sentences. Proofread your revised draft carefully, and correct any errors. Then write your final version.

WRITING APPLICATION B: Using Degrees of Comparison

Each year, players on professional sports teams vote for their MVP, or "Most Valuable Player." *Most valuable* is the highest level of comparison the team members can make and is an example of a third-degree comparison. However, there are two other degrees of comparison that you can use as well when you write. These are first-degree and second-degree comparisons. In the first degree, no real comparison is made. In the second degree, only two things are compared. In the third degree, more than two things are compared.

FIRST DEGREE	Carol is a *good* swimmer.
SECOND DEGREE	Carol is a *better* swimmer than Dennis. (Carol is compared to one other student.)
THIRD DEGREE	Carol is the *best* swimmer in this school. (Carol is compared to all other students in her school.)

Writing Assignment: On a separate sheet of paper, compare the skills of two or more of your favorite athletes, actors, singers, or authors. Use at least two degrees of comparison in your writing.

Evaluation Checklist: Reread your first draft. Use these guidelines to help you judge the content and organization of your writing.

____ I have used second-degree comparison when I compared two things.
____ I have used third-degree comparison when I compared more than two things.
____ I have included a topic sentence in each paragraph I have written.

Revising, Proofreading, and Writing the Final Version: Revise your draft based on your evaluation. Then proofread your revised draft. Write your revised draft in final form.

WRITING APPLICATION C: Avoiding Double Negatives

People, in general, do not like to be told "no." They like it even less when they are told "no" twice in the same sentence. Using a double negative is like saying "no" twice in one sentence. One of the negative words in the sentence is unnecessary and should be eliminated. You can usually correct sentences that have this error by removing one of the negative words.

DOUBLE NEGATIVE	Bill has *not* done *nothing* about the broken window.
SOLUTION 1	Bill has done *nothing* about the broken window.
SOLUTION 2	Bill has *not* done anything about the broken window.
DOUBLE NEGATIVE	Sandy *never* asked *nobody* to help her with that project.
SOLUTION	Sandy *never* asked anybody to help her with that project.

Writing Assignment: On a separate sheet of paper, describe some small task that you dislike doing but must do from time to time. Avoid using double negatives as you write.

Evaluation Checklist: Reread your first draft. Use these guidelines to help you judge the content and organization of your writing.

____ I have not used double negatives in any of my sentences.
____ My description follows a logical order.

Revising, Proofreading, and Writing the Final Version: Revise your draft based on your evaluation. Then proofread your revised draft. Write your paragraph(s) in final form.

UNIT 9 Using Pronouns Correctly

WRITING APPLICATION A: Choosing the Correct Pronoun

Have you ever hesitated when speaking or writing because you were unsure which pronoun to use with a noun? Perhaps you did not know whether to use *us* or *we*, or *I* or *me*. In sentences in which you have a conjunction connecting a noun and pronoun, your choice of pronouns may at times seem confusing. However, you can easily choose the correct pronoun by quickly testing each pronoun alone in the sentence. The pronoun that makes best sense in the sentence is the correct one.

SENTENCE Russell and (me, I) visited Toronto last year.

TEST 1 Me visited Toronto last year. (makes poor sense)

TEST 2 I visited Toronto last year. (makes good sense)

SOLUTION Russell and I visited Toronto last year.

Writing Assignment: On a separate sheet of paper, write about a place you attended with another person, such as a friend, a classmate, or a family member. Possible places might be a park, a shopping center, a theater, or a baseball stadium. Describe some of the things you did in that place.

Evaluation Checklist: Reread your first draft. Use these guidelines to help you judge the content and organization of your writing.

____ I have tested each of my pronouns to make sure it is correct.
____ My writing follows a logical order.

Revising, Proofreading, and Writing the Final Version: Revise your draft based on your evaluation. Make sure each of your paragraphs contains a topic sentence. Then proofread your revised draft. Write your revised draft in final form.

WRITING APPLICATION B: Using Possessive Pronouns

Although there are exceptions to almost every rule, there is no exception to the rule about using apostrophes with possessive pronouns: *Never use an apostrophe with a possessive pronoun.* Possessive pronouns that end in *s* are *his, hers, ours, theirs, yours,* and *its*. Careless writers sometimes incorrectly write *its* as *it's. It's,* however, is always a contraction that means *it is.*

EXAMPLES
1. *Its* coarse fur is usually brown or gray.
2. *Its* owners know when *it's* hungry.
3. *It's* camouflaged in the wilderness by *its* unusual skin color.

Writing Assignment: On a separate sheet of paper, describe something to your classmates so that they must guess its identity. Use the pronoun *it* to refer to your chosen "thing." Write clues that reveal specific details. In your last sentence, identify the thing you have been describing.

Evaluation Checklist: Reread your first draft. Use these guidelines to help you judge the content and organization of your writing.

____ I have used *its* as a possessive pronoun.
____ I have used *it's* only as a contraction.
____ My description provides detailed clues.
____ I have written all other possessive pronouns correctly.

Revising, Proofreading, and Writing the Final Version: Revise your first draft based on your evaluation. Make sure your last sentence identifies what you have been describing. Proofread your revised draft. Write your draft in final form.

WRITING APPLICATION C: Using the "*-self*" Pronouns

If one day someone accuses you of being selfish, you might be offended. However, if that same person accuses you of being *selvish,* you might instead just laugh because you know the word *selvish* does not exist. Using the "*-self*" pronouns in your writing can have the same effect on your reader when you misuse their forms. Be careful not to write forms of these words that do not exist.

EXAMPLES
1. They gave *themselves* extra time to complete the project. (Never *themselfs, themself,* or *theirselves.*)
2. Brad congratulated *himself* for finishing the project on time. (Never *hisself.*)
3. Phyllis and I introduced *ourselves* to the receptionist. (Never *ourselfs* or *ourself.*)
4. Always try to give *yourselves* a few moments to regain your composure. (Never *yourselfs.*)

Writing Assignment: On a separate sheet of paper, describe gifts you believe friends or relatives would give themselves if they could. Use the correct form of the "*-self*" pronouns in your writing.

Evaluation Checklist: Reread your first draft. Use these guidelines to help you judge the content and organization of your writing.

____ I have use the correct form of the "*-self*" pronouns in my writing.
____ Each of my paragraphs has a topic sentence and supporting sentences.

Revising, Proofreading, and Writing the Final Version: Revise your draft based on your evaluation. Then proofread your revised draft. Write your revised draft in final form.

UNIT 10 How to Use Capitals

WRITING APPLICATION A: Capitalizing Geographical Names

What is one of the first things you might do when taking pictures on vacation? You might focus your camera lens to get a clearer picture of a favorite spot. Focusing a camera lens is a little like capitalizing geographical names in writing. Capitalizing helps focus in on a specific place by calling attention to proper nouns.

EXAMPLE The tranquil St. John's River stretches halfway down Florida, from the busy shores of Jacksonville to the wetlands southwest of Cape Canaveral. Near Melbourne, the river melts into the landscape to provide a lush, marshy habitat for Florida's wildlife. Some say the majestic subtropical beauty of the St. John's is seconded only by that of the Everglades.

Writing Assignment: On a separate sheet of paper, describe one or more of the outstanding natural wonders in your state. Name specific lakes, mountains, parks, or large bodies of water. Write your description so that it will appeal to someone who has never visited your state.

Evaluation Checklist: Reread your first draft. Use these guidelines to help you judge the content and organization of your writing.

____ I have capitalized all geographical names that are proper nouns.
____ I have capitalized all other proper nouns I have used.
____ I have not capitalized the word *the* or any short preposition when it is part of a name.

Revising, Proofreading, and Writing the Final Version: Revise your first draft based on your evaluation. Then proofread your revised draft. Write your revised draft in final form.

WRITING APPLICATION B: Capitalizing Dates and Special Events

On most calendars, you will find days of the week, months, holidays, and special occasions. These words indicate specific dates or periods of time. What you will usually not see on a calendar are the four seasons. The seasons are important but are not as specific periods of time. In writing, the seasons and other references to time are treated in a similar way. Specific days, months, holidays, and special occasions are always capitalized. The four seasons are never capitalized.

EXAMPLES
1. In the winter, children look forward to Chanukah and Christmas.
2. Our Thanksgiving last fall was particularly special.
3. Celebrating the Fourth of July is an important summer event.

Writing Assignment: On a separate sheet of paper, write about your favorite season. Describe the special holidays that are celebrated at that time and some of the things you do to celebrate.

Evaluation Checklist: Reread your first draft. Use these guidelines to help you judge the content and organization of your writing.

___ I have capitalized all days of the week, months, holidays, and special occasions.
___ I have not capitalized any of the four seasons.
___ I have included details that accurately describe the season and holidays I have chosen to write about.

Revising, Proofreading, and Writing the Final Version: Revise your draft based on your evaluation. Then proofread your revised draft carefully. Write your revised draft in final form.

WRITING APPLICATION C: Capitalizing Titles of Artistic Works

Personal titles such as *Dr., Colonel, Ms.,* or *Mr.* are always capitalized and help make the names they precede stand out. In a similar way, important words in titles of literary and artistic works, such as books, poems, and songs, are capitalized to make them stand out. Less important words in titles are not capitalized unless they are the first word. These less important words include conjunctions, articles, and short prepositions.

EXAMPLES
1. Peter Taylor's book *A Summons to Memphis* won the Pulitzer Prize.
2. Alexander's favorite poems are "Velvet Shoes" and "Swift Things Are Beautiful."
3. "Rhapsody in Blue" will always be my mother and father's favorite song.
4. All his students were required to read "An Approach to Style," the fifth chapter in *The Elements of Style*.

Writing Assignment: Compare two of your favorite books. Describe what you like most about each book. Tell how each book is alike or different.

Evaluation Checklist: Reread your first draft. Use these guidelines to help you judge the content and organization of your writing.

___ I have capitalized the important words in titles of books, poems, and songs.
___ I have not capitalized conjunctions, articles, and short prepositions unless they are the first word in titles.

Revising, Proofreading, and Writing the Final Version: Revise your draft based on your evaluation. Check that you have described how the books are alike or different. Then proofread your revised draft carefully. Write your draft in final form.

UNIT 11 Learning to Use Commas

WRITING APPLICATION A: Using Parallel Structure

Both the World Series and a lecture series are types of series. However, you would not expect to watch a baseball game at a lecture series, and you would not want to listen to a lecture during a baseball game. In a similar way when you use a series of items in sentences, you need to make sure each item in the series is alike. If two of the things in your series are nouns, then the remaining things should also be nouns. If most items in your series are prepositional phrases, then the remaining items should also be prepositional phrases. This rule can be applied when using any combination of words in a series. Use a comma to separate each of the items in the series except the last.

EXAMPLES
1. I must take one teaspoon of that medicine before breakfast, after lunch, and during dinner. (prepositional phrases)
2. Literature, art, architecture, and music are my favorite topics. (nouns)
3. Please sweep, dust, and wax those particular floors before I return. (verbs)

Writing Assignment: On a separate sheet of paper, describe the things you have done to occupy your time during long car trips or long waiting periods. Use prepositional phrases in a series at least once.

Evaluation Checklist: Reread your first draft. Use these guidelines to help you judge the content and organization of your writing.

____ I have used the series comma after each item in my series except the last.
____ Each of the items in each of my series is grammatically alike.

Revising, Proofreading, and Writing the Final Version: Revise your first draft based on your evaluation. Make sure you have included topic sentences and supporting sentences. Then proofread your revised draft. Write your revised draft in final form.

WRITING APPLICATION B: Using Commas After Introductory Words

Not using a comma after an introductory phrase or clause is like driving past a yield sign without slowing down. Chances are that you will run into something coming in the other direction. Commas help create the necessary pauses that make your sentences understandable to your reader. Note how the following sentences are improved when a comma is inserted after the introductory phrase or clause.

EXAMPLES 1. To Paul Washington was the greatest president of all.
To Paul, Washington was the greatest president of all.
2. Whenever I chew my ears begin to pop.
Whenever I chew, my ears begin to pop.

Writing Assignment: On a separate sheet of paper, describe whimsical and fantastic gifts you would give to your family and friends if money were no object. Use a comma after each introductory phrase or clause.

Evaluation Checklist: Reread your first draft. Use these guidelines to help you judge the content and organization of your writing.

____ I have used a comma after each introductory phrase.
____ I have used a comma after each introductory clause.

Revising, Proofreading, and Writing the Final Version: Revise your draft based on your evaluation. Check that you have used correctly all punctuation in addition to commas. Then proofread your revised draft carefully. Write your draft in final form.

WRITING APPLICATION C: Using Commas with Interrupters

No one likes to be interrupted while speaking or writing. However, every person interrupts his or her own speaking and writing from time to time with short phrases called interrupters. Examples of interrupters are *of course, by the way, if possible,* and *for example.* These phrases accent the main ideas in sentences and are set off with commas no matter where they appear in the sentences.

EXAMPLES 1. *By the way,* Mrs. Bennetton will be stopping by tomorrow.
Mrs. Bennetton, *by the way,* will be stopping by tomorrow.
Mrs. Bennetton will be stopping by tomorrow, *by the way.*
2. *Of course,* the launch is still scheduled for 6 a.m.
The launch, *of course,* is still scheduled for 6 a.m.
The launch is still scheduled for 6 a.m., *of course.*

Writing Assignment: On a separate sheet of paper, write to a relative or friend you have not seen in a while. Describe some of the things that have happened recently that might interest that person. Use interrupters such as *for example, by the way,* and *of course* when appropriate to help you express your ideas.

Evaluation Checklist: Reread your first draft. Use these guidelines to help you judge the content and organization of your writing.

____ I have set off interrupters in my sentences with commas.
____ Each of my paragraphs has a topic sentence and supporting sentences.

Revising, Proofreading, and Writing the Final Version: Using your evaluation, revise your first draft. Then proofread your revised draft. Write your draft in final form.

UNIT 12 Apostrophes and Quotation Marks

WRITING APPLICATION A: Using Apostrophes

Before you can buy something that is owned by someone else, you need to determine who the owner is. In a similar way, before you make a noun possessive, you first need to ask, "Who is the owner?" If the noun that will show ownership is singular, add *'s*. If the noun that will show ownership is plural, add *'*.

EXAMPLES
1. Have you seen the writers' computers that are being used for word processing? (The computers are owned by more than one writer. *Writers* is plural. Add *'*.)
2. The secretary's notebooks are kept here. (The notebooks belong to one secretary. *Secretary* is singular. Add *'s*.)

Writing Assignment: On a separate sheet of paper, write about the variety of student interests at your school. Use both the singular and plural possessive forms of the word *student* in your writing.

Evaluation Checklist: Reread your first draft. Use these guidelines to help you judge the content and organization of your writing.

____ I have used *'s* with nouns that are singular.
____ I have used *'* with nouns that are plural.

Revising, Proofreading, and Writing the Final Version: Revise your draft based on your evaluation and on other rules of grammar and composition you have studied. Then proofread your revised draft carefully. Write your draft in final form.

WRITING APPLICATION B: Forming Contractions

One of the meanings of the word *contract* is "to shrink" or "to shorten." In writing, shortening words by omitting letters is called forming contractions. Apostrophes are always used in contractions to show that letters have been omitted from the words. Therefore, if you think you are writing a contraction but are not using an apostrophe, you may be mistakenly writing a pronoun instead. Several of the contractions often confused with pronouns are shown below.

EXAMPLES
1. I am not sure *who's* planning to attend whose party on Friday. (*Who's* means *who is*. Do not confuse it with the word *whose*.)
2. Miriam, I hope *you're* planning to audition for your sister's play. (*You're* means *you are*. Do not confuse it with the word *your*.)
3. *They're* obviously not responsible for their actions at this time. (*They're* means *they are*. Do not confuse it with the word *their*.)

Writing Assignment: On a separate sheet of paper, describe a club or organization to which you would like to belong but have not yet joined. Use some contractions in your writing.

Evaluation Checklist: Reread your first draft. Use these guidelines to help you judge the content and organization of your writing.

____ Each of my contractions has an apostrophe.
____ I have not confused contractions with pronouns.

Revising, Proofreading, and Writing the Final Version: Revise your draft based on your evaluation. Then proofread your revised draft. Write your draft in final form.

WRITING APPLICATION C: Using Quotation Marks

To signal a taxi on a busy street in New York City, you need to wave one of your arms. To signal for a turn when you are driving, you need to turn on a turn signal. In writing, you signal that you are using the exact words of a speaker by enclosing those words in quotation marks. Use a comma as a separator between the quotation and the expression used by the speaker (such as, *he said*). If you are only reporting indirectly what someone else has said, you do not need to enclose the words in quotation marks.

EXAMPLES
1. "This will be my last term in office," the senator said.
2. The senator told reporters that this term in office would be her last.
3. He warned Pandora, "Never open that box!"
4. He warned Pandora that she should never open that box!

Writing Assignment: On a separate sheet of paper, describe an interesting conversation that you have had. Include both direct and indirect quotations.

Evaluation Checklist: Reread your first draft. Use these guidelines to help you judge the content and organization of your writing.

____ I have enclosed all direct quotes in quotation marks.
____ I have used a comma as a separator in direct quotations.

Revising, Proofreading, and Writing the Final Version: Revise your draft based on your evaluation. Then proofread your revised draft. Write your draft in final form.

FRAME INDEX

Each entry is indexed by frame number, followed by the page, in parentheses, on which the frame appears. The references included in each entry direct the reader to Key frames. Additional information and related exercises may be found in the frames preceding and following those listed. Complete review exercises for major topics are listed in the table of contents.

REVISING AND PROOFREADING SYMBOLS

Symbol	Example	Meaning of Symbol
≡	uncle Tim	Capitalize a lowercase letter
/	my Uncle	Lowercase a capital letter
^	a stew (delicious)	Insert a missing word or punctuation mark
℘	our reunion picnic	Leave out a word, letter, or punctuation mark.
^	weather (a)	Change a letter
℘	my coussin	Leave out and close up
⁀	home made	Close up space
∽	blaknet	Change the order of letters
tr.	The picnic was special this August	Transfer the circled words (Write *tr* in nearby margin)
¶	¶ We decided to have a family reunion	Begin a new paragraph
⊙	We played volleyball	Add a period
^,	Uncle Tim, Lee and I	Add a comma
# ^	Irishstew	Add a space
⊙	these six stages	Add a colon
^;	County Cork, Ireland London, England; and Brisbane, Australia	Add a semicolon
=	white tailed rabbit	Add a hyphen
∨	Uncle Tims banjo	Add an apostrophe
stet	special summer month	Keep the crossed-out material (Write *stet* in nearby margin)